Y Blc

By Anthony Lynch

Chapter 1: "Lunatic Attendant"

I lay in my ground floor bed. This morning I was to start work and the prospect had been a good alarm clock. There were three hours to go and I had no distance to travel. The house where I had happily found a room was opposite the back of the hospital whose giant rambling and turreted structure all of the same dirty red brickwork looked down on the road and cut out all the light. Occasionally, a French window high up on a fire escape would be left open. Then a flash of sunlight might reflect into my room. That was all the sun it received. Heavy framed bay windows were one-third stained glass. If any light did penetrate these it was caught up in the brown folds of the pelmet, or lost in the muddy-milk muslin curtains that hung tiredly down. Brown wallpaper spread between brown woodwork. Gloss brown linoleum on the floor reflected the brown varnished dressing table and dresser. Even the counterpane was brown. My bed was a double bed. The easy chair wooden framed, and the rest of the furniture a card table. Mrs Baron collected two pounds a week from me for this, and by her almost total inability to smile endeared herself to me as little as did the room.

But it had not been easy to find a place. I had tramped the whole day yesterday from the plain filthy to the unjustifiably snooty. At the only place I fancied, the room had been let that morning. The landlady there was a big buxom woman whose ancestry spoke of southern climes. The house was brightly painted in and out. There was colour everywhere and everything shone with cleanliness. Her kids were scrubbed, her husband's baggy working pants were scrubbed and she radiated good health. It was a shame the room was gone, because her advertisement did not say 'No un-coloured people'.

And now I had found myself lodgings; a white landlady and brown home. It was no use wishing it was the other way round. My reverie carried me back two days, to Monday.

***

I had come to London from the green peace of the West Country to find and begin humanitarian work. My 1953 Tribunal as a Conscientious Objector directed that there could be no exemption, but allowed an alternative to national service after I had completed my three years reading history at Cambridge. The alternative service was to be humanitarian they said, and the alternative to that was gaol.

The West Country offered sufficient gaols but I could find no humanitarian work for unqualified men. So, arriving in the autumn sunshine of 1957 at Paddington, I bought a Nursing News and boarded a bus for Camberwell. Camberwell was a magnet, not through any particular charm of its own, but because there my girlfriend Paula was in a university hostel and it seemed now – and later proved – to be a good idea to find work where her company was not far away.

The situations vacant column of the Nursing News was heavy with opportunities to serve suffering mankind. But mankind seemed repeatedly to suffer in London boroughs of which I had never heard. Eventually "East Dulwich" caught my eye. That name was billed on the front of the bus.

"Staff required for male side of large geriatric hospital. Apply to Matron, St Francis's, East Dulwich," said the advertisement. Right, I would.

I did.

'Miss Angus?' cheerily I pushed open her door. 'I'm Lynch I rang you earlier.'

'Oh yes. What can we do for you?'

'You want staff. I've got two years alternative service, thought I'd apply.'

'Are you qualified Mr Lunn?'

(Qualified for what? I don't expect to start off as a doctor.)

'No Miss Argus, I'm sorry.'

'Angus. Miss Angus or Matron will do!' She looked down at her desk. I stood. No seat was offered. Her little bright peroxide curls bobbed on her forehead. Her cap and cuffs sparkled starchily. She pushed her glasses down her nose, tilted her head back and eyed me along her nose. Perhaps that way she saw everything through the pink and blue haze radiating from its tip.

'Ah well! Have you ever done any nursing Mr Lunn?' – She knew it was Lynch, but this was for her a matter of principle. I couldn't win.

'No Matron.'

'Do you know anything about the insane?'

An odd question that. Have all her staff gone so?

'No matron.' A small 'm' this time. I felt I should not be too subservient. 'But I've always been interested in mental disorders and have read a bit of psychology.'

'That's beside the point Mr Lunn. We want workers who aren't going to take fright just because some poor dears are insane.'

'Well I can work and I don't usually take fright.' I returned her critical stare to prove that she would have to offer more fearsome lunacy than hers to frighten me away.

'Perhaps I can offer you a job.'

She consulted her large blotting pad, leathercornered and of the purest unblotted white. There was no inspiration for her there. It seemed that she was anxious to have me, but could on no account tell me so. She summoned her wits to extend the interview as long as possible.

'You'll have to have a medical.'

'I have had one recently if it . . .'

'That's of no account Mr Lunn. You'll have to have *our* Medical Examination. It includes an X-ray.' The word "X-ray" was delivered in a vocal climax. This would put Lunn in his place. He was to understand quite firmly that people were not just *offered* jobs in this hospital. They were examined and by the most rigorous methods known to Matron and Modern Science.

I raised no objection to the X-ray.

A long pause. Her eyes scanned me and then the blotter, found nothing of significance to help her in either. She fixed her eyes in the middle distance. 'Are you determined to stay here for some time Mr Lunn? Because I've too many staff upping and a-waying all the time.'

'I should think so.'

'Well I've got a Very Special Block here which is a wee bit difficult to staff.' She made it sound as if it was merely the size of the doors made it hard to get people inside. 'Would you like to work there?' Pretty slim information on which to decide.

'Yes.'

'It's the Psychiatric Observation Unit; Y Block. It used to be just for pauper lunatics but nowadays it is not just paupers who are lunatics its quite well off people as well' She paused to let that sink in. 'We run it as an emergency wing to take urgent insane cases that are temporarily committed to us. We sort them out and steady them down and then they go off most usually to one of the big mental hospitals for treatment. It's very worthwhile work,' she added, 'the hours aren't too long.' She paused, reaching into her mind for benefits to offer me. 'The pay is slightly more than on the geriatric side'.

'Right. OK. When do I start? I'd like a day to look around for lodgings.'

'Why don't you live in Mr Lynch?' Now, if she hadn't got my name right that time I probably would not have noticed. But it seemed her niceness was hiding a catch somewhere. 'It only means about four pounds a week and all found including laundry.'

There's one catch for a start. Four pounds a week from about the six I would earn left only two for me to go mad on.

'No thanks Miss Angus.'

'All right, suit yourself. Start the day after tomorrow, 9 o'clock. You'll to go see Mr Webb in the secretary's office first, and he'll fit you up with a uniform and some white coats.'

'Thank you.'

'And a mackintosh.'

'Thank you.'

'Not at all. Mind how you go and you should be all right.' Pleasant but nebulous goodwill. Sounds a bit frightening. Ah well. Cinema and chips tonight. Tomorrow start looking for a room.

Suppose *I* was a nut case, would I have got the job? As far as I could see, yes. So long as I didn't drop my pants or shake my fist, or wave a chopper at the matron during the interview there could not have been any snags. I was now a Nursing Assistant; furthermore, I was a "Lunatic Attendant" as they called my job during the Depression.

***

I climbed out of bed and put the gas fire on. It was not cold but the fire added a little colour. A few clothes strewn about added colour too. Camp coffee and puffed wheat. Use the brown lavatory cabinet. Wash hands and face in the brown and black bathroom. Off to St Francis's Hospital, East Dulwich – The Psychiatric Observation Unit.

***

The road up to the hospital has plane trees on either side, filling the handkerchief gardens of the two rows of houses. Every tree, every house, is the same. How the people must be grateful for numbers or they would take ages to get home.

The Porter's Lodge directed me to Mr Webb. He had a large airy office, as big as a ward. There were two girls in it. One was large and plain and the other thin and plain. The thin one had hairy shins and soft brown eyes. She fancied Mr Webb and he had her smiles. He was tall, bald and horn-rimmed and filled in papers rapidly. Soon I was taken to a vast linen cupboard to be fitted. Fitted perhaps is not a good word. All normal navy blue serge suits had been taken. Freak sets remained for me. The best outfit left my ankles uncovered, a big knot of spare cloth at the belly and the waistcoat impossible to do up. The jacket was not too bad. I wrapped my own belt around the midriff and, leaving a parcel of my civvies with him for the moment, made my way over to Y Block. Lord help me and make these two years go quickly.

Y Block is a separate unit. Its two storeys are connected to the main block by an uneven and misshapen covered way. It is a piglet building sucking at the upturned sow of the mother hospital. I approach by the ambulance route; through a big double doorway into a high walled yard. The walls have spikes. Steps up to the front door. Wired glass in the windows. The handle turns but nothing happens. The door is locked. Ring the bell and knock, Lynch, they are probably having a tea break.

I was let in shortly.

CHAPTER 2: Y Block

Twice the key was turned in the lock before it opened slowly. Then my first impression was of the smell. Carried through the slightly open door on a waft of centrally heated air, it was a smell that I had never breathed before. Rubber and urine mixed with crude soap and floor polish; a tang of disinfectant fighting and losing against body smells.

'Come in quickly.'

I stepped in; the door was slammed to, and, keys swinging across his thigh, the man turned and rushed off to his right dragging green screens on wheels behind him and slamming a door again.

I stood on the mat.

The light through the door behind me lit up a small doorway; a little office was on the left; a ward, now screened off and locked, on the right; a corridor led down to the left where another ward was empty except for its green covered beds – about a dozen of them.

Green was a popular or at least a much used colour. These were no natural greens. Up to a height of four feet the walls were done in a dark green – the green that weathered copper turns before it goes black. Above, the green paint was lighter but no more pleasant. The floors of the corridors were in red tile, while polished parquet made the downstairs wards lethal for anyone unsteady on their feet.

'Are you being looked after?' A very short, tubby man addressed me. Silver hair, scarce and smooth, was laid out nicely on the pink scalp on either side of a geometrically precise parting. Baby soft pink jowls hung down beside a trio of immaculately shaved chins. Soft blue eyes looked out with bloodhound expression from behind jet black rimmed glasses. Silver catkin eyebrows arched interrogatively. 'I'm Nurse Dunning. Who are you?'

'My name's Lynch, I've come to work here.'

'Ooh yes, I've heard about you.' He delicately slipped his glasses off; a little authority in the action. Lightly sucking a side piece he eyed me up and down and down and up again. 'Ooh you've got nice hair, haven't you?' I did not answer that. I felt like an upstairs maid applying to the Duchess for a job. Dunning obviously felt a bit like a Duchess.

'Well my name's Billie.' It was said that way, "ee", no short crisp "y", 'and I'm a staff nurse here. We'll introduce you to Father in a minute, only they're having a bit of trouble in there at the moment.' He waved the most delicately done nails towards the locked ward. 'Come in here.' He sidled into a little room opposite the front door. Medicine cabinets and a sink occupied most of the room. There was a mirror over the sink. It was this, or rather what Billie could see in it, which claimed his attention. He was polishing round his generous nostrils with Vaseline. 'Little black specks,' he said. 'They're a bugger (pardon my language); don't know where they come from.'

The door, which Billie had closed behind us, opened and a stocky, iron-grey, crew-cut man strode in. He glanced quickly about, grabbed a bottle of gentian violet and daubed it over his wrists and the back of his hands, then rushed out again. Billie had paused, hands held drooped in front of his egg-shaped paunch. He watched the man come, perform and go. 'That was Father,' he said, 'Chief Male Nurse Howard; he's *quite* as mad as you see, but a *dear* really. Shall we go in and see him and everyone now?'

Billie must have felt confident in his make up by this time, and sure that trouble was over. Waggling his hips enough to make it noticeable under his loose hanging white coat, Billie led the way into the now open ward.

All the smells were stronger here. A committee of three with white coats sat behind a desk with Father at the centre, a cluster of blue pips on his shoulder. They commanded a view right down the corridor to the far ward and side entrance. Backs against the wall and knees notched into the lip of the desk-top, they glanced to right and left over the ten green-covered beds in the ward. In the left hand wall as the white coats sat, were two doors.

'Mr Howard this is Mr Lynch. He hasn't told me his first name yet.' A slight pout crossed Billie's face.

'Never mind Billie, give him a chance. How do you do? Hope you'll be happy here. Billie, you'd better get Allan to show Nurse Lynch round.'

'I can take him if you like Father.'

'No, I want you to do the bloods Billie.'

Billie turned, I think to hide tears of vexation. Nevertheless, he came back shortly with Allan. Allan was old, tiny, owl like behind gold-rimmed spectacles. Sparse white hair stood to attention on his head. His white coat reached down to his ankles. Though never appearing to put anything into his mouth he was always rapidly chewing; all his other movements were slow, even languid.

Allan's guided tour was a most uninspired affair. He showed me the private staff lavatory upstairs. Staff were pointed out and named.

'There are forty-one beds altogether.' His voice had just a touch of Irish, 'And mostly there's never more than eight staff on.'

I was most interested in the first ward downstairs where the "trouble" had been. I understood that this was the Admission Ward, and that troublesome patients as far as possible were confined here. The only sign of trouble now was on a bed just by the desk. Two bulky nurses, one polar bear coloured and the other gorilla, sat firmly one on either side of a tousled sweaty heap whose red face now rested on the pillow. Nothing was said.

Allan told me, 'He's been a bit naughty but we've settled him down. We gave him a shot and he'll have a nice sleep now.'

I learned later that Allan's use of "we" was quite misplaced in this and most instances. He liked to use "we" not in the Royal or Queen's plural as Billie did, but to include himself in anything in which he did not take part, but might have been expected to. Typical instances are "We won the war", "We gave him a good hiding", "We gave something towards a wreath", "We do a good day's work for our money".

At the first sign of trouble Allan disappeared. If he did not he was encouraged to leave as he tended to get in the way. His regular duty point was Ward II, which, being the ward by the side entrance, was empty all day. The kitchen was next to it and Allan made tea there. Occasionally he had a quiet patient with him who could make a better cup of tea.

Allan showed me the padded cells, which he referred to as the pads. These two lay off the Admission Ward - private booths, near to the ward's separate bathroom. From here came some of the smell of rubber. Thick, fat rubber walls, floor and ceiling bulged in on the small space. A rubber gutter ran round the bottom to drain outside. Light came from a wire-guarded dim blue bulb high up in the ceiling. Central heating came also from the ceiling. I stepped inside a pad. The door slapped and clicked heavily to behind me. Allan's watery eye peered at me through the minute porthole lens. It is hot, smelly and oppressive in here. I can hear my own pulse thump. O Lord, this would drive me mad to be in here for long. 'Is it often necessary?' I asked as he let me out.

'Oh, we don't use them a lot,' he said, 'but most weeks we get someone who wants to rest in here for a bit.'

Immediately inside the first ward were two little bare rooms without beds. Mattresses lay on the floors with a tumble of sheets. A West Indian gentleman snored on one and a Polish gent on the other. Both gave off a strange goat-like smell.

Father, or more properly Chief Male Nurse Howard, now directed me upstairs. Allan and I could stay upstairs he said and send the other nurse up there downstairs. Out of the corner of my eye I caught Billie fiddling with a syringe and pouting in my direction. Father had obviously spoilt his fun. Allan hadn't even left him the upstairs lavatory to show me. This had in fact been the first thing Allan had put on his itinerary. The reason, he explained, was that it was nearly eleven o'clock, and Father went there at eleven. Evidently, Father's bowel routine was something not to be disturbed. The whole staff were in dread of it.

The upstairs nurse, Haynes, the first young nurse I had seen – well, not over forty anyway – did not want to go down "to make tea for that bloody lot". He took his time about going down, and on his way advised me closely to watch days off, duty times, dirty jobs, coat pinching and a host of possible other areas of victimisation and persecution. Though he did not suppose I would get a rough deal, because if any nastiness was going *he* always got it. Even as he retreated down the narrow stone stairs he continued to spit his advice back at me – "watch out for bottom pinchers."

'Did I upset him?' I asked Allan.

'Oh no. He's like that with all of us,' he assured me. 'He's had a rough time they say; he worked in a TB hospital and his wife caught TB. She's supposed to be better now, but he thinks he might have it as well. He's been checked and there are no signs. He came here 'cos the money's better. But I don't think this work suits him.'

At either end of the upstairs corridor was a ward - one, a now empty dormitory, the other the Recreation Ward. Off the corridor between were various small rooms: a big washroom with half a dozen hand basins, a tiny kitchen, a bathroom, an interview room, the special private lavatory and a linen cupboard where the staff kept their supply of white coats. All these rooms and the dormitory were locked. We took up our station in the Recreation Ward, which contained a ping pong table, a piano, a television set, and numerous different easy, barely easy and damned uncomfortable chairs. Green paint of course prevailed, now encouraged by dark green polished lino on the floor. The smell at least was more wax laden here. But the fairly strong smell of a seaside urinal came through from the lavatory at one end.

Of all the wards this must have been the most miserable. Had I known then, when I first stepped inside it, how many long sad hours I would spend there, I think I would have left then and let the Army have me.

Stiff in my white coat and serge trousers, I stood with back to the door post. Allan lounged around and opened the sash windows. That is, he opened the windows as far as they would go, only four inches. Each was of heavy wired glass. Howard trotted up and darted along the corridor to us.

'Key for you Mr Lynch.' He passed me a big key on a boot lace and I tied it to my belt.

'You keep it on you all the time and never ever let a patient have it. As soon as you go off duty you give it in to the Charge Nurse. We don't have any mistakes with keys here. If this lot gets out we'll have the devil to pay.'

He darted across the room, grabbed a fallen and tatty book, shelved it, tutted and darted out again.

I felt more secure now with my key. Secure? I felt I was the gaoler. They're an odd lot I thought – the staff that is – but friendly. Somehow I had not really seen patients yet. They did not appear to be the dominant element. Later I learned the reason for this. "Little Tom" had been on duty the night before. He travelled a long way to work by motor cycle combination, and since his five children demanded attention during the day, night duty put a strain on his five foot frame. For that reason his regular policy was to issue a strong ration of sleeping draughts and pills to the patients. This enabled him to get his head down more frequently and so return possibly even refreshed to his family.

So now in the morning, the patients were quiet, docile and not obtruding into the life of the nurses. It would not always be so.

***

16

Allan strolled across to the lavatory and opened the door. 'This should be kept open so we know what's going on inside,' he turned to me without looking inside. A pair of long legs and flat feet belonging to an Indian gentleman straddled shakily on the pan. Scrawny arms gathered a white nightshirt and red corduroy dressing gown round the patient's body. His height and his unsteadiness and his complete visual inattention to the matter in hand contributed to his inaccuracy. He looked at us mournfully with brown and blood shot eyes while he peed resonantly onto the floor. Slowly Allan turned and like a ringmaster showing one of his animals, ordered the patient down who finished, stepped into his brown felt slippers and shuffled through to a seat behind the piano. There he continued to gaze mournfully but now nowhere in particular.

A tubby, pop-eyed and very clean young man jumped up. His broad backside bore the name 'St Francis' embroidered in red across the shapeless grey flannel. He ran across to the lavatory and pulled the chain before sluicing water on the floor and wiping toilet paper round the rim of the pan. Then he washed his hands, and washed his hands and washed his hands and washed his hands. Allan stopped him and retired momentarily for a big clean draw-sheet from the linen cupboard. The cleaner dried thoroughly with this and then took advantage to wash his face and dry that. The performance seemed likely to spread so Allan took the draw-sheet away.

'Shan't I change his slippers?' this patient asked.

'No,' said Allan.

'Should I fetch a doctor for him?' 'No,' said Allan.

'There's something wrong you know. That is four times he's used the lavatory this morning.'

'I know there's something wrong,' said Allan.

'Well, won't you do something?' His eyes nearly popped out of his head.

'No, we've got it all under control. Now just you sit down.'

He did temporarily, but was soon up again, first for a renewed appeal on behalf of the Indian patient and then, thwarted, to fetch a glass of water for another patient, to have a cloth to clean the windows, to have a brush to clean the floor. He was given the latter. But somehow the job was never finished before another urgent cause claimed the attention of this selfappointed social worker.

Allan had it all under control.

'He's not quite right in the head,' he told me.

'Yes,' I said, 'they told me I might find quite a few like that here.' The sarcasm was thinly veiled. It needn't have been veiled at all for Allan. It made no impression on him.

'Her Ladyship is late this morning,' said Allan.

'Who's that?' I thought perhaps he might mean Billie.

'Matron. Usually she's round about half past ten. If not, Deputy Matron comes round at eleven. Of course, she may miss a round but it's not likely.'

No sentence, however short, could make Allan's delivery appear rapid. The latest took about a minute and a half to utter. Not surprising then that as he trailed to a full stop there was a swish of skirts on the stairs.

Deputy Matron, fully seven feet tall and with Howard anxiously in tow, swept imperiously up to the locked dormitory ward, turned the handle and tried to walk through. Her extended black, polished beetle crushers thudded bang bang into the solid door, and by virtue of their slight advantage in length saved her nose from piercing the plate glass.

'It's locked,' said Howard, 'all patients out,' and wiped a grin away with the back of his hand leaving a gentian smirch there instead.

'Open it then.'

Absolutely simply for no reason at all she examined the ward minutely. Every bed and under it was inspected. The only misplaced item, a dirty tea cup on the table by the door, was swept invisibly into Howard's side pocket.

Her visit to the recreation ward was brief. Her nod to Allan and myself peremptory. She did notice the Indian patient in night attire however.

'Why's he in a dressing gown?'

'Going out this morning Ma'am. Cane Hill. If they're a bit frisky you know we don't let them dress for the journey.'

She knew, of course. The Indian did not look at all frisky.

The pop-eyed, self-appointed social worker approached her as she strode back down the corridor. On the trot he caught up with her at the top of the stairs.

'Could I have a word with you about the Indian, Matron?'

'Oh, why, yes.' She was embarrassed and flustered. 'What is it then?'

'In private I'd prefer.'

'It's all right,' Howard interposed, 'you can say what you like in front of us.' He clapped his arm reassuringly around the patient's shoulder and drew him firmly into a huddle.

'He makes a mess when he goes to business, Matron.'

'Oh we all do sometimes.' She silenced even herself, surprised by her ineptitude.

'That's all right,' said Howard, 'it's all taken care of.'

The pair moved off downstairs.

'He'd knock you over as soon as look at you,' Howard told her as they reached the ground floor. She would have been disappointed to know that there was not a grain of truth in that. For twenty four of her forty years perhaps she had been waiting and hoping for a man to knock her off her feet. Deputy Matron smiled showing beautiful teeth and a kind face.

Howard had to tell her that story however. It wouldn't do if she got into the habit of granting private audiences to the patients. That sort of thing was infectious. All the patients would want a go and where would discipline be then.

A couple of clangs came up a hot water pipe to advise that the inspection was over, and Deputy Matron had left the block. Tea came up shortly afterwards.

'What's the visitation about?' I asked Allan.

'Ah, we're responsible to the Matron you see, so women from the main hospital come and inspect us.'

'Do they know what they are about?'

'Ah yes, I expect so. They're not stupid.'

Some of them didn't appear to though. There was a touch of ignorance here and there, as if they were lost in confused male world. Some of the duty sisters who inspected Y Block had never before set foot inside a mental hospital of any sort. They didn't know what to do, or say, so concentrated on looking intelligent and spotting irregularities amongst the staff. If a Sister occasionally reported someone smoking on duty, the Matron would be happy knowing she had her eyes open.

The morning passed quickly towards lunch. In a place like St Francis's, lunch, or in fact any meal, assumed terrific importance. Appetite and table manners were a guide to diagnosis. Not the diagnosis that appeared against the patient's name in the register. That was just a label supplied by the duty doctor, a trainee psychiatrist from the post graduate teaching hospital up the road. The diagnosis supplied by the nurses was an assessment of behaviour. On each nurse's assessment rested his ability to run a ward or read peacefully when he was on duty. He had to know how far a patient could be left, and how far controlled rigorously. Bring a man to food and there you will learn much of him.

***

The first sign of lunch upstairs on this and many days was the arrival of Johnny, carrying a clean sheet for a table cloth. Mobile patients sometimes took lunch upstairs in the dormitory as well as in the two wards below. This generally was only if we had a full house.

Johnny, a high grade mental defective, asked to be let into the kitchen and the dormitory. He appeared an amiable patient. Cheeky and often quite noisy, his total lack of sexual development made him look very fresh and clean. His mental ability was quite high enough to have found him employment outside, as a labourer or commissionaire, but his 'personality was disordered'.

Now, that was a popular covering diagnosis to be found frequently in the Admission Ward register. Clinically it is of less use than privately however. Of anybody who offends it is soothing to say he or she has a personality disorder. In what order should their personality be?

Johnny irregularly drank too much, and alcohol had a quick and exaggerating effect on his behaviour. He was, drunk or sober, liable to fits of lachrymose depression. He was also liable to periods of hysterical gaiety. But there was no visible rhythm to this, nor any visible cause. There well might have been a quite ordinary causal agent. His mother may have angered him that day by serving up fish instead of meat; perhaps his bed was hard. It was difficult to say because Johnny was mostly very cheerful with us, and he did not have much insight. Since he came to us regularly every month or so, his biggest intellectual triumph was working out a method to get back in. He probably spent the whole of each term at Cane Hill Hospital puzzling out a method to employ as soon as his discharge came through. It always did. Johnny was balanced and secure in hospital. He didn't even show signs of institutionalisation. Granted, he was first to sweep up for dog-ends, but his face didn't bear the creases and dead pan expression of long-term patients in the asylum. Probably his breaks outside prevented this as much as anything.

It would have been better for the hospital authorities on his release to have fixed a time for him to be picked up again. This way considerable money and effort would have been saved. For a start, he could have been admitted regularly every two months. Rather than straining himself thinking up new entry methods, he would have gladly hung on for a while. Six admissions per year are cheaper than eight or nine. Then again, working his own way back meant the police force was disturbed.

Johnny had three main methods of entry. The commonest was to assume or really to be violently drunk and then accost a policeman. Accost is too mild a word. Johnny was a fairly big chap and he must have scared hell out of half the Metropolitan Police in his time. Usually he approached a policeman and with a squeaky roar brought his fist down hard onto the poor man's helmet. Preferred times for this were when the policeman was on point duty, or moving people along at a crowded event. Johnny had a great sense of the embarrassment in things.

Method number two was the social method. A good crowd, a public house and the presence of his mother were essential. Seriously at first, he would begin to argue and shout then work himself up into a fine condition of histrionics. Once he had achieved froth around his mouth and the attention of all the bystanders he would begin to assault his mother. Having contributed almost entirely to Johnny's characteristics, she did not take this lying down until he put her in that position. One gathered that, apart from an occasional black eye, he rarely hurt her. According to which pub he was in, if the landlord knew and liked Johnny, his action brought the ambulance and the Duly Authorised Officer. If the landlord did not know him or disliked him, the police were called. The DAO is employed by the Council and commits people to an observation wing until the medics and authorities make a longer-term decision. If Johnny was committed by the DAO, it was all very friendly. The papers were filled out in the ambulance, and information was exchanged. The DAO would know of any changes at St Francis's; Johnny may know who was due to be released from Cane Hill Hospital. This warned the DAO because ten to one a released patient would be back in his area soon, possibly needing admittance. If the police brought Johnny in it was a struggle all the way. Not that he struggled to get free, but merely as a matter of principle. He was inordinately proud of his mother because she had been "inside", but did not feel disposed to thank the police for it, when they must at some stage have been partly responsible. As soon as the police got him to us, Johnny pretended to have met his match and would subside gratefully onto the admission bed.

Johnny's third method was his quiet and miserable one; to be chosen if he wanted a bit of a fuss made of him when he came in. I suspect this method was employed only when his mother left him to fend for himself for a while. He would arrange for someone to call round to his house, or he'd go to a public place, and there begin to commit suicide. Waterloo Bridge in the rush hour was fairly good on a fine day. If it rained, he asked Aunt Margo to pop round; stuck his head in the gas oven and switched it on as she came up the path.

He had tried cutting his wrists but that was messy and difficult to time correctly.

So Johnny was back in, and everybody pleased to see him for a day anyway. He would sweep floors, wash up, carry dishes and do a good day's work – just so long as he got Paraldehyde as his nightcap. Without this he would sulk and avoid work.

'Hi Doddery,' he called to Allan. He had heard somebody else call him that. Johnny never initiated anything. 'How many you got for lunch then?'

'Seven,' I called back, 'up here anyway.'

'Who's your gentleman friend, Doddery?'

Allan introduced us and Johnny walked up the corridor to greet me. He welcomed me and hoped I should be happy here. Johnny made me feel that he owned the place, was its Managing Director, Founder and Patron Saint all rolled into one. I was, I suppose, a novelty to Johnny.

'Don't call me Doddery,' said Allan, 'it's not respectful.'

'No sir, three bags full sir, Mr Allan, Sir.'

'Now get on widge our table laying.' Allan always said 'widge' instead of with.

Clanging from the kitchen showed that work was being done. Shortly I moved along to see how the table was going. It was immaculate. The knives caught my eye; each had been deprived of its cutting edge and part of the edge was also bent out of line so that it would neither cut nor pierce. The forks were solid webs except for a sixteenth of an inch of tines at the end. No deep injury could be done with these tools as long as the eyes were not attacked.

Two white-aproned porters from the main hospital brought up the food in big churns. Meat was on a plate already cut, potatoes and peas in one churn, tapioca in the other. Doddery and I served out. As soon as all was ready we went along to the Recreation

Ward to collect our patients. Johnny had been keeping a guardian eye on them meanwhile.

'Lunch is ready,' Allan shouted.

'Grub up,' I translated.

'Chow chow,' Allan called to the Indian.

The pop-eyed, self-appointed social worker was the first up. He was determined to help a senile patient who didn't know where to come or what to come for. The pair of them eventually made the journey. Popeye's name was actually Smith. This was very disappointing. At the very least it should have been Anthony Howard Wilberforce Ashley Cooper. Not a bit of it. Plain Smith. Only child of mother. Father unknown.

I did not find that out from Allan. I asked him once during the morning about a patient's history.

'I don't enquire into their circumstances,' he said. 'It's none of my business.'

This seemed odd, but he was quite sincere. He never did. And he never had the slightest idea of what made a patient, or any person, tick. They were almost all normal and uninteresting to him. He was thus enveloped in a mental security that was enviable. I gathered that he lived for his off duty hours when he took poodles for walks in Chelsea. He always spoke of Chelsea with reverence; evidently he called regularly at certain smart houses and took their poodles out. Any opinion he expressed was not just his personal opinion, but also that of a lady in Chelsea.

Eventually, all were gathered to the luncheon table.

***

Upstairs, ordinary heavy plates were used. Downstairs the plates were glazed cardboard or *papier maché*. They were not disposable and extremely difficult to break. Whereas upstairs one porcelain plate was broken on average at each meal, below, if the plates had not been cardboard and the cups not plastic, most would have been broken each day.

Today, it was a senile patient who broke a plate. Determined to arrive nearer to it, either to spoon its contents directly into his face, or to allow the dribble from his mouth to fall directly onto the plate instead of the cloth, he grabbed it. His fingers clawed trembling to the edge and gripped it, drawing it up and towards him until the contents (potato and gravy) sluiced down his red flannel coat. Then he dropped the plate onto the floor.

Self-appointed social worker Smith was surprised and called out a little advice. He was not, however, on this occasion prepared to do anything. Tired by his efforts of the morning, Smith was now reinforcing Smith. He was choking food back excitedly.

'Never mind old man,' Allan called encouragingly to the senile patient. 'We'll soon clear that up.' That is, I would. Fragments had all to be collected and assembled, for someone might have saved a sharp sliver for a suicidal purpose. Then the red flannel coat was stripped off the old man and used as a floor and finger wiper. This, including squeezed up potatoes, was thrown directly into the dirty laundry bin downstairs. Seeing that, I made a mental note never to work in a laundry. Potatoes are the least obnoxious lumps that one may hope to find in a dirty laundry bin.

Smith was finished and offering to dish out the sweet. A pale and handsome young man at the end had not finished. His name was de Champs.

Motionless, he sat with his hands on his lap and gazed at the wall. Neatly dressed in a grey suit, only his red St Francis's Hospital slippers were out of place. His features, regularly set in a triangular face, below a very broad and high forehead, were delicate and fine. Large brown eyes with their complimentary lashes and hair made his skin appear pallid and transparent. 'Come along Mr de Champs, eat your dinner.' I laid a hand gently on his shoulder and felt his whole body stiffen beneath it. I took my hand away and sat down beside him; that I felt would take away any imperativeness from my position. He vibrated and remained rigid, staring ahead.

'Come on, it's good for you,' I said.

'No nonsense up here now,' said Allan, 'or it's away widge you to the padded cell.' At this he brought de Champs' head towards his plate; de Champs was rigid with fear and now as soon as he was touched he coiled up and squirmed to the floor, whimpering and begging, 'No, no!'

'Then eat your food.'

He shot back onto his seat and tried to gobble up something quickly, but soon was staring fixedly at the wall.

Allan spoke again, and again de Champs reacted with stiffness and trembling. Any word increased his terror, even words of encouragement. It was not just the threat of the padded cell. I doubt if he even feared this as a message.

Silence except for slurping from the senile patient. Other patients at the table gathered something was wrong and were uneasy.

'Yes – what do you want? I will,' de Champs answered a voice that no one else heard. He cocked his attention in panic towards a light bulb. 'No, no. I won't again.' And then a silly laugh.

This raised the hairs on the nape of my neck. His auditory hallucinations separated him from us. He was irrevocably in a world of his own. Not much fun there either poor soul . . . he was scared stiff.

Sometime later I met de Champs' father during one of his visits to Y Block. He was a mild, quiet but healthy looking man. He wanted to worship David, his son. But how could he when David was odd and when the world looked at his father and questioned if it was from him that the madness had come – and pitied both.

'He was brilliant at school,' his father said, 'particularly at languages. He speaks perfect French, German and Spanish.' I doubted it, for small truths are enlarged and adorned by any loving parent, and if that parent has to gild and spread the truth to cover the frightening reality of a son's sick mind, how far that truth is likely to be stretched. But I was wrong. Later, when David had a quiet spell, I tested his French as far as I could. It was streaks ahead of any other Englishman's French I had heard. Of his German and Spanish I had no doubt when he talked about those countries.

His elder brother and mother both committed suicide,' his father said. 'There were several years in between but it shook me up a bit.' Loneliness and bewilderment were in his voice too. Wasn't his wife obviously sick when he married her, I wanted to ask. Apparently not. Probably she was withdrawn and gentle, perhaps odd at times and childlike. 'She painted beautifully.' De Champs senior had my sympathy. There was no understanding this even if you were not involved. Involved and wanting to believe the ordinary and normal, what explanation could a man make for this to happen to him? Death is explicable at a physical level; even spiritually there are contrived and silly consolations; "God wants her for a sunbeam".

God cannot want a shattered mind.

'He'll look forward to coming home you know,' said de Champ senior.

'What will he do?'

'Oh, he has lots of friends he visits, and he takes them bars of chocolate and fruit.'

Good people of Wimbledon. 'Here's poor David again. I do so wish they'd cure him and let his father have a bit of peace. Come in David and have a cup of tea.'

Perhaps David and his father had some luck there. Many people paralysed to nastiness with fear would have shut their doors against him explaining, 'he's just not safe my dear. Don't you know he's been AWAY?' And privately, barely forming the words to themselves, "My Peter might have been like that. I could go like that myself. Don't think about it. Have a cup of tea. Why don't they find an answer?"

David never hurt anybody. He was picked up only because he was found wandering aimlessly and Ophelia-like far from home, wither he had gone on some uncompleted and forgotten errand. Crazed and shattered, there was little enough contact with the world for him. Even quiet, drug-induced remissions lasted for only a while; and then after starting a conversation he would change abruptly in midsentence to another and then a third. Then gradually it would not be you he was talking to but The Voice. The Voice is real; it is no echo of the conscience; it is not David talking to himself, conscience debating with conscience. David hears it. He listens and he answers. Sometimes it is cajoling and urges him to lie down or walk about, to eat or stop eating. Sometimes it is comic and tells David jokes or expresses itself with wit to make him giggle and snigger. But David will not share the joke. He is loath to confess that action of his is governed by The Voice because The Voice is real. It is his and part of his world. Here, in contact with this private Voice he is unassailable, remote. If The Voice is kind he is lit up with peace and temporarily inspired and soothed. If The Voice is harsh, he is subdued and sent cringing to a corner, humbled, shattered, down cast and lost because that thing which is nearest and most relevant to his world has let him down.

**

Last to finish eating were two depressed patients. Blank faced and slow in all their moves, they made Allan in comparison shine like quicksilver. He seemed to like them. He could out-talk them and outjoke them.

Clearing away was handled by the epileptic patients – distinguished in any ward by their scars. Hands and foreheads bore the white marks of sudden contact with the ground. Fits on the ward were rare as the staff controlled and timed the doses of anti-convulsive drugs, but trouble from these patients was frequent. The least disturbed in Y Block were always erratic. The two now clearing up would not clear the lunch away tomorrow for instance, nor again while they were here.

But it was not for having a sudden fit on the street that they were brought in, nor yet for being erratic and moody. If either of these two reasons were sufficient, the wards would have been ten times too small. The hallmark of Y Block's epileptic patients was their violence. This was manifested before and after the seizure despite the terrific final headache. Violence is frightening. How reasonable seemed ancient belief that there were devils inside the victim.

Sinews toughened with the exercise of so many spasms could rip the steel frames of our beds apart and tear canvas into shreds.

Coupled with this, the epileptic man, possibly because he can recognize his fellow sufferer, is frequently clannish. Whereas all the other patients may live in their private worlds, the epileptic shares part of his with others. This was even the case where epilepsy was only one of the complaints, almost as insignificant to his general behaviour as acne or dandruff. The epilepsy sufferers brought to St Francis's bore other burdens, psychoses against which no drugs were effective, and which made them incapable of controlling their seizures. The clannishness affected us very little in Y Block. Patients rarely stayed more than fourteen days, and with relatively small numbers to handle, troublesome groups were easily dispersed. But old time attendants told frequently of refractory wards in large institutions temporarily taken over by groups of such men. Thus, in our wards the epileptics were not given adjacent beds, and were encouraged to submit to recreation at opposite ends of the ping-pong table and preferably in separate wards.

Johnny supervised the washing up, and combined his duties here with the successful cadging of two "roll ups" from his suddenly good friends the epileptics. Johnny got on well with all the patients. He was to many of them proof that one could be normal in a place like this.

Y BLOCK

It was hard to be normal in a place like this, and the staff were generally poor evidence to the contrary.

***

Each twenty-four hours on Y Block was divided into three shifts, Allan told me: seven in the morning until three in the afternoon; midday until nine pm; nine pm until seven am. There was an overlap from twelve in the morning until three o'clock. The theory of this was that some staff could go off to lunch and others could go on escort duty. The fact of the matter was that Y Block for about two hours was crowded out with staff.

I wondered about the arrangements for staff meals. Miss Angus had said these were to be taken in the main hospital staff canteen; the cost would be deducted. Dutifully this first day I asked to be released and made my way through a labyrinth of corridors to the vast gothic barn of an eating place. Female nurses were packed onto benches against long trestle tables. The hardness of the benches – harder than that of any church pew – was in fact only matched by the pastry. Minced meat could be smelled throughout; it seemed that the woodwork of the floor was treated with its pungent greasy stain. I prised my way between two shapely looking posteriors. The backs were of different size and shape and bore little relationship to the faces of these two. There were no nurses present who would be instantly recognised as glamorous. Judging by the faces geriatric nursing did not attract the stunningly attractive; yet even dressed in both utilitarian and uniform clothing, their laughing and kind faces unaltered by cosmetics will have been a reassuring balm to their very elderly patients.

Somehow I survived the mincemeat to tackle the second course. This was apricot flan and was billed as "The Chef's favourite". It was apricot jam smeared on bullet-proof pastry. The patients' semolina, in retrospect, was a culinary luxury and gave less or no work for the hospital dentists. Extracting myself from the impinging bright blue buttocks and flashing pink elbows, I made my way back to Y Block.

There, I found the reason for the prompt arrival of the afternoon shift. The tiny downstairs kitchen was full. Some had made soup out of the lunch gravy; huge chunks of white bread floated and soaked up the brown liquid until they sank into it. Others, Allan to the fore, had gross beef sandwiches. Billie, either by virtue of speed, or neglect of the first two courses, was already at the semolina. No neat semolina for Billie; a little blob of strawberry jam brightened his, and he delicately ate his way round it, smacking his lips and leaving it till last.

Alone at the Admission Ward desk sat Howard, violet now from ear to ear and morally supported in his isolation by a mug of tea. Admission patients were all fed and somnolent. Billie had been round with the afternoon drugs and all was peace. Every day Howard sent his "children" off for lunch and they never got further than Ward II kitchen twenty paces down the corridor. Some came in especially early to obtain lunch while it was still hot.

I never ate in the canteen again.

No patients on our wards went short. Food, more distinguished by its quantity than its quality, was thrown away every day. The authorities must have thought a symptom common to all mental illness was gluttony. Only on the staff side was this the case.

The overlap time-table was fruitful for me to take stock of my superior nurses. Only the half dozen or so on night duty were not present now. Physical stock was easily enough taken. But the business of knowing them, their vices and virtues, was never really complete. And often one could only guess at what brought them into mental nursing, and particularly into this branch of it.

The staff all deserve mention, if only briefly, to throw some light on the strangeness of this environment. Some were not here for long; some became like pieces of equipment – old and out of date, but still used here because they were familiar and predictable.

Lakhani, a mixed Jewish, Afro-Indian, originally he said from Israel, was like this. Monotone in his habits and conversation, nothing ever disturbed him as far as one could see. He said (frequently) he had been a medical "stoodent" in Edinburgh as a lad. Now fat, and walking always as though with a vast legbuckling hydrocele, he was just past forty. Rolling menthol crystals into his cigarettes was the least of his vices. Picking his nose and breaking wind at both ends less acceptable. Funds and ability had conspired in his first year as a medical student to run out on him concurrently. To take up nursing was a line of least resistance when he had to work for a living. Mental nursing made less demands on clinical alertness or cleanliness, and a couple of private jobs caring for senile patients led him eventually to Y Block. Now totally predictable, he upset the whole Block two years later when he arrived for the early shift singing loudly and hurling pound notes about. Probably it was the singing that finished his career as a lunatic attendant. Neither patients nor nurses could stand that. The underpaid staff, however, would have kept quiet about the pound note chucking for some time had it been carried on in silence. Still singing, Lakhani was removed to the teaching hospital up the road. Some sympathy was gained for our staff for a while. The sympathy was not for the loss of a colleague so much as for the pointed lesson his loss gave. What a great strain we must all work under. The sympathy was withdrawn when it was learned that Lakhani had not given his undivided attention to the examination of dead bodies when a medical student. Somewhere along the line he had caught a very living dose of syphilis, which saved up its more subtle punishment until his middle age. Thankfully, he was unmarried and lived in. Six months later he was back nursing in the Geriatric Block where the strain was less. It also, of course, gave him no chance of swapping symptoms. At least he had originality on his side; in the Block's experience he was the only person to go mad first thing in the morning. Most people do it late at night or, if they are really self-respecting, certainly leave it until after breakfast.

Dobey and Riddle, gorilla and polar bear, were the two big men heard "settling down" a disturbed patient in the Admission Ward when I first entered the Unit. Dobey was kindly and belied his appearance. He was in nursing because he wanted to do something good and worthwhile. He was in mental nursing because the money was better. His personal problem that hampered his long and stalled career at St Francis's was that his bowels had the misfortune to urge him at the same time as Howard's, the Chief. This made him disliked by the Chief, who worked normal office hours, and since Dobey could not reset his bowels to go off at a different time he rarely found himself on early shift.

Riddle was harder, less kindly and even thicker in the head than Dobey. He was strong and mostly silent. Rumour had it that Riddle had been recruited to the ranks of mental nurses by an ex-patient from St Francis's, who drank in the same local as Riddle. Rumour embroidered it with a facility for narration that would have amazed the Irish Riddle himself.

'What are you doing now then, Paddy?' the ex-patient, also Irish, said, sipping his first tomato juice since release.

'I'm working in Tilers' Bake house, aren't I, until I get me driving licence.'

'Is it hard work then, Paddy? 'Ave another drink.'

'It is. I will. I'll have the same again. In fact, I'm thinking if I am unlucky and I fail me driving test

again I think I'll work for a nice soft number. Cartin'
sacks of flour about's not good for a man. Cheers.
Aren't you drinking then?'

'No, I'm on the waggon. Just taken the cure.'

'The cure, have you?' Well, I'll not make you drink
to go against that.'

Certainly, Riddle would not for the sake of
economy.

'You're a kindly sort of fellow, Paddy. Have you
thought about nursing then?'

'No, I've not. Is that what you do then?'

'No, but I've seen some likely looking fellows in
the hospitals I've had to be in for me cures. I should
think you'd do if you're not likely to be put out by a
bit of violence now and again.'

'Are they beatin' the drink out of you in these
places then?' Riddle's eyes glowed and his blubber
stomach shook with a chuckle at the prospect of
violence.

'Ah no, not at all. But you have to take the cure in
the first place where they've got a lot of loonies you
see.'

'Is that so? And these loonies take a bit of handling,
do they?'

'Oh, I'll say. And the nurses have to sit on them you
see until they quieten down a bit.'

More chuckles from the depths of Riddle. Violence
and a sedentary occupation all in one. What more
could a man desire? Riddle felt certain that he could
sit more violently than anyone.

'Well, if I fail me driving test I might have a go at that.'

'It's a steady job if you've got the nerve for it. St Francis's, that's the place to try. Emergency Unit they call it. All violence and sitting down as far as I can see.'

Riddle failed his driving test, which put paid to his other dream of being a short-distance lorry driver – between pubs preferably. He came to St Francis's and whatever interpretation others might have had for the job, he stood, or by choice sat, rigidly by his: sitting down and violence. He retained only two other interests in life: one the drinking of beer and two the taking of driving tests. He made use of his old Morris car each day to come to work, without L plates. Then, as frequently as possible, Riddle took the test again, borrowing a qualified driver and L plates for the occasion. He failed each time. Failure did not discourage him from using the car; it appeared to give him courage. There was a lot of responsibility on a qualified driver he thought, not to make mistakes. But people expected a little slowness and hesitance from an unqualified driver. So when there was a job to be done on the Block that demanded speed and directness metaphorically he kept his L plates on. Thus when a bed pan for an incontinent patient was urgently required – Riddle would sit, talking about and planning his next driving test, leaving the skilled job to a qualified driver, or other. And when the day's sitting down and violence was done, Riddle drove home without L plates, courageously rehearsing his next attempt at a coveted driving licence.

Walker was not to be with us much longer. Eighteen stone, black haired and asthmatic, he was off sick most of the time. His twin interests were watch repairing and union activities. He did no nursing. Short of reciting union rules now and again he did not do much at all. Even when Father was there he occupied the central chair at the desk. He put the patients' names on the bed board in beautiful copperplate, and similarly completed the register. Twenty five years in the place, he was barely missed when he retired permanently sick a few months after I first met him.

Elgin, Badcock, O'Connor, Manley – fly-by-nights, trying anything once perpetually – came, made no impact and were gone. But perhaps the impacts made on them were too great.

O'Leary and Raggle, the one absolutely unqualified, the other the most highly qualified, were the workers. If floors were to be cleaned O'Leary did them. He sweated and grunted and seemed just to enjoy the necessity here for cleaning up filth. Raggle, the Deputy Chief, worked hard as though that would increase his earnings to support his wife and three children. Like Dobey, he was doing the job because he wanted to. Unlike Dobey, he could have done a variety of jobs.

Semple, dark haired, slight and hook-nosed, had a mobile and generous mouth that was usually spread open in a wide crack for ribald and noisy cockney commentary. Third in the hierarchy, he was completely normal, worked office hours like his two superiors, Howard and Raggle, and advised the whole Block on horses, wages and financial matters. As O'Leary had half an ear gone, so Semple had lost the ring finger of his right hand. Both items had been lost when they were young men and less cunning in rough houses with violent patients. The ear had been bitten off quite cleanly. The finger had been so badly chewed and poisoned that amputation had been necessary. Both men came to nursing during The Depression.

Sandy Wilson, Whale and Big Wilson – a big, manic Scot – were also driven to nursing during The Depression. It was said Howard himself was tramping the roads at the same time until he received his call to nursing. His moves always had a deal of foxiness about them and he advanced in the profession. His wife was the night sister in the Geriatric Block and did some of the rounds to Y Block at night. Their days off were reputed not to coincide. Some had it that they had not actually met since their wedding. Plausibility was lent to the story because she had grown very redfaced and hard. She was twice Howard's height. Had he seen her recently in or out of her deep navy blue uniform he would surely have been frightened away. Whatever the truth, he certainly always travelled alone because his auto-cycle was not designed to carry a passenger. It would have been hard work for him to do so since an innate caution with regard to money rarely allowed him to put petrol in it. It was thus always pedalled into the yard of a morning. Some said (there will always be lots of some-sayers about those in charge) this was so that he could sneak in very early and quietly of a morning and find out what was afoot. That is an unkind and unlikely story. He knew that most nursing feet were up on the beds being rested at that time of day.

***

The staff finished their lunches and dispersed to the wards with cups of tea. Billie was getting made up ready to go out; that is, picking and scraping out the blackheads around his nose.

'Is he well looked after?' he asked Raggle.

'Who, and what do you mean?'

'Why, the Indian of course!' Has he had his you know what?'

'For God's sake, Billie, why don't you say? Has he had his phenobarbs, you mean? Why don't you say outright?'

'What, in front of the man?' asked Billie 'you must be mad?'

'You're unwell Billie.'

Billie didn't mind that in the least. Any suggestion of a female condition pleased him immensely in fact.

He was tucked neatly into a blue mackintosh and had the Indian patient's papers and clothes in a pale grey cloth bag on a string, preparatory to his deliverance to Cane Hill Hospital.

'You always get the cushy runs Billie,' someone said.

'Well, see Semple if you don't like it. He organised the trips today. Anyway it might not be quite so easy. That Indian can be quite a handful I can tell you.'

'Just because you tried to get blood out of his funny bone last week,' Raggle said. 'Anyone would howl at that.'

'Hope there's a nice driver on today,' mused Billy. 'It was a miserable git last time. Never said a word the whole way back.' Billie had a knack of changing the subject if he could not win.

'Come on, here's the ambulance; off you go,' said Raggle, 'and you can knock off now Mr Lynch.'

That was very decent of him. I had been sitting in a high wooden armchair just inside the ward by the admission bed, fervently but unsuccessfully praying that future shifts would not appear as long as this. All was quiet, and the early shift had been moving off bit by bit. They could do that if they did not take a lunch hour, which they all did – but took it on the premises.

I made upstairs for the linen cupboard and swopped the white coat for the blue jacket. Key handed in, 'Who'll let me out, please?' O'Leary let me out. Odd to be away in the middle of the afternoon. Had the dust not been settled by a splatter of rain, my arse, as they say, would not have been seen for it as I ran home.

Home was a very empty room. And dark brown.

CHAPTER 3: The Sadness of Morning

Mornings were to be my most frequent duty shift for some time as autumn turned to winter.

Morning in East Dulwich: a weakening sun squeezed by grey clouds against grey roofs; damp, never blooming laurel shrubs against the high spiked courtyard walls dripping soot-laden drops slowly onto the grey macadam; city noises far away where traffic hissed and rumbled on roads that ran purposely from living place to living place and work. But the road between the plane trees up to St Francis's is quiet. St Francis's is enveloped in its own seeming to be perpetual grey morning. A few clanks can be heard from distant kitchens embedded in the bowels of the hospital. The stench of dirty laundry wafts through the corridors that link Y Block with its ugly mother building, and the stench is occasionally wheeled about in wicker baskets by small men clothed in vast green gowns. But for the rest, the hospital is clad in a stillness that would not disgrace a cemetery.

Morning here epitomised the agony of St Francis's. The whole hospital appeared to be waiting in a perpetual dawn as a factory waits for a wet bank holiday to be over. But St Francis's waited in vain. For all the outside observer could tell, there was life there – bedridden, decaying life for the most part – and there were a few vague figures moving slowly from block to block concerned with their lives. Yet nothing appeared to happen. The expressionless red brick front of Y Block discouraged enquiry within. Its meagre damp and dripping laurels in the courtyard symbolised the sadness that was morning at St Francis's.

The sadness of the Psychiatric Observation Unit had many faces, each giving an impression of gloom that was hard to isolate and impossible to ignore. Whichever way one turned, one of the faces of sadness was apparent and, merging with a neighbouring sadness, oppressed the eye and damped the heart.

Y Block itself was always locked, and none of its sash windows to the outside world opened more than a hand's breadth. Wire reinforced glass throughout added to the security within, a security made claustrophobic and darkly private by the thick layer of yellow paint that blinded the lower three panes of every window. Those within the locked doors could neither see out nor be seen, unless they stood at the front door. Here, only staff members were allowed, and any patient wandering or waiting near the door was moved on to the artificially lit wards within, where the smells of urine, soap and rubber were undiluted by vagrant draughts from the outer world.

To this box of heavy smells and misery an unchosen multitude had temporary admission as patients. They brought their own several brands of sadness, isolation and unreality, surrendering with resignation or violence their attachment to outside normality. Once across the threshold they became "them", for the staff wore uniforms to protect their identity and developed an attitude or distinguishing characteristic to protect their sanity.

Each long-serving member of the staff had acquired some habit to separate him from the patients and the other staff. Key, uniform and liberty to come and go at will were not enough to preserve the self, though they sufficed as insignia of sanity for the outside world.

Howard, the Chief, the Father, carried more keys on his bunch than anyone else. He had his own keys to the Block, the office in the Block, the cabinet where the record files were kept, the drugs cupboard, the icebox where the tea, coffee and bread knife were kept, the petty cash box, and the central drawer of the desk in the Admission Ward where nothing in particular was kept. Keys, the rattling of them and irregular darting movements to confirm their appropriateness for a particular lock, were his professional preoccupation. If all was locked and he knew all was locked then things were right and he was happy in his job. Time then to worry about his skin and to daub gentian violet over the backs of hands where the skin was already stained and cracked.

Semple's escape and individuality was intellectual. That was the duty rota which he completed in final detail -although the first draft was made out in precise longhand for months in advance. It was a complicated chart showing opposite the names of the nursing staff their times on and off, overtime worked, holiday due or pay due in lieu of holiday. Semple was happy for staff to ask for changes in their duty times for he could justifiably spend another hour or two at the desk. It was obvious that Semple would have preferred to spend his life as a racecourse organiser or superbookmaker. He juggled with the figures for time on and off duty as happily as he did the odds on and against horses at every race meeting reported in the newspapers. It was no easy task to satisfy the reluctance of the rest of the staff to come to work, yet Semple worked marvels manipulating the rota so that they came to work when they were least disinclined to. Nor was he absent when a morning rough-andtumble developed. True horse lover that he was, he would climb on to the back of the patient as soon as he was brought to bed, slide a towel under the patient's face where his teeth could grip it and gently jockey the patient until he was stationary. Never did Semple do this unkindly, and never without realisation of what he was doing. It was merely that Semple would have been much happier if all the patients had been valuable horses and the staff their valued grooms.

Other staff mannerisms were less endearing. Dobey of the untimely bowels was so long about his business in the upstairs private lavatory that he was open to easily proved charges of idleness. Whale was the only staff nurse who lived in at the nurses' quarters and permanently had a key to Y Block. He did not need it, but having acquired the custom of having it on the pretext of always being available to help out in an emergency, he rejoiced and simpered in the extra dignity it gave him. He could and did waggle his way in and out of Ward II's side door more frequently than necessary, just to show that he, Whale, had a key of his own and was therefore saner than all the rest.

Big Wilson had his own mug for tea.

Some obsession gives security. Keys, rotas, bowel habits, a special, very large mug for morning tea, all of them provided tracks along which the particular nurse could put his mind. Once his mind was on this track it became easy to ignore the patients; it became easy even for the more enquiring mind to cease asking questions about the charges. For there were no answers to be gained from them. They were by their existence a threat to the sanity of the staff. Better to tend them to the limit of your capacity for tenderness but shunt your mind off on tracks of its own. Their patients' tracks were twisted, the direction uncertain and he who followed was in peril. The helplessness of the staff to understand the mysteries inside the skulls of these unfortunates while being committed to observing them and attending them, caused sadness. To be shut off from them and to shut oneself off from them is safety or else all weep senseless tears together.

Weeping would not help, nor any stray expression of emotion. Y Block was full of behaviour: the exaggerated behaviour of the patients was what brought them here. The staff observed behaviour: from unprovoked tears to unprovoked maniacal laughter; from rigid immobility of gaze and posture to wild and irrelevant violence against things and people. So the staff observed and indulged themselves in as little expression of emotion and as little behaviour as possible. Any antic was seen as a reflection of a patient's antic. And as each day was full of patients' antics their attendants had to be careful to choose for themselves antics which only staff could have. Keys, rotas, a special mug for morning tea, clockwork bowel relief in the staff lavatory were privileged, staff-only antics, sad only in their uselessness to the patients.

Time in Y Block was an odd and artificial standard. Shift succeeded shift succeeded shift. Season followed season marked more by the incidence of smog-affected lungs and the stifling power of the central heating than by the flutter of autumn leaves or the burst of green spring. Holiday times came round, duty hours changed, blood samples were drawn on some days, visitors came on others, patients were not escorted to their treatment hospitals on Sundays, and clean white coats for the staff were delivered on Fridays. Patients were admitted at all times. There was a never-ending supply of patients, some new to the Block, others creating the illusion of a lunatic cycle by their periodic admissions. There was nothing to look forward to in Y Block. However hard one worked, however industriously one observed or however quickly the duty doctor diagnosed and arranged the transfer of patients to their catchment area hospitals, the well of misery did not dry up. There was no prospect of treating let alone of curing the maladies brought to us for inspection. The most rigorous enquiry yielded no believable hope of understanding, preventing or remedying any of the diverse conditions of madness.

Hope was not abandoned in Y Block but sadly minimised. Ambition for the staff became a win on the pools; aspiration a good share of the frequent pots of tea; hope a quiet shift and an increase in the pitiful wages; happiness a short wait at the homeward bus stop.

Life in Y Block was a sequence without relevance; a catalogue of staff with small habits and voluntarily constricted personalities; a catalogue of patients each of whose odd identity was unsecured by any necessary position in time or space. The shroud of compassion that hung in the air was deliberately pierced by small routines; unimportant orders of events were imposed to give distraction that alone could relieve the density of frustration which lingered between violent scenes and threatened anarchy. There was no sensible future, and morning time in Y Block emphasised its absence.

CHAPTER 4: Early Shift

I lingered in the corridor running past the Block's side door, waiting for Whale to mince along from the far end which gave out onto a yard containing the boiler house and nurses' quarters.

'You're early this morning Nurse Lynch.'

I shrugged inside my navy blue serge uniform. The trousers twisted round and the collar slid up under my ears. Too much shrugging, I thought, and the trousers will drop off and the jacket part at the seams. Delicately, Whale parted his white coat and carefully withdrew His Key by its leather thong from his pocket. He squatted slowly in front of the keyhole and spied through it.

'All clear.' He hurriedly inserted and turned the key, beckoned me through and sidled closely after, the knuckles of his big hand guiding me in the small of my back.

'You have to be *so* careful,' he said. 'There may be one waiting to make a bolt for it.'

'Shouldn't think it needs a bolt; the double lock ought to be enough.'

'Oh! You're a schizy one, aren't you? I mean a patient, waiting to make a dash, funny boy.'

'Yes.' I would have had to be barmy or stone deaf not to know what he meant. Every time he went through that door he keyhole-spied first. Every time

53

he said to whoever was entering with him, 'You have to be <u>so</u> careful.'

Five minutes peace in the linen cupboard upstairs manipulating ivory buttons and their split ring fasteners into a white coat; then with clinical dignity downstairs to the Admission Ward.

'Help with the breakfast nurse. Have you got your key?'

'Yes. Yes thanks Mr Howard, and signed for it.'

In the Admission Ward breakfast was porridge, bread and marmalade and coffee. In Wards II and III, where the patients were ambulatory and ate at tables, sausage, stiff fried egg or glutinous scrambled egg were delivered – as was the porridge – in cans from the main hospital.

'Eight patients in here,' called Howard as I retreated to the kitchen pushing a trolley. Two women in green smocks dished out the food in the kitchen. Mrs Scott and Lucy were let in every morning to serve breakfast and to do the washing up. Mrs Scott supervised and was then let out. Lucy did the work and was chaperoned to the staff lavatory to scrub there; after which she was chaperoned to the ward lavatories, bathrooms and padded cells to disinfect, wipe and scrub as necessary. Chief and most regular chaperone was Corrigan, a bellicose, ruddy-faced and noisy Irish nurse. Lucy worshipped Corrigan. Her blue eyes gazed at him in admiration from under a straggling forelock of blond hair. Corrigan stood at the doorway of the tiny kitchen, guarding the women within.

'What you got in this morning then?' asked Mrs Scott, squeezing a dishcloth into the sink to douse her just disposed dog-end.

'Mostly alcoholics,' said Corrigan. It was not true, but he liked to stir up Mrs Scott.

'They're all the bleedin' same, mean! But thank Gawd my husband's not a bleedin' alcoholic. He's just a bleedin' idle waster, fonder of booze than anyfink else.'

'Now, now, don't be like that Mrs Scott. He's keeping you and feeding you and working for you isn't he, Mrs Scott?' Corrigan's eyes glinted with amusement as he baited her.

'Not bloody likely he isn't. What the bloody hell do you fink I come here for if he was workin'?' her voice rising in shrill response. Her steamed-up spectacles slid down her nose and she swivelled on her bandy legs to plonk a cardboard plate of porridge onto the trolley.

'I thought you came here to see me,' said Corrigan.

'Just your mark that is. Like me old man. Good for nuffing but lip and big 'eaded and a bastard.' '*Mr* Corrigan you shouldn't,' interposed Lucy. 'You shouldn't go on like that upsetting Mrs Scott. I'm surprised at you.' But her adoring eyes belied her and Corrigan was cackling and mutedly hooting with glee. He so far forgot himself as to begin pushing the trolley back to the Admission Ward himself instead of leaving it for me, as was his wont.

We fed the patients. Dobey buttered and spread at the trolley, for no knives at all were allowed in this ward. Corrigan delivered a plate with readymarmalade bread to each bedside locker. I took porridge and yellow plastic cups of coffee round. I sat on the edge of a bed to spoon-feed an old man who had in his senility become a permanent wanderer. In his second childhood he was beyond filial control. The police had collected him, half dressed, zigzagging and tottering amongst the traffic of Victoria Street.

'It's the bloddy Boers,' was the only particular he was able to give.

'Where do you live Dad?'

'It's the Boers, son. Get me away.'

They got him away to us. Saliva, hardened white, stuck the corners of his mouth together. His massive plate of upper teeth rattled on the spoon and then on the pottery spout of the feeder as he sucked and wheezed at the coffee. Brown, bony fingers creased and re-creased the fold of bed clothes at his chest. Dribble coursed through white stubble to swing elastically from his chin.

'There's a porridge and a coffee left here,' Dobey said, staring at the trolley with an expression of disbelief. 'Have they given us one too many?'

'No,' Howard called in reply as he darted to the lavatory door to check inside. 'Laxton spent the night in the pads. He can come out now and go to a side room.'

'Has he been making trouble?'

'No. He couldn't sleep. Kept talking and singing, wandered about and tried to make his bed up on the floor so Little Tom offered him the pads for a quiet night. He sometimes won't sleep even if you give him a whole bottle of dope.'

Howard muttered further comments about Little Tom giving all the dope to the senile patients so there was none left for Laxton, and streaked off to the padded cells. Howard peered through the observation lens, held back the spring bolts and motioned us to go in. Laxton grinned and allowed himself to be shepherded like an amiable black sheep in white nightshirt to a side room.

'Did you have a good night?' enquired Dobey.

'Ah did. But they was funny voices that was speakin' to me last night. Ah don't know what ah'm goin' to do about them.'

'Never mind. You settle down here in your new suite and we'll bring you breakfast.'

'But they're after me, man. They've got it in for me ah tell you.'

'They've got it in for all of us,' said Howard, sympathetically joining Laxton on his side of the conspiracy. Howard felt it best at all times to appear to share the patients' problems, then there was less likelihood of the patient acting against him.

'Yes man, you're right. But they got it specially in for me.'

Fortunately, Howard could not begin to persuade Laxton that Howard was the more persecuted because Semple came through to say that there was one on the way in.

'Who's bringing him in?'

'DAO Peter Marshall,' said Semple. 'Don't know any more than that 'cos the duty doctor took the call. He's already in the office so we won't have to ring over. Must be bloomin' keen coming in this time of the morning to look at the case notes.'

Howard grunted; issued instructions for breakfast things to be cleared away and darted round to make sure all locks were locked.

Dobey grinned his lazy gorilla grin and congratulated me and himself on the luck of Peter Marshall being the committing officer on this occasion. Marshall had been a nurse in this very unit. Thus, he knew all the routines and would never bring a patient in at meal times or at change of shift. He was well liked and his achievement of a superior position had not roused the envy of the staff. He was regarded as one of the Unit's own staff, an "outside man", extending its power beyond the gates. Marshall was regarded in a sense as some sort of purchasing officer, on free range in the madness market. If he brought us a good patient all were pleased. If he brought us a rowdy or violent patient he did so apologetically, assuring everybody that County Hall had decreed that only St Francis's was equal to the emergency.

Routine preparations made, we sat around waiting. Observation; that was the job. Little to observe at the moment, however. Seven patients rested in their green covered beds, their several heads turned or hung, or rigid or recumbent. Howard dragged screens around the admission bed.

Lucy appeared at the ward door, bucket in one hand, and disinfectant in the other.

'Where's Mr Corrigan?' she asked.

'Upstairs in the Rec,' I said.

'You can't do the downstairs lavs now,' said Howard. 'We've got one coming in.'

'I know I can't,' she replied. 'I always do the staff lav first anyway. I want Mr Corrigan to let me in to it.'

'He's upstairs,' said Howard. 'He always is when one is coming in.'

Lucy turned. Her legs were large yet quite well shaped up to the skirt of her green overall; but Lucy's backside was vast and, adding to the effect of being mostly backside, her pink dimpled elbows hung and wobbled in imitation like two infant posteriors below her rolled up sleeves. She was heard calling for Corrigan as she climbed the stairs.

An ambulance backed up to the front door. Semple let Marshall in with his patient, a short, thickset man of about fifty.

'I've brought Mr Leonard Spot,' said Marshall. 'He wants to come and have a rest for a bit.' That was to let us know that Mr Leonard Spot would give no trouble – that he had been persuaded that St Francis's could analyse his complaint and give him peace. Frail hope, yet the only method to lure Leonard Spot into our security. He stood motionless by the admission bed behind the screens.

'If you'll take your things off, the Doctor can have a look at you; then you shall have a bath,' promised Dobey.

No answer from Spot. He stood slowly turning his head to scrutinize the bed, the floor, the screens. He looked at us and we had a good look at him: small eyes, crew-cut hair, a lined but impassive face, expressionless gaze and clenched lips.

'Come on now, there's a good chap. Undress and hop into the bed.'

'There shouldn't be much trouble getting him to undress,' Marshall called from the desk where he was filling out documents. 'He seems to enjoy taking his clothes off.' Marshall turned to Howard sitting at the desk's centre, 'He's depressed.'

'Yes, I could see that. Where did you pick him up then?'

'From home. His wife called the doctor and the doctor called us. He's been taking his clothes off everywhere. According to Mrs Spot – who's not the brightest of God's creatures – he has not spoken more than a dozen words in the last six months. But he will undress. He works for Kennington Borough and she says two blokes on the gang have brought him home four or five times 'cos he's undressed at work.'

'What does he do for a living?' asked Howard. As if to answer, Leonard Spot – now having with massive deliberation completed his striptease – announced:

'I'm Piggy Spot, Dustman.'

'Jolly good,' I said, beckoning to the bed, 'now if you'll lie on the bed…'

'I'm Piggy Spot, Dustman.' He took a few leaden paces forward, every movement in the slowest possible motion, and declared his identity and occupation again outside the screen. He turned and directed a slow gaze at each object and person in turn, found no one to challenge his declaration and so permitted his white naked bulk to be steered to the bed.

Until after the ritual bath, patients awaiting examination lie on a blanket on the admission bed, with the loose edges of the blanket folded over them. Piggy Spot stretched out on the bed but disdained any covering at all. Dobey called out body markings which I recorded on a scrap of paper.

'Vaccination left shoulder; tattoo – anchor and serpent – back of right hand.'

'That's all?'

'That's all. You've got a lovely clean body haven't you, Mr Spot?'

Mr Spot showed no pleasure in this compliment. He showed everything else: the undulations of his greyhaired chest, the flaccid mound of his stomach. His ruddy face and brown hands. All appeared to belong to a man in blue denims, not to the white body facing us with such solidity now.

'Not an operation scar or anything,' said Dobey, checking conscientiously in unlikely places. 'Both testicles there, I suppose?' he added, parting Mr Spot's legs. No reply from Mr Spot. Clearly Mr Spot felt reply quite unnecessary. Was not his body exposed voluntarily and deliberately at any time and in any place just to prove to unbelievers that he, Piggy Spot, was in fact a complete Dustman?

Mr Spot remained passive through the medical examination. Yes, his heart was there back and front; tongue entire though not to be poked out more than moderately; lungs capable of standing up to more than a two-fingered tap; and that rubber wheel on a stick would need more expert manipulation to excite knee jerks or wrist flexion in a man as solid as Spot.

The rubber coils of the sphygmomanometer received sideways glances but it was endured while the dustman's blood pressure was checked. His eyelids offered no resistance when the doctor's thumb raised them to peer within with an ophthalmoscope. Mr Spot's solidity extended to every part of his anatomy. His expression indicated, if anything, that the doctor would find nothing behind his eyes or between his ears, view and poke as much as he would.

Mr Spot declined to answer questions about his health. Mr Spot did not incline to speak at all. The duty doctor indicated that he would like to talk to Mr Spot in the office. At length, the naked and static figure was persuaded to its feet; a nightshirt was stretched over Mr Spot's broad, thick shoulders, the sleeves flapping above his brown hands, the tails decorously covering that which he was so persistently anxious not to have covered. A red corduroy dressing gown and matching slippers completed Mr Spot's coverage. He was led off at funeral pace to the office. Dobey and I left to run the bath. The Admission Ward bathroom had to be unlocked and draw sheets obtained as towels. Dobey unlocked and went for the bath key, a heavy bent iron spanner, which, since it was a lethal weapon, was kept in the locked dispensary drug cupboard. Mixing water to the required temperature necessitated strong engineering work by the attendant.

Upstairs, on my way from the linen cupboard, I found Corrigan standing guard at the door to the staff lavatory. This was a narrow room on two levels. A washbasin stood just inside the door and, beyond that, six steps rose to a second door behind which was the 'throne'.

'Come here,' said Corrigan to me. 'There's a sight you won't often see in here.'

Expecting to see Semple arranging a bouquet of flowers for Matron or some similar improbability, I stepped past him and peered within. A pelmet of stretched skirt, knickers and two pedunculated backs of thigh were all I saw as Lucy bent over to scrub the steps.

'There's a lovely sight,' said Corrigan hee-heeing with delight. 'A lovelier backside you couldn't hope to see; and you never will see in here.'

'There's a lot of it, certainly,' I admitted quietly.

'It's marvellous,' Corrigan glowed and giggled. 'You're our only bit of sex in here, aren't you darling Lucy? We don't have any other real women in here,

63

which is why they're all mad,' he added by way of instruction for me.

'You been lookin' up my skirt,' said Lucy, and turned her large blue eyes in admiration upon him; 'I heard you laughing. You dirty old nurse.'

Corrigan shook with happiness and clutched his belly to prevent it rolling out of control.

I clattered downstairs. The water was ready for Mr Spot. Dobey and I sat on the edge of the bath to await our patient.

'Lucy worked here long?' I asked.

'Quite a time. About six years I think; since she had her nipper.'

'Oh, I didn't know she was married.'

'She's not. That's why Corrigan got her the job just after the baby was born. He helped her find lodgings in Peckham too.'

'That was decent of Corrigan.'

'Yes I suppose so. He *is* the father of her little girl though.' Dobey paused for that to sink in. 'Don't say I said so. Corrigan doesn't think anyone knows, but Lucy said so. Corrigan doesn't even think she knows. But though she is simple, she's not daft, if you know what I mean.'

I was not sure if I did know what he meant, so I went off to see if Mr Spot had finished with the doctor yet, or vice versa.

Low urgent mumblings came from the inside of the office; questions asked in cultured tones and answered by uncultured silence. Eventually, the door opened and Mr Spot was shown out. He was stark naked.

'I'm Piggy Spot. Dustman.'

'So you said', muttered the doctor wearily, and passed me shirt, gown and slippers from the floor whither they had been abandoned.

Having finished his matinée strip, Mr Spot had nothing else to say.

CHAPTER 5: Straight-Jackets, Curtains, Other Matters and Patients

Time dragged or jerked on through the smog mornings of winter. Events and shifts blurred together like a host of dark slides projected by some stuttering magic lantern. It was easier for me now merely to observe and not to *feel* all the time. A thin hard protective veneer had crystallised from the salt tears of sympathy. This protection was not permanent, nor very durable, but it served to prevent the mind being obsessed exclusively by the conditions of the patients.

The job itself could not occupy a mind. The most intellectually strenuous exercise was stocktaking: a task which was never correctly completed. Practically every week, typewritten lists of equipment came over from Mr Webb and his adoring secretary, requiring confirmatory counts and checking against the contents of Y Block's linen cupboard and sluice room.

Bed sheets presented no problems. Semple kept a comprehensive laundry book, in pencil, and sheets not accounted for were entered as "dirty linen gone to laundry" when the need arose. That is where they usually were. Rubber sheets equipping every bed, and two spares only, made their computation easy. The draw-sheets covering them were used for such a variety of applications – from table cloths to bath towels to floor cloths – that the "remainder gone to laundry" technique had to be employed. But Y Block disgraced itself by being listed as short of one straight jacket at irregular intervals. This clearly was a sinister omission on Mr Webb's stock records. It was responsible it seemed for most of his stock checks. Underlined and sometimes typed in red at the end of each linen list was: "Straight-jackets, canvas x 6.

Y Block had only ever had five. Checker nurses with a misguided sense of honesty recorded the five only on Mr Webb's list – a brazen thing to do. Checker nurses who believed in seeing things as authority meant them to be seen, or who disliked idiot enquiries, recorded the expected six straight jackets.

As a result, some weeks Mr Webb was satisfied and all his fears allayed. Other weeks, Mr Webb (and perhaps his adoring secretary) were thrown into tremors of alarm. A straight-jacket, canvas, one of six, is missing from the Psychiatric Observation Unit. Was it worn out with cruel over use? Could it be that a patient had been sent to another hospital wearing it, or worse still sent home in it? Had a member of staff smuggled it out to use in equipping a private madhouse he ran as a hobby? Was it even now at large, awaiting use against some private citizen who might unwittingly try it on for size? Judging by his earnest phone calls to the Block, and his disinclination to believe explanations for its non-existence, Mr Webb's imaginings may have been terrible. They would perhaps have been deserved had he ever seen the straight-jackets.

All five of them were folded and piled upon the floor in the linen room. Here they gathered dust, and footprints, as their pile provided a comfortable step to reach white coats on the top shelf. Thick grey quilted canvas formed the substance of each jacket. The sleeves were long tubes of canvas, much longer than any arms, and ended in purse strings which gathered the canvas together. More string gathered together the back, the whole being designed in such a way that once the patients' arms were inside, a few knots behind immobilised him completely between head and legs. These fearsome restrictors were, however, almost entirely useless. None would fit any but the most skeletal and frail in physique. Their tailor must have known their purpose and thought that the only violent patients were children. Or perhaps, for they were very well sewn, he had delivered them as display models, and expected real patients who needed them to be sent to him for a fitting.

Mr Webb's fears should have been allayed. The jackets were used only in one event – that of a fragileboned and shrivelled old man who needed protection in his dementia. Though not entirely the most comfortable type of bed jacket for sleeping in, the "straights" had advantages. With the strings at the back loosely tied, a flat expanse of quilted canvas protected the old man's chest. Porridge, tea and marmalade were more easily wiped from this than from his wrinkled skin. His arms flailing slowly while he slept received no bruises from the bedhead or locker. The aimless swipe at a nurse when he awoke was cushioned too by the quilted sleeves, and his wandering, tearing fingers were made harmless by the cull-de-sac sleeves.

Even had the straight-jackets fitted, younger, lustier men were better confined in the padded cells until sedation was effective. There were no "straight trousers" and consequently no other protection of or from stout legs, kicking with an accuracy belying their owners' complete disorientation.

Count the stock. Linen checked, descend to the sluice room and check the hardware: sputum mugs – one dozen assorted shapes and materials; kidney bowls and hand basins – two of each, all enamel; bedpans – three stainless steel, two enamel; bed bottles – six, all of thick rubber. The latter were shaped like a wellington boot to fit a rabbit, with a broad flat-soled container at the end of a long upangled leg piece. They were designed to ensure accurate and splash-free urination, which they did provided it was limited. Unfortunately, the bladder capacity of our patients was frequently greater than the designers had allowed for. The sluice room reeks - of urine and faecal matter from the soiled laundry stagnating in two galvanised dustbins; of carbolic soap from Lucy's bucket and brush in the sink. Never were three smells so incapable of drowning one another. Each held its power in an individual key. No one ever forgot to close the sluice room door.

Count the stock and observe.

Three days to Christmas the calendar says, but nothing here gives any indication of it. The proportion of homeless people we have as "guests", and the number of bronchial old men wheezing and whining their time away in pulmonary and cerebral congestion prove winter has taken up residence in London. No jolly cards, no decorations are found here. No pleasant chat of presents bought or expected livens the wards; except that of Lucy and Billie. Lucy has told the early shift and Corrigan that she is knitting him something simple. It is a muck-brown scarf long enough to protect more than his overworked throat from the cold. If its length is an indication of her love, then she does indeed love him long, and well below that centre of virility which rumour insists provided the other love of her life – her little girl. She loves Corrigan to half way down his bulbous calves in fact. Billie has no one on whom to express his love. So Billie has bought himself some curtains for his new flat. Recently rehoused on the penultimate floor of a tower block at the Elephant and Castle, Billie has made sure his flat will be distinguishable by its curtained windows – from London Airport at least. Before choosing the material, Billie brought samples of a selected range for the late shift to inspect. The gaggle of design talent wolfing back lunch in the kitchen allowed Billie to persuade himself against a green velvet.

'It's rather *demure* though isn't it?' asked Billie of ears forced tightly shut by the pressure of food in their owners' mouths. 'But I would have to put liners in them you see, and I can't get all that sewing done by *next* Christmas, let alone this.'

'What's "liners" then Billie?' Corrigan asked through his potato. 'I thought them was underpants. Ha! Ha! You're not going to hang your underwear up at the window? Don't want Peeping Toms looking through your lingerie do you?' Corrigan looked round for approval of his wit, but found none as Lucy had gone.

'Oh, you're just ignorant and *coarse*,' said Billie. 'Don't know why I talk to you.' He made a little "moue" and extracted a sample of printed fabric from his pocket. Less than handkerchief size, it contained part of what might have been an enormous black comma. A white area ran adjacent to this, hotly pursued by some inches of a clearly massive whorl of orange, which gave way at the sample's edge to the beginnings of great things in green.

'There's a sort of cerise comes into it too. And the pattern is absolutely, oh . . .' Billie waved his hands in extravagant arcs and twists and billows, '. . . well, you couldn't describe it really.'

Because of its defiance of description, and because the beauties not revealed on his meagre sample lent themselves to even more creative imaginings, Billie plumped for curtains of this fabric. With unusual decision he trotted away to request use of the phone – 'shall only be two ticks Father, but I must order it now before it's gone' – and lay plans for what hems, pleats and pelmets he might use. Billie's concern about the chosen material being already sold was, alas, unfounded. His progress with the curtains occupied all his conversation while he worked late shifts and sewed in the morning shifts, and was only slightly less constant a subject after he had brought a curtain in on night shifts to finish it. That was well past Christmas.

Observe. The Block's trappings of Christmas are those of any winter morning. O'Leary has started the day in the way he favours most, with violent physical exercise. His white coat abandoned, blue uniform waistcoat unbuttoned, sleeves rolled up and necktie wildly askew, he is doing the floor in Ward II. All other staff supervised patients who did the floors. O'Leary preferred the exercise for himself, scorning the patience he felt was required to guide others to do a task he enjoyed. By his zeal, by his demoniacal pursuit of every blemish or dull patch on the parquet floor he might have been mistaken for one of the patients, except that he wore a tie and a thick leather belt and braces and had a key. These four items of dress were "staff only", being regarded as too easily adaptable for assault or self-strangulation or escape. Open necks were no hardship for patients in the heat of Y Block, but trousers requiring a permanent grip of one hand to stay up were a constant irritation to those not stout enough, or possessed of other methods natural or tailor-made, to prevent trouser collapse.

O'Leary called for two alcoholic patients from the Recreation Ward. They were invited to take off their jackets and then, equipped with broom, dustpan, a gallon tin of yellow sticky paste and a Squeegee, O'Leary locked them and himself into Ward II. Patient one swept while patient two moved beds and O'Leary fiddled with the wireless mounted high on a wall to get the loudest possible output of "Family Favourites", "Morning Service", "Weather Forecast" or "The Week in Westminster". Frequently, one of the young nurses had previously turned a knob to get some rock 'n' roll – Presley and Chubby Checker – or even Doris Day. The programme did not matter so long as reception was loud. As soon as it was as loud as frenzied manipulation of all knobs could make it, O'Leary climbed down from his chair and was ready to begin.

Patient one was the "paster" who threw daubs of the yellow goo in front of the rag-covered Squeegee. Patient two was the "pusher" who removed beds from the line of O'Leary's lightning-speed attacks. With the larch handle of the Squeegee gripped tightly in both hands, O'Leary hurled himself and implement violently over the floor, first crashing round the skirting board and pipes before working at enormous rate towards the centre of the ward. He indicated the direction in which a bed or locker should be moved firstly by banging into it followed by his loud commentary on what he had hit it and why. The second patient worked up a gigantic thirst during his removal efforts; the first was reduced almost to delirium by the anxiety of properly anticipating where he should next project a lump of paste. Progress round the room quickened in tempo until the roar of beds, the slap of paste and the slither of Squeegee and O'Leary's boots rose high above "Goodnight Irene" from the Weavers or "The Week in Westminster", which rather slowed the pace of the team. By this time, O'Leary did not so much handle the Squeegee as the Squeegee possessed him. Its savage lunges dragged O'Leary after it, arms stretched out of their sockets. Alternate flicks of paste landed on the floor; the rest were shoved equally between and under counterpanes and O'Leary's boots. Crescendo and climax were reached in the centre of the ward. Here, from an unfurnished area of parquet, rose a solitary iron pillar. The Squeegee led O'Leary into a merciless attack against it. Not until the sweat stuck O'Leary's forelock over his eyes did the performance end. Then, almost to the applause of his two aides, nodding with modest approval, he returned his equipment to the sluice room and began to solicit tea. Howard came through from Ward I, confirmed with O'Leary that he had finished, and switched off the wireless.

Peace descended on the locked, empty Ward II; its skating rink floor reflecting the dim light from the half-blind windows. O'Leary and alcoholics, now up in the Recreation Ward with cups of tea, stood silent and critical while Allan in dilatory fashion saw to it that any visible floor there was swept to the gentle strains of music from the BBC Third Programme. No activity here to gladden the heart. With O'Leary's mad performance below setting a standard of normality, any patients observing upstairs must have been cheered beyond measure. Up here there was a slow motion tension, a spiritual paralysis. The Recreation Ward was like a chess board filled with carved or cast players from different unrelated games. Each player remained fixed in his posture or made the move relevant to his game. Allan, like a judge from a dog show called in to direct a theatrical production of an Ibsen play, kept up a calm pretence of knowing what it was all about as he directed the players.

'I like the big ones sitting down,' he said, 'and the rest over there where I can see them.' He indicated the far right-hand side as he stood back to the door. There, three windows in a row allowed some light to filter in, and occasionally even formed squares of sunshine on the linoleum.

Little Tom came in, as was his wont, to demonstrate patients to me. Whenever his duty coincided with mine he sought me out to give me instruction; I was an ear into which he could pour his facts.

'Catatonic schizophrenia,' said Little Tom, poking his large schoolboy glasses back up his nose and talking quietly with Irish accents into the fountain pens and biros of his breast pocket.

'Yes,' I acknowledged, and looked towards a man of indeterminate age standing stock still by the television set. He held the handle of a broom in his right hand and looked intently nowhere, which for him at that time was directly ahead.

Little Tom approached him, gently guided him backwards until he stood against the wall, then he raised the patient's left hand until it hung above his head as if about to scratch. Little Tom stepped away to talk to me and the fountain pens again.

'You see. He'll stay like that for ages.'

'I know,' I said, 'but why? What is it?'

'Catatonic schizophrenia,' he repeated.

'Yes,' I replied. 'They used to call it Dementia Praecox.'

'Not a good name for it. It's not precocious senility.'

Little Tom, when not tending his five children or tampering with his oily motor cycle combination, was, he said confidentially, writing a book. He had not got very far, but it was going to be an index of mental diseases. Conditions, alphabetically arranged were to be described in detail from his own experience.

'You see,' he said, 'I've been a mental nurse for ten years. I've seen all sorts. I know what they're like, when they're like it and when you've got to be careful of them. How many psychiatrists know anything except what they've got from books?'

Although the question was rhetorical, I conceded that possibly very few psychiatrists had worked for any significant time with the insane. 'It's a lot to ask them to do after years of medical training,' I said. 'You want them to work as nurses or attendants in a unit such as this?' That question was not rhetorical but Little Tom took it as such.

'He hasn't moved yet,' he said, nodding towards the entranced figure against the wall. I wanted to know

76

more about Little Tom's attitude. I felt that there was some sense in what he said. Apprenticeship is not fashionable these days, but it would appear reasonable that any professional should spend some time actually serving at the bottom, without authority of any sort, before acting at an executive level. For the doctor in hospitals such as St Francis's encounters particular difficulties. In the Unit, he is often at least subconsciously resented by the nurses because he is not and never has been "a worker", "one of us". He has not, it is assumed, had intimate every-day contact with unsound minds. As treatments and understanding are still limited, the doctor's qualifications appear irrelevant. Little sign is given that detailed knowledge of a person's functioning in health or in sickness contributes to prevention, diagnosis or cure at the roots of mental illness. The authority implied in a medical qualification promises to the patient or his family hope of understanding, perhaps even remedy, and creates great disillusionment when that hope is dashed – when even the doctor does not know.

This clearly is no argument for unqualified practitioners of any sort to be involved with people with psychotic conditions. Yet if a man has the courage, interest or dedication to try and help those who are sick in their very beings, it would seem of practical value to reduce some parts of his scientific training. In its place there could be added firstly apprenticeship in the worker ranks of a psychiatric unit, and secondly supervised laboratory research into some of the biochemical and physical aspects of the functions of mind. Only massive study of what happens in the human organism will unlock sufficient of its puzzles.

There appears sometimes almost to be a fear, certainly a reluctance, to know positively how the mind ticks. It is as if discovery would remove a godly mystery, make the sacred familiar. Just as it is unlikely that all knowledge will be known, so it is unlikely that intricate and versatile mechanisms would, when understood, become contemptible. Reality is more marvellous than imagination. For those who feel that there are some borders of knowledge beyond which God-fearers must not go, their faith remains intact. The ultimate question mark – their religion – is not *what* but *why*. To relieve our catatonic fellow human being mute against the wall, we do not need to ask why it should be that he is deranged but what events and bodily processes brought him to this state. He is still a wonderful piece of work even if suffering some mechanical defect.

Little Tom strode again to the patient (called Knut), and arranging his hands on the broom rehearsed him in some forward steps and sweeping motions. With a gentle shove he then set the patient off on a straight course across the ward. Mr Knut went on like an automaton until he came up against the wall. No sign of him turning, so Little Tom turned him and Knut went through the same motions again in a track adjacent to the first. After two or three bouts, with the sweat breaking out on his brow, he was brought to a halt. Little Tom gave him a cup of tea and lifted his hand into the drinking position. Knut felt the wet on his lips and drew the liquid into himself. Drops of sweat trickled down his nose and into the tea. Little Tom sat him down, temporarily placing one of Knut's legs in a grotesque position to show me how long it hung there before slowly sinking to the floor. Knut's face remained impassive throughout. Motion for Knut, when it occurred, appeared to be decided upon by mechanisms far from his skull. Outside forces that achieved a new position in one of his limbs appeared then responsible for impelling the nerve signals to other parts of his body. Action was not derived from within the thinking patient but was inflicted on him. The thinking, living Knut seemed as remote from his own body as the moon from the seashore tides.

'Classical condition,' said Little Tom. 'I'll put it in my book.'

He did not mention his book after this. Perhaps the exigencies of an alphabetical layout prevented completion of the "Observers' Book of Lunatics". A for Alcoholism was an auspicious start but B presented immediate problems. A perversion or two suggested themselves: there were Bigamy and Bingo to be considered, but Little Tom had no time for the former and did not regard the latter as a category of mental illness. Catatonia solved, possibly even had been selected to solve the problem of section C. Depression and Drug Addiction looked after D so there was no need for Dementia Praecox. The more likely cause for the book not being completed was that Little Tom found more satisfaction in the planning than in the achievement. The categorisation of patients was a safety valve to Little Tom, as that sort of activity is to many of us. Incomprehensible things listed and documented lose some of their fright. Unpleasant facts put in order become acceptable as members of a whole system. It becomes possible to view the fact and worry about which category it should go into, rather than what caused its existence as an unpleasant fact. Not in Little Tom's activities, but at the pinnacles of psychiatric science, categorising is sometimes a boring vice analogous to the publishing of history books which contain nothing but dates.

Observing my patients' recreations, I drank my fourth cup of tea of the morning and gave part of my attention to the Daily Mirror of previous date. This was the Recreation Ward's only concession to journalism.

CHAPTER 6: Christmas Morning

Christmas Morning. The night shift exited at double the usual speed.

'Newcastle for the Cup. What's about then? Buy now, pay later. Ugh. God save the Queen. Ugh. There's no place like home.' The monotone roar of unrelated phrases filled St Francis's Psychiatric Observation Unit. The vocalist, Mr Morse admitted on Christmas Eve, was one of the regulars. He was hypomanic and his tones for all speech were those of a street newspaper vendor. Morse had jobs intermittently, but by quirks of fate they were never entirely suited to him. If he could have obtained permanent work – day and night as an extra in a football crowd – he would have earned his keep. His shout, projected from a roughened throat, long and skinny below a tiny head, was as shouts in crowds the world over. Sparse hair, on a parchment scalp, was kept permanently in a damp lick over his forehead. Pale blue eyes bulged tightly from their sockets. His head, as though not to fall behind his eyes on their outward course, jutted forward and strained continually on his neck.

'Stop me and buy one. A stitch in time. Newcastle for the Cup…' Morse was relentless. Raggle gave him a broom as soon as he stepped through the door.

'Go and sweep up, Morse; there's a good fellow.'

'What's about then? Don't call me. I'll call you. Six to three on "My Mother." Brass farthings. Who's going to win the Derby milk shake?' Morse began to sweep odd patches up and down the corridor and at random in Wards I and II. Where there was nothing to sweep up – and that was mostly where he chose to sweep – he took one of the tobacco tins that served as ashtrays on the Admission Ward desk and emptied it onto the floor. Then he was able to sweep out a dogend and pocket it.

Sweeping, together with shouting, was an activity in which Morse could be permanently engaged. There was no end to the mess he could make; a swept up pile arbitrarily divided, was pushed in separate lots to new positions in clean floor areas. He was O'Leary's nightmare. O'Leary ushered him into the downstairs washroom because there the floor was concrete and unsuitable for the Squeegee treatment that O'Leary gave to the parquet floors.

Morse's most recent occupation had, in fact, involved a great deal of sweeping and a tremendous harvesting of dog-ends. As a cleaner on Waterloo Station, his abundant small piles of litter occasioned no obvious remark. His vocal accompaniments did. Often heard above the clank and grind and puff of trains, his repeated clamour claimed an attention from the public which porters and ticket collectors rightly felt belonged to them. With a deportment and presence that spoke of knowledge, capability and determined strength, Morse was approached by passengers:

Y BLOCK

'Which platform for the 10.30?'

'A stitch in time. "My Mother" for the Derby. Stop me and buy one. Ugh.'

The ultimate grunt was not interrogatory. It replaced a laugh and helped to shift phlegm from his throat.

Morse received his cards after a fortnight and planned or at least appeared to be going in the general direction of a jolly Christmas with his married sister. However, his married sister's husband was mindful of his own normal, sensitive auditory apparatus. He was also mindful of the front room carpet which took unkindly to being swept. Therefore, he suggested, by direct reference to County Hall, that Mr Morse should go away for Christmas. And so Mr Morse came to us. We would not find out if he enjoyed it particularly, because he rarely gave any sign of disappointment or distress. Mr Morse always had a ready phrase unsuitable for any occasion, with which to reassure his listeners.

Christmas morning in Y Block was to be no tidy affair with patients tucked respectably in bed while the staff worked up seasonal spirit. Like other mornings, its sequences happened in varying disorder. But there were more happenings now and more behaviour; an effect exaggerated by minimum staff and maximum patients.

'The birds that bloom in the spring. Watchoo got I ain't got? Ugh.' Morse swept a diminishing pile of ash and matchsticks out of the washroom, along the corridor and into the Admission Ward.

'For God's sake take him upstairs,' Semple said to Allan, who stood by the ward admission bed airily appearing to be useful, but failing entirely. An admission case due, Semple wanted neither Morse nor Allan about. Allan was the particular handicap because he had access to more places where he would be in the way.

'Come along widge you then,' said Allan to Morse, following him upstairs, for Morse being that much quicker on the uptake was half way there before Allan had stirred himself to speak.

I was making beds. Since all bar one of them was occupied in Ward I, the task consisted now of straightening and folding the ends of the green counterpanes neatly at the feet.

'Are you making the beds Nurse Lynn?' Whale asked me. It was more of an instruction than a question.

'I am.'

'Because we've got one coming in you know. We can't all knock off because it's Christmas morning.' He minced across the ward to remove a sputum mug from the top of a locker. Whale, an Ulsterman, was six foot six inches tall; "queer as a clockwork orange" in Semple's phrase. He mixed his frustrated queerness with sadism. Billie hated him as much as Billie allowed himself to hate anyone. The occasional alcoholic patient's suggestion that Billie and Whale should get married was unlikely to be realised. Whale in any case preferred younger men, always hoping to have one in tow as a sort of apprentice-nurse-fiancé.

Y BLOCK

His early sibilant advances to me – 'Please Nurse Lynn, would you carry my needles for me and I'll show you how to do the bloods,' – disappointed him because I did nothing more than carry the needles and watch him. Upset because I did not crave his advice, offer to accompany him to lunch, request his strong hand upon a recalcitrant patient, he affected to despise me. So good was he at affectation that quite shortly he did. Then his great satisfaction was to find wet beds for me to change and faecal matter to wipe out of the padded cell.

'Would you stack the dirty laundry in the dustbins Nurse Lynch? *Someone* has put it all on the sluice room floor.'

'No,' Semple, busying himself with the admission tray, intervened, 'we've got one coming in. We need Nurse Lynch here.' Whale pursed his lips and moved away.

'Where's Wilson?' Semple asked.

'Having his other mugs of tea, I shouldn't wonder,' said Whale and glided out to sulk in the office.

Big Wilson was a Scot. Had he not worn a white coat his presence in Y Block would have been explained (as was Morse) by a short entry in the patients' register: "Hypomania". He was as big as Whale but he roared, while Whale simpered. His voice was loud and raucous, straining the Scottish accent until it broke up in a guttural tangle of "rrrs" and "ochs". He never spoke but shouted. He rarely acted, but shouted for someone else to act. Wilson's idleness was legendary; he "worked" morning shift as often as he could and never stayed beyond one o'clock. His large white tea mug was distinguished by its size and a great black W painted on the side. Wilson spent most of his time ordering the kitchen staff, Lucy and Mrs Scott, to fill his mug "wi gude strong tea, and make it hot and snappy." He was a bully but, to be fair, he did not enjoy cruelty for its own sake because that would interrupt his tea drinking. Physical force was a kind of repartee for him. If he was involved in an argument, or what others of lesser rank engaged in as discussion, he struck when his roaring had to be interrupted for a swig of tea. His mighty fist beat the table, his big foot stamped the floor and, should the irritator be within reach, he swung a back-hander to his ear. If it was a staff ear, he'd clip it in an almost half friendly fashion; if it was a patient's ear he'd bruise it, stinging against the skull. He took all patients and most staff as a personal affront. None in his view was ever sick or ever reasonable. All were bad, wicked, stupid and, at the best, play-actors. By what miscalculation on Semple's duty rota Big Wilson was on for Christmas morning, no one except Semple knew. Wilson was even more than usually furious.

The new admittance was a lonely Polish gentleman who was up in London from his industrial midlands town for the Christmas break; very quiet, but pursued by demons of which he would say nothing explicit. The police brought him in; an act of kindness since all attempts for him to find lodgings had failed. It was not that hotel receptionists and landladies minded giving him a room. But they were uncertain how to accommodate the various invisible people that Mr Skolka told them were following him everywhere.

Skolka endured his physical examination with dignity although he was a shade reluctant to part with his clothes until I assured him that he and they would be safe in here. The duty doctor, kindly and patient, lured him through the stages of a systematic check. The final stages Skolka almost seemed to enjoy. He stood naked behind the screens and with eyes shut succeeded in touching the tip of his nose with alternate fore-fingers. Outstretched hands were steady and he barely swayed on raising first one leg and then the other. Sensibly, as this procedure lasted some while, the doctor congratulated Skolka, promised to see him on Boxing Day and left, wishing us all a happy Christmas.

Big Wilson, who had been grunting at the desk while the examination stretched on, had gone with further very audible complaints to fetch another mug of tea. As he returned, I was folding the screens away and waiting to take Mr Skolka for a bath. He was still naked but concerned only to peer round the ward, quietly checking to see that no pursuers had followed him here, that there were no hidden threats in the room. Skolka's hand was on the knob of a side room door, wherein he would have found nothing more dreadful than a West Indian gentleman curled up on a mattress bed, when Wilson rushed up. Transferring his brimming mug to the left hand, Wilson clipped Skolka's ear with his knuckles and called to me:

'For Christ's sake, what bloody fool's letting this bloke wander around here? What d'ye think this is? A bloody hotel? Y'buggerrrs! Y'll have the devil to pay if this one gets the run of the place.'

'He's all right,' said Semple. 'He's just reassuring himself.'

'Well it's your bloody pigeon!' Wilson swigged his tea and left again, no doubt to have his mug refilled.

The damage was done. Mr Skolka had flinched but said nothing. He stood now with his back to us in front of the large wooden kitchen chair between the folded screens and the admission bed. I approached him.

'OK Mr Skolka? Your bath's ready.'

No answer. I led off to the bathroom hoping he would follow. He did not move. Semple went up to him.

'Come along Mr Skolka, the water will get cold.'

Semple laughed cheerily, 'Come on now. You don't want to miss your Christmas lunch do you?'

Skolka half turned, a hand dropping limply to an arm of the chair.

'That's right. You come on and have your bath and then you can have a nice lunch.' Skolka made half a slow step towards Semple and the bathroom. Semple closed in. The chair shot forward in Skolka's grip. The point of one leg smashed into Semple's left shin. He swore mightily and, giving himself barely half a second to wince, swept the chair out of Skolka's grasp. He embraced Skolka tightly and fell with him onto the bed. As I skidded across the ward, Semple's hug was broken and he was pushed away, landing in a monkey-like crouch on the floor. Together we leapt back onto Skolka, flicking him over onto his belly, his hands pinned to his shoulder blades. Whale padded in.

'I heard a noise. I've brought a towel.' He twisted it round the patient's wrists and began to tighten it until the cable-like strictures blanched the skin and bit into Skolka's wrist joints.

At this point, an alcoholic epileptic patient in a far bed began a seizure. The rattling and creaking of his bed and his convulsive writhing gave an idea to a slightly effeminate and grossly hysterical youth nearby. He leapt out of bed with a great cry and, landing on all fours, supplied a most rapid and serpentine exhibition of a fit.

'Oh for God's sake shut up and get back into bed,' Semple shouted at him. 'We'll deal with you in a minute.' At the promise of early attention the hysteric allowed his fit to subside. With tortuous limb-waving reduced to intermittent presentations and his yelps diminishing in volume, he allowed such order to his jerks that it seemed as though they, in the natural course of his affliction, had jerked him slowly back to bed. There he eyed the ward with expectancy and interest in case further symptoms and signs for his repertoire should be happily revealed.

'It's a good job the others are all drugged to the eyeballs,' said Whale, still twisting his towel, 'or we'd be in real trouble, I can tell you.'

This recalled Semple's attention to the body he was sitting on. He had the knees; I had the less comfortable feet beneath me. Semple saw that Whale now had one knee in the small of Skolka's back, and was gloating over the winces he was wringing out of him.

'OK! That'll do! We can manage now. Will you go and see to the EP (epileptic patient), Brian?' It was not often that Semple used a first name, but he realised that he had to offer Whale some sop if depriving him of an opportunity for sadism. Whale peeled himself away and went for drugs and a hypodermic.

'My old man said follow the van,' Morse announced his arrival. Allan was with him.

'Oh Jesus wept,' said Semple. Allan blinked at him like an incredulous owl with silver hair and a white coat.

'Well, he's disturbing the patients up there in the Rec. I tort he'd be better down here. You see I can't keep my eyes everywhere. His shouting about disturbs the others. I tink he should be down here.'

'You're not paid to bleedin' well "tink",' said Semple in pained crescendo, 'for Pete's sake!' He turned his gaze to Morse. 'Will you go back upstairs and not come down again 'til after lunch? Be a good chap and stay helping Nurse Allan all the time.'

'Stop me and buy one. Ugh. Newcastle for the Cup. What's about then…?' Morse shouted Allan back upstairs.

'Where's Wilson?' Semple called after Allan.

90

'Not upstairs,' came the peeved reply underneath the Morse shouts.

'Cor, bloomin' heck, what a staff. Why don't you take this up for a career?' Semple asked me.

'I don't think I've got the vocation.'

'Who *has* got the bleedin' vocation I'd like to know. Look what I'm lumbered with today.' We lifted Skolka, now withdrawn and quiet, into the last available bed. 'You'll have to have your bath tomorrow Mr Skolka,' Semple admonished him. 'You shouldn't have been a naughty boy; we're only trying to help you.' Semple wagged his forefinger at Skolka and we walked back to the desk.

'Just look what I'm lumbered with today,' Semple continued: 'There's bloody Wilson started it all. He only uses his right hand and his throat. He's either swiping somebody and swigging his tea with his left hand or bellowing like a castrated bull. Then there's Brian Whale. He'll work all right, but prefers it if it hurts somebody. Got to watch him else he'll turn some poor bugger into a colander one day when he's doing the bloods.' Semple was getting quite warmed up in his Christmas moan. Yet every statement was terminated with a laugh that proved his good temper. He was not very good himself at getting blood samples from vein to syringe. But he did not poke and jab the needle about for fun; he just could not see very clearly where to put it when working at close range with his spectacles on. 'As for Allan, he takes the cake for thickness. "I tink he should be down here",' he mimicked. 'He's not paid to think. If he was he'd get sweet FA in his wage packet. Cor crikey, I don't know.' Semple ran his three fingered hand through his hair and sloped out of the office.

'Get the Hysteric up,' he said as he left. 'He'll be better having something to do.'

'Fully clothed or just dressing gown and slippers?'

'Gown and slippers.'

I fished out the red corduroy gown and brown felt slippers.

'Here you are Barnaby. Pop these on and you can eat along the corridor in Ward II.'

He looked as I imagined Dicken's *Barnaby Rudge:* *t*hin face, half concealed by lank hair, his long bony frame and pigeon chest were a Dickensian caricature. Yet he was invested with a spasmodic theatrical vigour, and a suggestibility which enabled him to be a percipient understudy of those around him.

The Admission Ward was now quiet. Whale finished serving out the drugs and told me that lunch was ready and wasn't I going to get it on the trolley and serve out in here. Because we couldn't all have a holiday. And there wouldn't be any staff coming for a while because *some people* were having lunch at home. And he, Brian Whale, was not going to do *everything* on his own.

I trundled down to the kitchen to serve the sliced cold chicken and roast potato, the Christmas pudding and custard, all on cardboard plates, to Ward I; the same with more trimmings to Ward II where a clean white sheet was laid as a table cloth and the patients had already been shepherded down from the

Recreation Ward by Morse. On the appearance of the patients – in dirty hospital slippers and crumpled St Francis's trousers, - some were seen clutching dogends and bundles of newspaper which Morse had swept up and brought down with his broom.

Big Wilson was alone in the Admission Ward. Now all was peace. Whale counted drugs in the dispensarycum-washroom. Semple sorted documents in the office. Allan observed the progress of Christmas lunch in Ward II.

Here, as an alternative or extra to Christmas pudding, there was bright red jelly. One or two Asian gentlemen helped themselves to the pickles and gherkins with their cold chicken. Barnaby disdained such condiments for the first course. He saved them for the jelly. Brown onions and green gherkins adorned the red of his jelly. Then, with half a pot of yellow mustard pickle slapped on top, he admired the colours briefly, mixed and ate.

'By God, the lad eats with relish!' said a smiling Irish alcoholic opposite. 'Give the lad some more.'

Allan pootled through to the kitchen. More jelly, more condiments. The mixture as before. Proud and sweating, Barnaby polished off a second helping and enquired about a third. In view of the expense of the extras it was refused. Also, even Allan, had the glimmer of an idea that should Barnaby be sick, he might have to clean it up.

***

Howard came in at one o'clock to let Semple get away for lunch with his family. With the late shift not due in until three this day, Big Wilson fumed continually. Father left him to fume on his own in the Admission Ward. Wilson was in any case a Charge Nurse and should have been capable of running the whole shift.

I stood idly flicking through an old newspaper in the corridor. A luckless Irish boy, in appearance totally without muscle and labelled a paranoid schizophrenic, lay in the bed next to the desk. He had very little mind left at all it seemed. He spoke to Wilson.

'Don't you keep looking at me.'

'What's the matter then, eh?' Wilson rose and dug him in the ribs.

'Stop hitting me, you are hurting me.' The boy's voice began to rise in alarm.

'Be quiet, do,' and another punch on the boy's chest.

Screams of fright followed, and as Wilson stooped, roaring obedience into the boy's face, the boy's arms came up to protect himself. A thin twig of an elbow brushed Wilson's face.

'Och, yew'd go forr me would ye?' Wilson swung his knuckles into the boy's ear. In stupid panic, the boy almost returned the backhander given by Wilson. That was it. Wilson had the boy round the head and dragged him out of bed.

'To the padded cell with him. By God, the bugger went for me,' roared Wilson to the help which had now arrived. Howard vainly tried to get Wilson to go away but he would not. He must be in the forefront of trouble like this. He must be justified. The lad was dragged kicking and scratching and screaming to the padded cell. He let out with a bare foot at Wilson as he was pitched on to the rubber floor. Enraged, however harmless this barefooted gesture might be, Wilson brought his fist down on top of the boy's head. As the thin, crouching figure moved slightly, Wilson's fist did not make contact with the skull, but his forearm did. It snapped with a crack. I do hope the boy heard and knew what it was. Wilson howled as loudly as his victim had done, breaking the concert of his complaint only to boot the ribs of the supine youth. We practically lifted Wilson out of the cell.

Thus Big Wilson did not have to remain on duty for the whole shift. And he had six weeks holiday with one of his tea-drinking arms in plaster. We laughed like drains at every rumour of his discomfort. Father, who had not seen the entire incident, smoothed it over. Early in the New Year, when the boy's parents flew over from Dublin to collect him, the bruises we had so carefully washed this Christmas afternoon were fading. Howard's story twisted facts to give a believable balance to them so that anything the boy said could be put down to the delusion of his sickness. 'One of our staff was injured in an attack your poor son made,' Father told the parents. 'But, of course, it's a risk we take. Be on your guard when you take him home.'

Three o'clock brought release. My landlady Mrs Baron had her daughter and son-in-law closeted in her back parlour-bedroom for lunch.

'Come in,' she called, 'and have a drink.' Her ivory smile was already loosened by a glass or two. I yielded to the invitation. There was nowhere else to go. 'A merry Christmas' I said.

CHAPTER 7: Mrs Baron's Kingdom

Mrs Baron's kingdom was a large, dark downstairs room. French windows opened into a glass-roofed kitchen. If possible, less light penetrated into the brown recesses of this room than into mine. The daughter and son-in-law sat twiddling the maroon cut-glass stems of their goblets, anxious to get Mrs Baron back to the flat in Canning Town for tea.

'You'll all have a drink before we go?' Mrs Baron asked. 'There's only whisky left.' That was clearly an inducement to the son-in-law whose fingers and lips were still sticky from the port which had formed aperitif and lubricant to the turkey and plum pudding. Mrs Baron did not want to go without showing her daughter to me; nor did she want it to escape the sonin-law's notice that she extended a welcome to all sorts and conditions that may be found in a lodger.

'Mr Lynch works in the mad peoples' hospital over the way,' she explained, 'poor bleeders. It's a job I shouldn't like.' Her ivory smile spread itself again. That was twice since I had known her. The three empty bags of skin that formed her chins hung down like leather satchels. Each was concentric with the three rows of pearls that hung on her brown dress.

Daughter Joyce was a "professional person", Mrs Baron had said in her introductions. That meant, I was relieved to discover, that she worked in an office. She had the bulk and maturity of middle age to qualify her for other activities, but did not seem to have the drive or indiscriminate acceptance of people needed to be able to recruit women in a business venture for men.

'I suppose you get a lot of foreigners in there?'

'Oh, I don't know . . .'

'And they'll be the ones that give you most trouble too, I know.'

'Not particularly, no.'

'Some live near us,' said Joyce with decision, as though that in itself was conclusive damnation, 'don't them, Ronny?' Ronny so safely brought into the conversation agreed and left it again.

'I 'aven't anything against them,' Mrs Baron interjected with some splutter and mismanagement of her false teeth, 'but I couldn't use the lavatory after one.'

Whether that difficulty might have been a moral or a physical one I never found out. It was a last word as far as Mrs Baron was concerned. Already coats were being donned and Ronny was fiddling with his car keys. I withdrew with appropriate wishes to my room. There, I made a cup of coffee and gathered my parcels from home onto my lap in the wooden-armed un-easy chair. I put Christmas off as long as possible; warmed each leg before the gas fire; lit a pipe. And then unwrapped. Slippers from Paula. Food parcel from home. Welcome gifts, even though the slippers were brown. I would, I thought ungratefully, have preferred them in ritzy red leather. There was so much brown around this room, and the whole house in fact. Come to think of it, it was a pity Mrs Baron didn't have a few West Indian lodgers about the place. They would have satisfied her predilection for brown and they would have brought some gaiety to this drear place.

Mrs Baron was a dried up mixture of a woman, I mused. Aged and drooping, the widow of a bookmaker, she had seen better days. Nights she had probably seen more of still, until recently. Her prime together with her husband's income had been spent in the seedy, expensive nightclub world where the only criterion for admission was money. Her face was creased and stained with long continued cosmetic use; lips brown with nicotine. Now in crotchety widowhood, her solace was a nightly bottle. Not that she mourned her husband. He had gone on a trip to Australia – partly business she said – and had been killed in a car crash. A telegram told her this news, which she believed instantly. Perhaps she wanted to.

The other telegram that marked her life she did not believe. She tore it up and said "nonsense". It bore the news that her son was missing, presumed killed, over Germany. Everyone acted in the feeling of his death except her. Four years later he arrived home unheralded. Mrs Baron only told this story once to me. But the manner of telling left no doubt that it was true. And somehow she looked as though she had never been rewarded for those four years of faith. The son never having been dead, was not unusually glad to be alive. He left soon for the States and prospered there. She had no grand children to rock upon her knee. No second fruit to show for her labours.

Now and again she wrapped herself up in a brown coat with brown furs and slipped up to Victoria. There some jewellery was pawned; pearls and diamonds never to be reclaimed, never to be grieved. They had been stored against such rainy days as these. Gifts from her husband, they held no sentimental value because they had been expensive peace offerings after his even greater expenses with younger women.

Mrs Baron was dry, and hankered after the fat whisky days before the war. So, slowly she counted her nights away with the pearls that would buy the whisky, in the company solely of one silent budgerigar.

**

While Paula was on holiday, Mrs Baron was practically the only human contact I had off duty. She rarely stirred from her room until mid-day, and as my hours could be erratic, we met seldom. That was no great hardship for she enlivened the house as much as a brown ghost might have done. I missed Paula. Off duty hours were spent largely together. In the gay common-room of her university hostel, there was a happy, swirling skirted life remote from the Block: a balm to spirits jaded by the discord and unreality of St Francis's. But now I was alone. Friends away on national service; neighbours as anonymous as only city neighbours can be; social activities excluded by virtue of an erratic working life – I had arranged to fill these blank days into the new year by working the late shift.

This extended from lunch time to nine o'clock at night and eliminated the awkwardness of early rising. Although I had done some spells of late and night duties, most of the time Semple had kept my name down for mornings. It was, at the beginning, so he could keep an eye on me, and later because perhaps he felt I was not quite so idle as some of those who insisted on being put on the early shift. Theoretically, each nurse worked early, late, night – one week of each shift – and then back onto early duty again. That system, though beautifully easy to work out on paper, was so disruptive to any stable pattern of living that many staff rejected it.

Apart from filling the time, I found late shift more congenial because waking at six stretched my inventive powers to the extreme. The paper boy came too late to rouse me by a bang on the ground floor window of my room. Mrs Baron was no sharper than myself first thing in the morning. Alarm clocks, however resonantly placed in jugs or saucepans, evoked no response from me.

The technique evolved to get me out of bed on time was alas fallible, or at least not ultimately convenient. One-and-a-half pints of milk drunk (half-a-bottle was spilt on the bed) before retiring created an urgent need for relief by six in the morning. For some days I was up with the first buses. Then the scheme failed. Bladder muscles previously anchored firmly to the sleep centres of my brain shifted their hold to the source of dreams. The white sheets became the sought after stalls of a public lavatory and in imminent danger of wetting the bed monumentally I woke only three hours after I had gone to bed to relieve myself appropriately.

Late shift then had its advantages. 'You are emotionally disturbed, Lynch,' I told myself. 'You are not,' Good Sense being on my side replied, 'but you value sound sleep and there are limits to your bladder's extensibility and it too dangerous to use it as an alarm clock. Be warned. Be dry.

CHAPTER 8: Room for Recreation

The afternoon shift lacked the bustle of the morning. Beds were all made, floors mirror-clean; there was no work for those patients capable of work other than the laying of tea at four and supper at seven. As soon as lunch was over, the patients who were not still confined to the Admission Ward were sent upstairs to the Recreation Ward. By three o'clock, when morning staff had all gone, and when those patients due for transfer to a treatment hospital had been escorted away, St Francis was generally a quiet, sad terminus.

The passengers gathered in this waiting room. Some - usually those who had never been up here before, entered at a trot with heads held high in expectancy. Across the threshold they sagged slowly to postures of resignation. For those who were sufficiently perceptive to the surroundings it was like coming onto the stage in a theatre with one person in a white coat for an audience. Rehearsals were for ever about to begin. But each actor had the script for a different play, and no script was complete. Snatches of soliloquy are heard from a tall, lean man gazing into the grey outside. Another follows his stage direction to walk rapidly across the room; but he is brought up short; the rest of his part appears not to be written and he slumps into the chair that a depressed Welshman has just left. Others sit round the television set waiting for the tuning pattern to break into a programme.

Something will happen eventually, unless it is a Monday. Tuesday and Saturday are bath and shaving afternoons, Wednesday and Sunday visiting days. On Thursdays the Occupational Therapist pays a fleeting visit, accompanied for strength in female numbers by the Psychiatric Social Worker. At any time a Psychiatrist may wish to interview a patient in the tiny room off the upstairs corridor. But never on a Monday. Nothing of the outside world leaks in here on a Monday. Even spring, making fitful efforts outside to break through the grit of winter, wafts no more than the perennial sparrow-chirp in here.

***

Long Monday hours I sat, back to the wall, observing. Reading was frowned upon by officialdom, though the chance of ever becoming oblivious to the surroundings was remote.

Next to me a short, smart looking young man sat craning forward with elbows on knees and hands clasped tightly in front of him. Olive complexion, fine teeth and smooth dark hair combined to give him a handsome Mediterranean appearance.

'What do you do this job for, Nurse?'

'About six pounds-ten a week net,' I laughed.

'No, I mean why do you do it?' The young man (Carey by name, and in accent also as English, even as Cockney as Semple), nodded his head towards the pathetic figures sitting round the room. 'Don't it drive you mad?'

'It's a bit of a strain sometimes. But the job has to be done.' I rarely admitted to a patient that this was my National Service; for I felt that if there were small ways in which I could ease some confusion, or soothe with charity some minds in the day's work, it would be better if the patient felt that it followed from principles held by all nurses not just me. It was too easily seen that some of the attendants were not following a vocation; too easy to dismiss the action of one attendant because he was an oddity – doing the job because he had to, because if he did not they would have him in the army. Also, from time to time, there was abundant evidence that such a job could not properly be a vocation. The Whales and the Big Wilsons certainly could find no other job that would invest so much power in such unintelligent persons. Yet even that was partly the fault of the system. Pay, as with any profession that may be supposed to be partly an exercise of love, is meagre. As a consequence, selection is unselective. Those who apply have only to show no obvious impediment to their joining, and they are welcomed into the service. One supposes, or hopes, that eventually, when more is known about the causes of mental illness, the system will change to meet the conditions. Change will then work down from the top. Yet meanwhile, even within the rigidity of a state controlled enterprise, it should be possible to have a few more men and women, well paid, to work in units even such as this. Without white coats to separate them into "them", and with progressive opportunities to experiment by leading patients in heavy manual labour, in physical training, sport, art, even in light study, nothing would be lost in the way of observation. There might even then be a gang of "lifesavers" ready to greet advances in knowledge half way when they come. If not, anything that threatens the kingdom of the mental nurse will be fought tooth and nail and tongue and book of union rules. It is understandable that that should be so. The people working here get more kicks than kindness from those outside. They want to hang on to whatever vestige of security and tradition there is in a disturbing occupation. Those few to whom power is important would perhaps gladly accept a larger pay packet instead, as a token of their social worth. Those who nurse in the hope of helping would like something to do. They would like some positive activity to offer their patients who are bound up in the business of their own brains.

The stigma attached to mental maladies began to go when the term "nervous breakdown" was invented. "My husband has been working too hard; he's had a breakdown and gone into hospital" covered all those cases from the worn out, sleepless, worrying, undernourished, under-cherished people whose confidence and spirit were sapped, to the previously dismissed "mad as a March hare". Then, in the guise of enlightenment, yet seeming to come from a compulsion for atonement, the wicked, the idle, the social misfits and the plain bloody minded were given or sought the excuse of mental sickness and nervous breakdown. So, full circle, the stigma is back. It is now not so good to admit to a nervous breakdown because that covers a few of not understood ailments and a multitude of sins.

The mental nurse is the sorter and guardian of the nation's unsolved sicknesses. He is a target for occasional violence inside, and abuse from the outside. He is subject to endless assault on his senses and reason, unrelieved by feelings of achievement or the consolation of respect. He has little help from authority; even the most optimistic or gullible nurse, male or female, fails to hope that any government will invest energy, enterprise or money to match the size of the problem. No wonder Mr Carey asked, 'What

do you do this job for?'

***

Cartoons for the children on the television. Mr Carey half-way through the ninth game of table tennis with the Welsh gentleman. Carey served with energy and some skill. The Welshman stood solid, stiffnecked and almost immobile opposite him. For the game to rise anywhere near the heights even of pingpong, Carey had to make certain that his serve hit the bat of his opponent or else the ball did not come back to him. Winning, Carey came and sat down again.

'What do you do for a job, Mr Carey?'

'Me? I don't have a job at the minute. I live with me old woman, don't I?' He grinned as though life with mother was better than any other sort of job he had heard of.

'Well, you seem very happy. What brought you to us?'

'The police brought me in because I had a nervous breakdown.' He eyed me askance to see if that information would go down without difficulty.

'Oh, I see. What happened then?'

'I was unconscious in the park. I'd been on Benzedrine. Had the bottle in my hand. They took me to the general hospital first.'

'Trying to do yourself in were you?'

'No, me an' me mates take that, you see, to keep us awake. We've got a sort of Society. Meet at night and that. It's a religion really.' He grinned. He had quite a likeable earnestness about him.

'You've got to have something to believe in, haven't you Nurse?'

'Yes.'

'Now, me mother, she's an old pro and you can't believe in her. And then all these churches and that, they don't do anything.'

'So what does your Society believe in?'

'Evil.'

'What the hell do you mean, "Evil"?' That the conversation had continued so long on a rational plane was surprise enough in this place. That it had taken such a sincere and sudden turn to lunacy was a double shock. But Carey had not delivered his creed with intent to shock. He was leaning forward earnestly now, intent to tell me more, not assessing my reaction from a distance.

'Evil, destruction, blood. We cut our wrists and write our names in blood. We agree to be as evil as we can; to worship the Devil. You see, there must be some power in the world. You can't have a world without anything to believe in.'

'But what about a power for good? What about beauty, creation?'

'They don't *do* anything!'

'Supposing I told you I work here because I believe in life, and in doing something rather than destroying.'

'It won't do you no good. You won't enjoy it. No one will take any notice of you.'

'Is that what you want then, notice taken of you? 'Cos it won't be for long if you go bunging back the Benzedrine.'

'No. But it's a great feeling and you are awake longer to do things. Evil things.'

I stood up to busy myself about a cup of tea. Carey followed me, heaping description of evil upon evil. Robbery with as much violence as possible. Wrecking cinemas and dance halls. Beating up believers. The ultimate kick of shedding a little of his own blood and gobbling down Benzedrine in nocturnal rituals.

Later, when all patients were stowed away in bed and the lights were out, Carey – assigned to sleep in the Admission Ward by the wise precaution of

Raggle – had obtained the ear of a neighbour and was still pouring forth news of his religion.

I checked in the patients' register. The column for provisional diagnosis gave Drug Addict/Psychopath. Which caused what, I asked myself, and where on earth could we send him? He needed training as well as treatment. Age: 26. I had thought him about 17. Where and what would be the future of Carey?

CHAPTER 9: Bath Day

A Saturday afternoon; one of the two bath days that marked the course of the week. In theory, only those patients due to go out on a Monday or a Tuesday morning had to be bathed on a Saturday, but I preferred to give baths to as many as were in the Recreation Ward as possible. It kept me occupied and, in general, appeared to have a therapeutic effect on the patients. Distracted minds became absorbed in their toilet; the sad were momentarily cheered as they contemplated steam rising in wreaths around the light bulb; shattered minds became intent and integrated while they studied between their toes. Few are disinterested in their own bodies so that their personalities while bathing were for a while as normal as those people having their Saturday baths anywhere.

O'Leary, sharing the shift with me, was a keen scrubber. He had quite positive ideas on the use of the long-handled brush and liked to give each patient a good going over. He certainly was speedy and very thorough without hurting the naked body reddening under his systematic ministrations. The brunt of his vigour was borne by the deep water that filled the vast old-fashioned upstairs bath. Within ten minutes and four patients of O'Leary starting, the bathroom would be awash and the duckboards likely to float out of the door. Feeling some of the therapeutic value of the bath for the patients, to be lost by such rigorous activity, I, as always, volunteered to look after the bathroom while O'Leary kept his eye on the Recreation Ward and the electric shavers.

'Don't take the bloody thing to bits,' he called to a timid, well-spoken man having his turn at the electric shaver.

'It's broken,' he said.

'No, it's not. It's loose in the socket.' O'Leary bustled over and pushed the pins home. He muttered abuse against new-fangled gadgets in general and electric shavers in particular. This was a new acquisition, a gift from "The Friends of St Francis's" and welcomed by most of the staff as a blessed relief from some of the manual shaving that had to be done. It brought to an end the long sessions before bathing when each patient was seated in the washroom while I, or another nurse   lathered and scraped. No safety razor ever left the hands of a nurse since the blades were easily secreted and became weapons for those at risk of suicide. Stubborn bristle in the wrinkled chin of an old man took ages to remove with a conventional razor. Acutely paranoid patients had often to be held down in the chair while the business was completed, and even then a nick or two produced enough blood to frighten others. But for the energetic O'Leary, the advent of the electric razor took away something glorious from his life. On morning shift he still could help the visiting barber with haircuts when they were prescribed. But since most of those were performed on staff, there was no great outlet for him there.

'Come on Johnny,' I said. I'll let you in to run the bath. You can give it a scrub if you like.'

'I've already done that,' said O'Leary.

'I'll do it again,' said Johnny, 'then I can have mine.'

Johnny, our regular high-grade mental defective had been brought in at lunchtime. On this occasion he had assumed monstrous inebriation which had vanished as soon as the duty doctor had written "Alcoholic/Psychopath with and/or with Diminished Responsibility" in the patients' register.

Johnny had his bath, then cleaned and filled it for the next. I hid the big iron tap-key under the bath and took my chair in to supervise the next volunteer. This was Mr Mullins, a mild but eccentric schizoid man – mainly showing distraction and severe neuroses. He was shattered when he was brought upstairs after his admission. There was no sureness about any part of him. Restless and pointless, his distractions allowed him no peace. He knew something was wrong but attributed it mainly to the world being slightly out of gear; which it was for him. I do not know if he ever got better but I know that, small consolation though it may have been, he found some peace on bath days. Whatever the reasons were, and Freudians could put a pretty unpleasant complexions on those, he tookgreat care with his toilet. Mullins was scrupulous. Congratulated afterwards, he was pleased and proud, and became for one moment a whole child instead of a shattered man. His pride would have had no expression had I bathed him rather than let him do it for himself. Good years are built out of small moments. It is a pity that those we offered came so late and were so small.

Johnny brought clean draw sheets in and took away a bundle of dirties. As he left, a fat, white-skinned and red-freckled man pushed his way into the bathroom. He was depressed; the liveliest thing about him was his name, "W Spark", printed in large awkward letters on sticking plaster stretched along the ear piece of his horn-rimmed spectacles. Blinking and slowly puffing in the bath, he gave each armpit long and rhythmic attention. Eyes screwed up, he groped for the soap; I passed it to him and as he took it into his left hand he let out a punch with his right. It caught me on the chest so that momentarily my balance was lost; feet slithered on the duck boards and my knee came up with a bang against the iron rim of the bath. Cursing, I leant in, grabbed his wrists and dragged him to his feet where he was in a less, and I, in a more secure position. I had a great urge to punch him hard in the midriff, to wind and hurt him as I was hurt. Not because I am a saint but because already Mr Spark had withdrawn into his inner gloom, I desisted. I remained standing while he dried and went back wordless to the Recreation Ward, then I told Raggle of Spark's temporary ignition.

'Yes, he does break out now and again,' said Raggle. 'There's no telling when or why. Lord knows what's cooking inside his skull. Watch it though. We don't want a rough and tumble with him. He's been in trouble with the police for unprovoked assault.'

'It's OK – O'Leary is up there with me. I don't think there was anything personal in the punch anyway. Perhaps he felt he'd been waiting too long for the soap.'

'He's going out on Monday.'

'Voluntary or certified?'

'Certified this time. He's been away, as a voluntary patient about half a dozen times before, had his shock treatment and insulin therapy. Won't go this time, so he was certified yesterday. That may be what has upset him if it's got through to him.'

"Certified". The word sounded like a death knell, an order of demolition on a sound but haunted house. Apart from Spark's own sadness was this implicit confession of failure on the part of knowledge; the waste of an efficient body because it's guiding mechanism was tangled up. Such contemplation was not conducive to good spirits, but was inevitable, particularly on bath days. So many of the bodies stretched out in the bath were fit and healthy. Physiques and complexions rarely gave the impression of belonging to athletic owners, but they did speak of sound constitutions. It seemed sometimes as though the patient was crying out for some disease to make him suffer, to give him some excuse for rest and withdrawal, but the body denied him this and the brain took on the burden.

Mr Nelson, another on the bathing list, illustrated this. He was a Jamaican with a superb, slim body. 'Nutty as a fruit cake,' said Billie, popping his head round the door to make sure he was missing nothing.

No signs show. Clean, lithe limbs bear a few pinkwhite scars at knee and elbow. A small patch of curly hair adorns his chest. He is civil and, with us at any rate, smiles a lot, though Big Wilson, Semple and even the ever patient Raggle do not get on very well with Nelson. *They* want to know why he was let into the country when he was so obviously mentally disturbed. It is no good prattling to them of civil liberties, British Subjects, or how often the colonies were populated by English adventurers (psychopaths?}, social outcasts and the bad sons of the rich. They feel that the admission procedure to an overcrowded island should be a little more selective. On their count, five marks would go against the immigrant if he were black because he would be unlikely to fit into the social structure as *they* want it; ten marks against criminals and the insane. Semple and Raggle would award points of equal value for the candidate's record in his own country, and for the possession of particular skills or a profession. The Irishmen on the staff (always at least 50 percent of the total) do not seem to bother themselves particularly. To them, the patient is a "black bastard" if he is black and annoying, an "English bastard" (or Irish or whatever) if he is white.

Mr Nelson was committed to us as soon as he got off the boat-train at Waterloo. He had spent the journey in a way not entirely agreeable to his less social English travelling companions. Shortly out of Southampton, he borrowed a *Times* and a *Telegraph* with urgent thanks and serious apologies to the owners. These were ripped up into streamers so that he could decorate the carriage. Which he did. Messy, but artistic touches were added by orange skins over the electric light bulbs. By this time, he was almost alone in the compartment. If this had been his objective, all his behaviour would have been explicable – even reasonable and amusing. But company or no, he was not affected. Taking his shirt off, he now screamed obscenities at a non-existent person in an unoccupied corner. This was too much for the solitary lady in the opposite corner who had so far determinedly sat through the performance. Convinced that the abuse was directly aimed at her, she left, protesting and saying, 'Such a pity when we did so much for them during the war.' Men

were called.

Poor souls.

Most had tried to hide in other compartments, to reassure themselves that this bizarre thing was not going on. The last lady to leave sought them out and implored them to do something. Her position as director of operations was at this stage a little handicapped as our friend the Jamaican was now without his trousers as well. Madam could not let the other people see that she had seen him naked as the day he was delivered. Quite natural that – because the others would accuse her of being curious. Which she was. So would you be if you had reached the age of sixty and never seen a man naked. She actually expected him to have a little fig leaf over it? She did not expect him to have an erection and possibly did not know what it signified.

Led by a gentleman who had been to a minor public school, a few men started to pacify Nelson. This angered him intensely and he had to be sat on. Thus the whole matter was brought to Waterloo.

Nelson's father in Jamaica had done a smart thing. He had found his son expensive and difficult to live with. He had started too many fires to be a reliable asset to the family. So Mr Nelson senior saved up towards the single fare to England. His son was a British subject. It was quite likely he had caught one of the diseases British subjects are open to. Therefore, his father would help him to Britain to seek a cure under the National Health Service. Soon, because friends had contributed, he was able to say, 'My son has gone to England.' And eventually, people asked after him kindly because they forgot his brain was bad; and the old man was able to make up stories that brought prestige.

On the day Mr Nelson arrived at Y Block, someone might have lain too long after a road accident and perhaps died because his ambulance was Nelson's taxi to St Francis's. People like Big Wilson were angry. And other more reasonable people.

Nelson, droop-eyed and drugged, bathed. He was as clean and trim as a black scalpel. Poor chap was not wanted on either side of the Atlantic. No one could help him. His disease was not infectious but he was spurned. He begat a child in a Brixton brothel, came back to us a year or so later, and was then lost to St

Francis. Is his child the carrier of Nelson's illness now?

***

I was told to do the postman last. It was understandable as he stank. He had been to us years ago they said, with a flower in his buttonhole, full of extravagance and tales of wealth and contacts in high places. He used the name of Henry Ford then. Even Billie, on duty at the time, smelt a rat. Plausible though his stories were, the fact that Henry Ford was dead upset them a little. This, coupled with the fact that the postman's cerebro-spinal fluid was loaded with spirochetes, unbalanced belief against him.

Now, his delusions were a pleasant thing of the past, as was the pleasure that caused his pain. Syphilitic gummas rotted against his shins and arms. He walked as though about to topple over from the apparent exertion of rubbing out marks on the floor. His time was done. The best hopes for him were that he should die of an aortic aneurism rather than rot away.

I helped the shuffling old postman along the corridor and checked that O'Leary was needing no help getting the upstairs ward to bed. Then I scrubbed the bath out thoroughly and took a bath myself. Billie noticed my pink freshness as we went off duty into the cold grey night.

'If you've just had a bath you want to wrap up warm you know, else you'll catch your death.' He looked solicitously up into my eyes as a mother might look up at a daughter who is growing into a big girl.

'Oo! I say!' A thought had just struck Billie, and he put two delicate fingers up to his fleshy red lips. 'You haven't just bathed after the postman have you?'

'Yes, Billie, but I cleaned the bath out first.'

'I jolly well hope you did and no mistake. He's got a right dose of the pox I can tell you.' Billie looked alarmed and then tittered: 'We shall very soon know if you've got it. You'll be beside yourself with grandeur. Positive *grandeur*.'

'You're an old woman, Billie. That bit about picking it up in the bath is an old wives' tale.'

'It's not so old neither.' He patted the smooth silver hair at his temples, 'We shall see. Grandeur. Positive *grandeur*.' He patted the air once with his hand as if pushing away a dog's nose that was just going to lift his skirt, and made off into the night chuckling. I did learn a little later about tertiary syphilis and its effects on the brain and other bodily parts.

CHAPTER 10: A Shadow of Doubt

I had been off the day before and so collected my pay packet this Saturday noon as I passed the Porter's Lodge. Pay day was Friday, when the staff of Y Block and the Geriatric Wards queued during their lunch hours. Nursing staff, male and female, lined up along one of the long, linking corridors that led to the main hospital. At the far end a small glass annex with in it wheelchairs and gymnasium apparatus sprouted off. Here Mr Webb and his adoring secretary with the hairy shins handed over the slim brown packets and took autographs in a large green ledger. Upwards of three-quarters of an hour one might wait to progress to the head of the queue. Green-coated Cleaners held out their palms for reward along with Staff and Charge Nurses

That queue was a symbol of service. Work for and serve your patients, then go and hold out your hand for money. However trivial and childish pride may be, it certainly exists and no good is done by denying its existence. Probably no staff expected to be thanked for their week's work, yet to expect them to line up like Oliver Twists was not a healthy reminder of their subservience. It would not have been a very much more costly or complex problem to have the wages ready at the Porter's Lodge for all staff as they clocked in.

This day, however, I later wished I had been around to collect the money in the usual way. While wearing

121

a white coat, one automatically buttoned the pay envelope into the back trouser pocket. However, while wearing the blue serge jacket of off-duty dress, it was natural to put the money into one's wallet and then the jacket breast pocket. On entering the block, jacket was exchanged for white coat in the locked privacy of the linen room.

I changed and made my way down to the kitchen for a bite to eat before starting the afternoon's bathing. Dobey, Riddle and Allan were there, wolfing back lunch before going off duty. In the Admission Ward Father was talking to Elgin, who had just come on for the late shift. Elgin was a short, smooth and dapper little man. This was the end of his first week at St Francis's. He had, he said, been a private nurse before. He added to the mystery which uncurious colleagues allowed to surround new staff, by advertising the existence of an invalid wife. She was, he said, permanently confined to a wheelchair; paralysed below the waist.

'But, she is a real *lady*,' Elgin told Howard, 'and I do everything for her. Change her and everything.'

Howard made his sympathetic fatherly noises and contemplated the gentian violet patterns concealing the veins on the backs of his hands. Raggle came through the office to take charge and send off the morning shift. One by one Dobey, Riddle and Allan changed in the linen room, gave in their keys and quietly left. Other morning workers had already left when I came on. Little Tom supported by Billie, Elgin and O'Leary, were keeping their several eyes on downstairs events. Father would go shortly. He kept his white coat in the office, as did Raggle, who stayed until five and then, if all was quiet, handed over to Little Tom. Raggle seemed to like the job and always did his share of Saturday work, making it possible for Semple to go off to the races, or Little Tom to come in late if he wanted to take his wife and five children shopping.

Upstairs, Lakhani shared duty with me. He was very generous in this matter, allowing me the lion's share of all work without the least grudge or interference. He sat at first in apparent content, rolling his menthol cigarettes in the Recreation Ward. Unusually for a Saturday afternoon, one of the teaching hospital's trainee psychiatrists had come in to do some interviewing and case work. He had given Lakhani a list of patients he wanted to talk to in the upstairs consulting room. Raggle had also given him a list of patients requiring baths before going out on Monday. Between the two lists and the litter of cigarette rolling apparatus on his broad bandy-kneed lap, Lakhani made a fine old mess of things. It would have been better if the psychiatrist had interviewed his patients in the bath. For that is where each one was when wanted; and as he grew increasingly irritated with delays, I hauled the patients rapidly out of the bath and sent them rough dried to drip over the consulting room floor. Last in to see the psychiatrist was Lakhani, after furtive tapping at the door. It was not revealed whether his visit was to apologise for sending the penultimate patient in twice – before and after his bath – or to seek advice about his own mental condition. With hindsight, recalling his later aberrations, I incline to the second opinion.

At about a quarter to nine I went to my jacket in the linen room to see if there was an odd sixpence in my pay packet. Little Tom was collecting the weekly contributions for the staff tea kitty. The pay packet was gone; stolen from the wallet as selectively as its other emptiness made possible.

'Have you seen a pay packet lying on the floor in the linen room?' I asked each of the on-duty staff in turn. Only staff had access to this room. It was never left unlocked. There was not a glimmer of guilt from anyone. Little Tom expressed incredulity, firstly at my leaving it there in the first place, and secondly, about my being sure it was gone. Lakhani sympathised and reminded me that he had been a medical "stoodent" and the same thing had happened to him then. Elgin felt, so he said, that he was too much of a newcomer to be able to help in my enquiry. O'Leary tugged at the lobe of his half-ear and fetched a brush to sweep under the bottom shelves of the linen room in case it had got under there. He found nothing but was immensely pleased to have found an excuse for a spot of sweeping so late in the day.

'You sure you didn't drop it anywhere else?' he asked. I was positive, so O'Leary sadly put his brush away. Billie clucked a great deal, and when he finally understood that the pay packet had been stolen, and quite positively by one of the staff, dismissed them all. 'They're all a lot of heathens. You can't trust one. Be on your guard, that's what I should be.'

'Yes, Billie,' I said, 'but at the moment one of them is more heathen that the rest.'

'It might have been someone on the morning shift,' he said, as if that took some of the unpleasantness away. As far as I was concerned it multiplied the unpleasantness almost precisely by two. Dobey, Riddle and Allan were three with opportunity. Raggle and Father had opportunity, yet I found it impossible to believe that they would take it. I never knew who did. The loss of the money was annoying, but the little bit of doubt about these nurses and the chip of faith knocked from me disturbed me more.

·CHAPTER 11: Visiting Afternoon

On Wednesdays and Sundays Y Block admits the existence of a world outside the Psychiatric Observation Unit. Reluctantly, and always with a sense of foreboding, visitors are received. They announce their arrival at the Porter's Lodge, who rings through to tell us. Ambulatory patients are told to wait on the locker seats in one of the dormitories. Round the beds of those few patients in the Admission Ward who have visitors, we arrange the green screens on wheels so that they shall have some privacy. But a flap is always left apart so that observation can continue. We guardians fix our faces into the most benign smiles that we can muster and stand in various attitudes of being occupied with something else, but ready to help if help is needed.

Children are left outside. Wives, parents, daughters, sons and brothers come in two by two. Present bearing, they seek consolation and find none. Questions on their lips and no answers; looking to give love but finding it harder even than loving their own reflections in a distorting mirror; hoping at least, at last, to be seen to be good relatives.

Even perhaps the most hardened of attendants found visiting afternoons hard to bear. A sad charade, a mad pageant, where private agony was a public spectacle, bringing home to each of us the almost absolute mystery of insanity. Whale and Howard looked omniscient, like High Priests officiating at a ritual which only they could understand. Semple occupied himself with whatever clerical work he could find. Billie rushed about talking *sotto voce* to everybody as though the show was about to begin and he was the principal lady.

Two 'til four, smile and look hopeful.

Two 'til four, grope for the right words.

Two 'til four, pretend there is no agony; pretend that there are no tears in that wife's eyes; pretend that it is only a matter of a short time and all will be understood; look like love in a white coat, for that is all we have to offer. Big Wilson, who firmly believed for five days a week that the mentally unsound should be "put down like dogs that are no good", thought on Wednesday and Sundays that something "should be done about it". For at the spectacle of normally functioning people suffering for their afflicted kin, small pieces of Wilson's protective beliefs were flaked off. Seeds of thought sprouted briefly in the raw patches where the beliefs had flaked away; sentiment watered the seed until visiting time was over. But there was no light from above to encourage worthwhile growth in such a poor ground.

***

A typical Sunday brought visitors to only three or four of the patients in the Admission Ward. Though many wives sought out their peripatetic and insane husbands, some patients may well have come from far corners of this country or others, and too recently to be tracked down by their families. The patients who stayed in the Admission Ward for more than a couple of days were frequently without wives, relatives or friends of any sort. Those old lags we knew and knew never to have visitors, were sent up to the Recreation Ward if possible. Here, their loneliness was emphasised less, their chance of creating a disturbance reduced. Here the television might break its customary pattern and provide entertainment. The grand piano was very rarely opened but an oldfashioned radio fixed to a wall was occasionally switched on – usually by a younger member of staff – and the sounds of popular music would revive some of the solemn patients. But there was a risk here – a thumping good melody from Elvis would get feet tapping, which led to feet stomping and an angry visit from Father.

Noisy patients slept in the side rooms; very noisy ones in the pads. Bed patients were propped up, their antics and eccentricities reduced by sedatives.

The women brought flowers - to occupy their hands and to give a visible purpose to the visit.

Here was a tearful little old woman. Grey-haired and bandy-legged, she walked with a slight stoop. She sat on a low armchair dragged up to the side of the bed, her shoulders barely as high as the pillows. Her husband, Dicky – a huge, white-haired, not sedated mass in the bed – dwarfed her, his great red face turned down to her as she offered him flowers. 'Here, dear; I've brought you daffodils.'

'Take the bloody things away,' he shouted.

'They're no bloody use to me. I'm not dead yet.'

'No dear.'

'Instead of picking bloody flowers, why don't you spend your time finding out why *they've* got me locked up in here.' He pointed a thick forefinger up and over the screen towards the desk where Howard and I stood.

'Yes dear. Well, the doctors and everybody are trying to find out what's wrong.'

'There's nothing bloody wrong with me. I've told you that. So why waste time picking flowers? I've told you about that before too. I'm bloody always telling you about something or other. I'm bloody always having to tell somebody something about something or other.' He only spoke the truth.

'I shall speak to the doctors again afterwards Dicky dear. We'll see what can be done.'

'Don't bother to see about what can be done,' he mimicked her as best a lion roar could mimic a mouse's squeak, 'bloody effing well get me out of here, I say.'

'Would you like to go to where you had a rest last time? I don't think we can afford the private place again?'

'I don't want to go to any place,' he mimicked her tones again. 'What the hell do I want to go to any place for, you stupid old cow? There's nothing wrong with me. I could run this place. They're all a lot of stupid idiots. Why am *I* in here, you stupid bitch? You stupid bitch. Tell me that I say, you bitch.'

'Shut your bloody trap,' she screamed back. 'You're shut up here because you're bloody nuts. And here's hoping to God they bloody well keep you here.' Her accents were vigorous but still thinly refined. Her outburst did nothing to staunch Dicky's abusive flow.

Now her anger gave way again to the puzzlement and tears she had had so long. Years as a companion on her husband's journey from robust normality through robust eccentricity to robust abnormality had turned on the taps of her restraint. She had never publicly returned even a word of her husband's abuse before. Now she was ashamed.

We ushered her out for a moment, telling her that he was due for his medicine. He was not, in theory; but he got it. Something was needed or he would break up the ward. Already he was out of bed chanting, 'Get the bitch away, away. Get the bitch away.' Howard talked to him with a hypodermic needle. Ten minutes later, the screens rearranged, his wife came back in to contemplate the tragedy she had married.

He's drowsing now, she thought; nothing wrong to look at except he has got too big since he was a young man. All his face bones are grown large. His hands are vast. His Adam's apple nearly the size of a teacup. Surely something has gone wrong inside. Something she could understand and tell her sisters about.

'No,' the psychiatrist had said.

Again and again she asked. She knew he was not the same now, physically, as he was before; but although he was big she supposed he wasn't abnormal to look at unless you knew him long, long before.

He had been extensively psychoanalysed because they had been fairly well-to-do. For the psychoanalyst it had elicited several guineas and much peculiar matter for speculation. He had also earned himself a punch on the nose during the final session. This he found physically disturbing, but it expanded his clinical diagnosis a little. He stretched his label for the case to "Chronic hypomania with strong aggressive bouts and complete lack of insight", collected his fee and left it at that.

'Oh dear,' the patient's wife said now with relief, 'he's asleep. I suppose I might as well go.'

Her loyalty would not end. Heaven was a place, she thought, where husbands snapped out of it and where time was lived again.

Dicky used to write long and violent letters to The Times and sometimes they were published. He used to have friends in those days who joked with him about his latest hobby horse. He had no friends now.

***

Behind further screens a lean, ascetic bearded figure stretched out on his bed. Obsessional and sternly suspicious, he was a forbidding spectre-prophet of a man. He had friends. He was Jewish, a kosher butcher by profession. It was thought he might have homicidal tendencies as he had been overheard on frequent occasions talking to himself of plans to kill someone.

Undeterred, four jolly fat men in black arrived to see him. Though they were double the regulation number allowed at the bedside, they overcame

Howard's scruples with warm smiles and happy argument. Moving as a team, they trotted into the ward and took up positions on the Prophet's bed. None of them relatives; they had heard of his plight and had come to cheer him up with kosher titbits, biscuits and fruit. Soon afterwards they made arrangements for him to leave. He did not have the appearance of gratitude for these endeavours, but we were sure he was grateful. He went to where they, his friends, took him with far less fuss than he would have gone with us.

It was good to see Jew solidarity in action.

***

The third patient to be visited does not get all the benefit of his guest, who is his wife. His case is of such interest that the duty doctor and his chief from the teaching hospital have decided to ask his wife in for a chat. They have come down especially on visiting day to see her. When she appears and is ushered into the upstairs visiting room, bawdy remarks are made about their purpose. The patient is a Polish gentleman. Classified as a paranoid schizophrenic, he is in physically good health. His command of English cannot have attracted his wife. Maybe the powerful, mysterious glazed look in his pale blue eyes did that, coupled with his size.

She is gorgeous. Big and blonde and every curve under control without the aid of a corset. Everyone except Billie and Whale is excited.

'No wonder the head-shrinkers want to chat to her.'

'Which one will be taking down her particulars?'

'If she coughs they'll get crushed in that small office.'

This, naturally, was the moment when the headshrinkers were offered tea.

'I saw right down her dress,' the tea carrier reported. 'Smashing!'

'Bet *they're* not real,' said Billie, with a note if not a full chord of jealousy in his voice. 'It stands to reason, it isn't possible. Good heavens, men *are* stupid. If they were real she'd topple over, obviously.' 'Go on Billie, you're jealous.' I patted him irreverently under the nipple. 'Start exercises lass and grow some.'

The psychiatrists' discussions were on an altogether superior plane. The case notes contained a fair deal of chat about previous illnesses, afflicted siblings, education and financial background and then got down to it.

'Are sexual relations between you and your husband normal?'

'Yes.'

'How often do they take place?'

'About once or twice a week but less just lately.'

'Have you noticed any change in your husband recently?'

'Well yes, he's got a bit odd.'

'In what way – with regard to sex?'

'Well, it's a bit difficult really.'

'Go on.'

'Well, once the lights were off and we were naked he'd leap back up and switch them on again.'

133

'Then what?' (I bet he never bought paperbacks. No need with this sort of entertainment.)

'He stood on the bed and made me kneel on the floor. He made me promise to be faithful to him and to worship him and to kiss his feet.'

'Did this continue?'

'Oh yes, only then he didn't believe me and said I was making love with somebody else and voices had told him.'

'Have you?'

'What?'

'Made love with somebody else?'

'Good Lord no. Not since I've been married. He's enough for me and no mistake.'

And so the conversation, reconstructing itself from the case notes goes on. Meanwhile, her husband, thank the Lord, does not know his wife is here. He would be a bit of a handful if he knew. Four policemen were needed to bring him in. He had gone for his wife seemingly for rather more than his conjugal rights, because she was well able to cater for those; and she, frightened out of her wits and evidently most of her clothes, had gone for the police. They had extended a courteous welcome to her. So eager were they to listen to, and look at her full story, by the time the wild Pole was apprehended he'd broken up their happy home and was starting on the landlord's place below. Still in the nude.

He was an unusual case for us because very few of our schizophrenic patients were married. An article by a psychiatrist at that time argued, on that evidence, that singleness and isolation were contributory causes of schizoid behaviour. Which is as may be. It is almost certain, however, that by and large, women don't go for violent, deluded, hallucinating men when they are thinking of marriage. And men, preoccupied with their visions and voices, tend to neglect the fair sex and all that fun.

Perhaps this sick Pole was a genius; perhaps he was a late developer. It might have been wise, however, to run a Wasserman on him to test for venereal diseases, along with some other analyses.

***

In one of the side rooms lay a man named Harris whose recently adopted profession was faith healing. He was serene and quiet now, but his evangelical bouts were so unpredictable and noisy that he was, for our peace, confined where his cries could be muffled by a closed door when necessary. It was for his safety too. For though an occupation such as Harris' demanded a good degree of self-confidence, his claims alas were larger than his talents. And he largely chose the wrong clients on whom to work his miracles of credulity. Mr Harris was convinced he could make teeth grow at will. He invited some gentlemen in a public house to knock a few of his out and then watch. They did. They were sceptical enough not to believe that new teeth were springing up when all they saw was blood. Then, having had their sport, they uncharitably had him removed to St Francis's. He came peaceably with the DAO and St

John's Ambulance men, who told him he would find plenty of opportunity here to heal. He was again disappointed, finding only that he was on the receiving end of observation and a service that had not the faintest article of faith in its ministrations. But Mr Harris was undaunted. He felt convinced that he was normal or supernormal, and that his stay here was only one of those trials any man of vision must endure before the world accepts him.

His daughter came on a Sunday visiting day. Her faith in him was profound. He grey haired and unshaven, lay on the thin floor mattress in his rough night shirt.

She was lovely. Natural auburn hair fell in shining cascades onto her shoulders. Clear, delicate eyebrows on a white forehead arched over long lashes. Her sapphire eyes, perhaps a shade too pale, gazed softly down on her father, while her white skin contrasted like the flesh of an apple against her light green summer dress. She was tender, sweet and pathetic.

'Father's all right, isn't he?'

'Well, that's what we've got him here for,' I stalled, 'so that we can check up and advise treatment if necessary.'

'He's got a few daft ideas but he's all right really, aren't you, Dad?' She crouched on her haunches beside him.

'They are not daft ideas, I tell you Anne. I've proved it, I can heal. I can make hair and teeth grow.' He opened his mouth to reveal deep red, blood-clotted empty sockets.

'See them growing?'

'No. No, Dad, not yet.'

She turned away and tears slid down her cheeks. I wanted to be able to say that we'd put him right but I couldn't do that.

She fiddled with the sapphire engagement ring on her left hand and I wondered about her fiancé. Is he going to run the risk of having unbalanced children? These things are often inherited. Again and again the madness can be traced back. Or will he leave her to bear her cross alone?

She left her flowers and went.

***

Shortly, the bell sounds through the wards and visitors leave. They are relieved. They have done their bit. No one can say they are not dutiful. Sometimes they leave with a hurried instruction to the nearest nurse:

'Please see that he doesn't take his false teeth out, won't you? He's broken four pairs already.'

'Thank you Nurse for looking after him I'm sure you earn your money.'

To which we inevitably respond:

'Oh, he's all right.'

'He'll be better soon.'

'We've had worse than him you know.' Words for your comfort like the flowers you brought; to hide behind; to give us the look of purpose. Like you, we wait for understanding.

The door shuts behind the sigh of the last visitor and we are left with bits of their lives in beds around us.

They are in our care. In our key-jangling omnipotence we will send them to Cane Hill, St Ebba's, Horton or one of the other asylums.

Passing the parish church on this Sunday evening, I recognise the familiar music of the hymn "Thou whose almighty word" and I pause at the open door to listen to John Marriott's words:

Thou who didst come to bring
On thy redeeming wing,
Healing and sight,
Health to the sick in mind,
Sight to the inly blind
O now to all mankind,
Let there be light.

CHAPTER 12: Night Shift

In comparison with morning and late shifts, the night shifts could have islands of peace but weeks of dark, gloomy content. Though the emergency admission rate would be high between eleven and two o'clock, the night was rarely disturbed after that. The DAOs and police respected the larger of the small morning hours and left us in our isolation then.

The night was heavy. The great green-lagged pipes of the central heating system simmered and clucked softly along the walls. The heat mounted until just before dawn when it dropped as though to give way to the sun. A regular monotone routine guided the Block. Three attendants sat at the desk in Ward I, another in an armchair in Ward II, while the fifth member of the shift had the upstairs dormitory ward to himself. All other doors were locked. Three small pools of light, one over each desk or table in the wards, were reduced to the smallest diameter when the overhead bulbs in their green shades were pulled down on adjustable flexes to within inches of the working surfaces. The neuroses and psychoses of daytime were concealed in the drugged murmurings and snores of sleep. Occasionally, a cry came from one of the padded cells where a blue light burned behind its wire mesh high up in the ceiling. Staff moved, when they had to move, on rubber soles squeaking softly against the parquet flooring. Talk was low and ventriloquial with labial stillness.

Two visits by the female Night Sister were timed at one o'clock and six-thirty. Her last morning round caught the Block already awake; the one o'clock visit was heralded from far away in the Geriatric ward by the echo of a closing door drifting along the linking corridors. For this visit she let herself in at Ward II and just creaked along to the Admission Ward before creaking back again with barely a nod to the Charge Nurse.

Night shift started at nine with a cup of tea and continued with cups of tea until two. Admissions apart, only one attendant was required to work. The third man in Ward I, who could not plead the dignity of blue pips on his shoulder, made tea for the others. He also cut the patients' bread for breakfast, buttered it, and brewed a great urn of tea to rouse them with. Even with a full complement of patients, these jobs took no more than an hour. One felt then that the whole night was free for reading. Libraries of books could have been read. Except during the lonely stint in Ward II, where it was not the case. Colleagues resented another one reading. When they had finished flicking over the evening papers they sat in contemplative quiet, with occasional desultory conversation until two. Then, blankets spread over unopened beds, they slept if they wished until fivethirty.

Sandy, who always took Ward II when on night duty, did not sleep. He sat on the second step of the stone stairs leading up from the downstairs passage. Here he could see along to Wards I and II and smoke his cigarettes all night. He warned the others of the approach of irregular visits, and answered the office phone should it disturb the heavy stillness of the night. He did not eat.

'No thanks, Mr Lynch,' he said, blowing a wreath of smoke into the stairwell, when I asked him if he wanted relieving to go to supper, 'I just like to stay here with a cup of tea and a fag.'

Only Whale went to the staff canteen for supper. Come hell, or a high admission, at eleven-thirty he minced off.

'I think he's got a boyfriend over there,' said Sandy, not unkindly but merely as a statement of fact. 'When he comes back you can relieve Herring if you like as I don't want to go.' Sandy's ghost-like hand gestured to the floor above.

Herring was at first a constant night-time figure on Ward III. He sat at the table, pipe clenched in a broad, flat, pugnacious face. Thin lips spread out in an oval slit to one side of his pipe when he spoke. With thick bowed legs appearing to be joined directly below his barrel chest, he moved slowly on tiny feet and pigeon toes. Steel grey, ball-bearing eyes scrutinised a notebook and various papers before him.

'Here, Thingamabob -what's-yer-name,' he would say when I brought his tea. 'My son will do all right don't you think?' He indicated columns of figures in his notebook.

'Yes, I'm sure. What does he do?'

'My boy's in the electrical business,' he paused and pointed an ash-speckled finger at a particular series of pencilled items and amounts. 'I've been doing some calculations and he *should* do all right.'

'Good. That's fine.' The computations were meaningless to me but Herring clearly liked to share his confidence and pride with someone - even if he could not remember his name.

'Yes.' He tilted his face back to prevent the smoke fanning under his heavy eyebrows and into his eyes. 'He's got three electrical businesses now, and thinking of a fourth. I look after the financial side.' He nodded and proved his claim by muttering up a further column of figures as I left.

As winter passed, I didn't see Herring on any of my night shifts again. Occasionally, he passed me with a nod and a grunt coming on in the morning as I went off. Then I heard he was off sick and was taking some of his holiday, so I forgot about him in my preoccupation with the job.

* * *

The comings and goings of staff were, in any event, rarely a matter for question. Elgin left after his first spell on night duty. 'It's for my invalid wife,' he said. I thought briefly that it might be to spend my pay packet, but, unfortunately, I could not be sure if it was he who had stolen it. I hoped it was, so that I need mistrust no one else.

Shepherd, a small, tubby, shiny-faced man with bald head and spectacles that made his eyes appear like bright blue lakes way back in the depth of his head, retired during the summer. He had worked in Y Block for fifteen years and looked forward now with boyish eagerness to his new job in the city. He was to be a messenger at one of the big banks, just as soon as he and his wife were back from their umpteenth consecutive summer holiday in Bournemouth. The banks will rarely have had a more cheerful messenger rolling round the city. Though not given to exerting himself too much, Shepherd had an enviable temperament. He smiled and was unruffled by any fiasco. He slept on night duty with the ease of an overfed bulldog. He appeared equally glad to be going on or coming off duty, as though life was in any case a hobby. I was sorry to see him go, and was surprised that there was no ceremony to mark his retirement. But Y Block hardly noticed his departure. With so many people in and out, patients and staff, the Block was unmoved by departures.

Big Wilson, broken arm now healed, found himself very quickly on nights after he returned from his protracted convalescence. Whether Father and Semple had had enough of his blustering daytime lunacy and wished to preserve the peace they had enjoyed during his absence, I do not know. Certainly, the morning shift's gain was our loss. Though his roar was reduced to a fume and splutter for the night, he griped and groaned and cursed for his tea. He expected sympathy and a perpetual hero's welcome since his injury, and was not bright enough to realise he would never get it unless he changed his job.

My nightly supper break was an hour locked in the kitchen preparing and eating from a limited repertoire of cheese dishes. Cheese was delivered in vast quantities supposedly for the patients' supper, but only a fraction of it was eaten. So it formed the basis of many meals, all of them on toast, some with the added luxury of tomato, and others with egg in various forms. For want of alternatives, I ate cheese until I was heartily sick of it. But I always took my break last, and reappeared at the end of the hour with the final cup of tea for the staff.

Wilson, of course, was oohing and aahing and hissing for his tea before the hour was up. And then it had to be in His Big Mug. Sometimes, shamefully, I childishly baited him.

'Do you pay twice as much into the tea kitty?'

'Are you being bloody cheeky?'

'Yes. But I was also asking a question.'

'When you've been in the service as long as I have and worked your way up to Charge Nurse, you'll expect a large cup of tea.' And more in the same vein.

'Oh, I see. It's status then. I thought it was greed.'

'Away with you.'

That was Big Wilson's standard answer. With him it was conclusive. It was logic, it was repartee, and it was wit. When, out of annoyance, I served him tea in a normal cup, his stampings and ravings were marvellous to see. It served some purpose though, because when Wilson was on duty after that I was despatched to look after Ward III where stretches of privacy and peace combined to make the night shift bearable.

Outside the dormitory ward at the head of the stairs, there was an ivory bell button in surrounding brass plate; this was for the staff to use in the case of emergency. Unless it had to be pushed and its rapid clangour summoned help from below, one could expect little disturbance in Ward III. The scheduled cups of tea arrived, and the sit-in for supper break. Apart from these diversions, the whole floor was under the observation of one upstairs man. Only the dormitory was lit and lived in, the other rooms being dark and locked. Down each of the two long walls of Ward III were seven beds; in the middle, separated by a low partition, three pairs of beds stood head to head; two more beds flanked the lavatory door in the far wall. When numbers were high in the Block, this was the first dormitory to be filled, for the bulk of patients were then out of the way of the downstairs affairs. By consulting bed board and register, one learned quickly the names of the twenty-two patients, even though the list changed within a week. It was well to know who was who for a grunt from one bed might indicate a bed bottle was needed, while an identical grunt from another bed meant the occupant wanted a smoke.

Of course, smoking after nine o'clock was strictly forbidden. But when I had been conscious for a while of grunts from a figure sitting motionless in bed, staring fixedly at me through the gloom, experience showed that a smoke was better than further sedation for him.

'What's the matter Mr Devlin?'

'Can't sleep. Dying for a smoke.'

'Where's your tobacco?'

145

Mr Devlin's finger, steadied now from the alcoholic tremors that shook it on his admission, points to a battered tin in his locker. I take it, tease some of the coarse brown tobacco (half an ounce issued per smoker per week by the office), select a paper and roll him a thin cigarette.

'Do you want to lick it?'

'Ta!' His tongue caresses the adhesive strip and his fingers seal the magic cylinder. I light it for him.

'Roll one for yourself, Nurse.'

'No thanks, I've just had one.' Tobacco, like cheese, was supplied in generous quantity so that the staff who fancied it could have their half-ounce too.

'Look, you'd better whip along to the bog to smoke that, else your neighbours will wake up.'

'What time is it?'

'Three.'

'Oh! Right.' The night-shirted figure of Devlin slides away to return shortly and make determined efforts to sleep. He is comforted by our small conspiracy; I feel less of a gaoler and more a nurse.

***

An occasional early riser pads softly down to the lavatory. Shortly, Allan – tea boy for the night – brings up a tray swimming in tea with plastic mugs practically floating in it. Half a white cupful is for me. I rise temporarily from bed or armchair to rouse the ward.

'Wakey, Wakey. Here's your tea.' Snores break into murmurs.

146

'Come on and get out of it. Those who want tea show a leg.'

When everybody is manifestly alive and awake, I go to collect the teeth.

Every night teeth and glasses are locked in the kitchen. The duty alcoholic could not get them because he did not know the names on the beakers of teeth. And some of the senile patients would answer to every name. They wanted everything that was going. That was all right apart from two things. One, Mitchell might erupt because he thought "dirty old Smith" had been wearing his teeth. Or two, dirty old Smith started drinking his tea with four dental plates in and choked. So I fetched and delivered the teeth, encouraging the owners to fish them out of the beakers as I proffered them. Dripping cold wet teeth in place, all except the most senile patients were ready to drink their tea and hop out of bed.

This was *their* ward first thing in the morning. Beds had to be made and the floor swept. Elsewhere, O'Leary and others did all the work themselves, which seemed to me a bad thing since it consigned the patients to a whole day full of internal agony and boredom. Here, they could nearly all lose themselves for a while in work. To add stimulus to the occasion, I ran the bed-making on competitive lines. The two or three patients who finished first and with neatest beds were awarded a prize: admittance to the kitchen to wash up the tea beakers. There were few who did not compete strongly to earn this reward; for the right to go into the kitchen and do more work was proof to a man of his good sense. There was a little prestige and individuality in being trusted. Runners up in the bedmaking competition combined efforts to change the bed linen of senile patients whose time was fully occupied solving the mysteries of trouser legs and buttons.

Initially, by mad mischance, my technique of work therapy did not obtain official blessing. The Night Sister, on this occasion the Deputy Matron – she of the long nose and even longer feet – caught me running the competition from my bed. Urging the patients on with cries of encouragement, 'Come on Mr Devlin, Mr Umcabo is beating you. Ten to one on Old Irish in the far corner,' I did not hear Madam arrive. Madam in any event did not like me. She expected staff to stand to attention when she entered a ward. There followed not even the least perfunctory nod to the staff who did. Those who did not were fixed with a malevolent stare. Warned of Madam's approach, I let my back take the brunt of her visual assault while I occupied myself lying on a bed reading a chart and encouraging ambulatory patients to make their beds. This morning I was not warned.

'Nurse!' Alarm, indignation and vast superiority were in her voice. She rocked slightly back in the doorway while her big black shoes came to an astonished halt further into the ward.

'Will you get off that bed Nurse! You've no business to be there. *You* should be making the beds.' She turned, snorting, to march downstairs. Big Wilson, a good six steps behind her on the way up had seen nothing. Such a titbit Madam did not wish to share with him. She snorted again and was let out of the Block.

The next morning after duty I was summoned to the Matron.

'I've had a report from one of my Sisters, Mr Lunn.' Hey ho. Here we go.

'Yes, Miss Argus.'

'Angus. Miss Angus. Or Matron will do.'

She would want another go at calling me Lunn and then we'd be all square and could settle down to business.

'I'm told that you were forcing the patients to make their *own* beds yesterday morning, Mr Lunn.'

'I was encouraging them to make their own beds. Yes.'

'Is that so?'

Now, I experienced a few moments of the over-theglasses stare. Attack Lynch, else there will be more to follow.

'I find this is very good for morale and has some therapeutic value.'

'Night Sister doesn't think so.'

'But I'm sorry, Night Sister doesn't know the first thing about it really. She's not running that ward of twenty disturbed patients. I am. While I am running it I must do it my way, subject to the approval of the Charge Nurse on Y Block.'

'Is that so Nurse?'

She'd lost. More over-the-glasses looks.

Counter-attack.

'But Night Sister tells me you were lying on the bed.'

'Yes. Sorry.' No good trying to escape that. Even if everybody does it, it's no good to tell her and ruin it for them. Apologise again. Make a feast of it.

'Yes Matron. Yes Miss Angus. Very sorry. Won't let such a thing be seen again.'

Too right I wouldn't. Come to think of it, why hadn't Allan banged on the pipes? This was always the signal to stub cigarettes and leap about a bit whoever was coming up stairs.

'Well Nurse, it mustn't happen again. Off you go now.'

Next time Night Sister came round in the morning, I was standing exhorting the patients to further effort. Her thoughts were apparent in her looks. Fifty-fifty. Nurse Lynch not on the bed. Good. Nurse Lynch not making the beds himself. Bad. But she decided to let it rest there. The male staff here are a bit jealous of we women I think she thought, and left.

Morning staff arrived.

Out into the cold fresh morning.

Puffed wheat and bed.

CHAPTER 13: Death in the Night

Although on night duty I generally managed to steer clear of skirted authority from the main hospital building, even upstairs the peaceful tempo was sometimes disturbed. In one week of grey rain-soaked summer nights, three patients died in my ward. That was evil luck. Though that it was luck at all I half feared I might have to swear in a court of law.

Normally, patients thought likely to die were kept downstairs. Someone slipped up this time. Perhaps Howard had put them up there to annoy Whale who was on night duty that week. But I do not think even the canny Howard can have known, although he could smell death a day or two off. These deaths were sudden.

The first occurred in the bed right by my desk. Its occupant was a mental defective of thirty-two named Albert. As such, he should not really have been with us. A home for the mentally sub-normal rather than the deranged would have catered for his needs. However, he had had a bout of 'flu and became truculent while having a holiday at home. The rest of his family were not bright enough to deal with him, so he was sent to us. The rest of his family were MDs too, of higher or lower IQ. His IQ could almost have been calculated before birth.

151

With my reading interrupted by the sniffing and snoring of Albert, I put my feet up on the desk, wrapped a blanket around them and dosed off. At about four o'clock in the morning Albert's snoring became very loud. He was congested and full of a heavy cold. Gently, so that I should not wake him, I rose and turned his head on the pillow to help him breathe freely. I did not wake him. He gave a snort and died. His sudden loss of movement was frightening. I ran to the alarm bell and gave it two short clangs. Whale was off his bed and up in a flash, followed by O'Leary and others expecting a rough house.

'The MD's funny,' I said.

'My God, do you have to ring the alarm bell?'

'Well, he's dead I think.'

'O'Leary fetch the doctor.'

Whale went off for a hypodermic, came back and gave the patient a shot.

'What's that?' I asked.

'Fruit juice to pep him up a bit.'

Was I supposed to laugh? I wanted to know, but Whale had so few pieces of medical knowledge, he would not share any.

'He's dead.'

'What caused it?'

'Heart attack, I should think.'

Oh my God. When I turned his head I must have frightened him and he died. Oh Lord, I'm a murderer and I'm sorry.

Later, my conscience was relieved when I learned that he had died from oedematous fluid on the lungs. That puzzled me. I felt it should have been diagnosed before. Then I realised that despite the difficulties with a snuffling MD, probably it had. It was just that, as with many other defectives, he was congenitally weak, with poor resistance to illness. For Albert, perhaps 32 was a good age to have reached.

He lay a flaccid, waxy mass, indubitably dead. Whale said so. The doctor, briefly appearing in trousers, pyjama jacket and mackintosh, said so. I did not feel too good. I had been so tangibly present at Albert's sudden death that I felt still in some way responsible.

'The Lord have mercy on his soul,' said Whale. Pontifically, he drew down Albert's eyelids and called for the paraphernalia to lay him out. Dobey brought it. With relief I turned away.

'Where are you going Nurse?' Whale, erect and straight faced, like a Bishop endeavouring to balance an undersized mitre on his head, slowly swivelled towards me.

'I was going downstairs. I thought if you and Mr Dobey were up here laying out Albert, I ought to be down below.'

'You *thought*! You don't have to think Nurse Lynch I'll do the thinking. *I'm* not laying him out.' He clasped his hands in front of him and nodded to the corpse. It was as if the priestly rites were done, and now Whale was absolved, nay, even barred from further contact with the body.

'Come on,' said Dobey when Whale had made his exit, 'we'll have it done in a jiffy.'

It took a long jiffy. The mass of Albert was heavy to move quietly on the bed. And Dobey discovered a sinus between Albert's anus and scrotum.

'Look,' he said, 'he's a two-sexer. A herma-whatsit.'

'I think it's just a sinus of some sort,' I said. But Dobey was convinced that Albert had harboured the genitalia of both sexes and went to report to Whale. Whale was not the least bit interested.

'Oh yes? Have him laid out before the early shift come on.'

Dobey's assistance at the laying out was slowed down by such official disinterest in his discovery. 'All these years I've been in mental nursing,' he said, 'and that's the first hermaphro-whats-it I've seen. And no one takes the least bit of interest.' He shook his head sadly and was reluctant to have the matter finished.

Dawn shufflings and tea sippings were beginning beyond the screens before we completed the task.

***

I was just as unprepared for the second death in Ward III that week. A slight, unhappy Irishman called O'Connor left us that night. I remembered talking to him a morning or two before.'What's the matter, Mr O'Connor? You're taking a hell of a time with that bed.'

'I'm not up to it anymore.'

'Oh nonsense, you're heaps better than you were.'

He should have been. O'Connor was an alcoholic and most of these men were comparatively bursting with health after a few days on our vitamins.

'Oh no. I'm no good and never have been.'

'Dear, oh dear. We aren't going to have a basin full of self-sympathy now, are we?' O'Connor could be really pathetic when he tried.

'It's no wonder me wife left me.'

'Yes, that's possibly true. You must be a right bloody bellyache to live with.' O'Connor brightened considerably at that. He loved to be agreed with, even to his own detriment. Perhaps he liked to be considered an impossible case.

'You're right doctor.' He must have been pleased. He well knew I was not a doctor. But that sort of upgrading was reserved to show appreciation or to soften up before a favour was asked.

'Never mind Paddy. A few days with us and you'll be OK.'

He didn't stay a few days with us. He died in the night, quietly and without waking. The post mortem report said that advanced alcoholism had aggravated pulmonary tuberculosis. I don't think the disease so much as killed him as depressed him until death seemed the easiest thing. He had tried to fill a sad and empty life with drink but it had only washed it into even greater sadness and emptiness. He was tired and gave up.

In Mr O'Connor's case I did not find him until about twenty minutes after he died. You don't go putting the lights on and waking everybody up each ten minutes to see if they're alive. Although I was sorely tempted to do so for some nights following.

We left him, eyelids closed, behind the green screens that gave privacy to patients admitted, visited or dead. The morning shift laid him out.

***

My last night that week yielded to a bright morning. It was fine. A summer sun streamed through the wired glass windows and shed its brightness and shadows on the linoleum. Motes turned and glinted and solidified the sunbeams. I took tea round myself.

The senile patients always slept at the far end of the ward near the lavatory. If any had the courtesy to ask for a bottle this made a shorter trip to empty it; it also meant a shorter walk for the patient if he was strong enough to get out of bed.

So the old folk received their tea last.

'Wakey, wakey!' Must vary that cry one morning, I thought; it's beginning to grate a little. I propped up the old men in bed and, as soon as their eyes opened and their hands came up, put a plastic beaker of warm tea into their grasp. Everything went well until the very last bed. There, as the old man put the tea to his lips he dropped back dead. His head banged against the metal tube of the bedhead. Blood trickled from a gash in his temple then congealed. His skin was thin and transparent like greased parchment.

'Good Lord!' I ran to the stair head and pressed the bell push and put screens around his bed while help came.

'Been at it again, Lynch?' asked O'Leary.

'Looks like it,' said Whale, who took this as a final and personal insult in a week of insults from Lynch and Ward III.

'Well at least we won't have to lay him out. The day shift can do that,' I said.

'Oh, they'll love you. They asked me to thank you for leaving Mr O'Connor,' Whale sibilates.

We slipped the deceased patient down into the bed and once again the duty doctor was called. He eyed me oddly as he passed.

'Hi vampire,' said Billie as I went off duty.

'Why do you do it if you don't want the bodies?' asked another nurse on his way up to begin laying out. 'Well, it keeps you in practice. I do them in. You lay them out. You need the practice.'

'You can stuff it.'

'No. That's what you'll have to do,' I thought with the irreverence that tiredness brings.

***

Death that week had become familiar. By the time the old man died on his last sunlit morning, the surprise of death for me was reduced. His manner of dying in old age struck me as a good way to go; clean and sudden with a cerebral haemorrhage; no time for pain; no panic moments hovering before death; zip! The curtains are drawn. Please may I go that way.

Nevertheless, despite the new familiarity with death, I was not unhappy to be on day shifts for a while following.

CHAPTER 14: Inside outside

A hot morning with pale grey skies held the promise of later sunshine. Summer had been for months reluctant to come, and now wished to impress on the sweltering inmates of the Unit that it was never too late to begin in earnest.

Father was letting the staff in. The draught through the door as he opened it dried the latest coat of gentian violet spreading from his neck to tint his iron grey crew-cut. He smiled and tutted and said, 'Good morning; it's going to be a hot one,' to each person entering.

'Ah, Mr Lynch,' he said, clicking the door to and double checking the lock, 'perhaps you could show Mr Verity around when you've got your white coat on.'

'Yes, surely.'

'Mr Verity's come to work here,' said Father, darting into the Admission Ward. There by the desk stood an immensely tall young man. A lock of thin, curly hair bobbed down against a narrow forehead and brushed the rim of his wire-framed spectacles. A long nose ended in the oblivion of a walrus moustache which drooped round a drooping mouth and chin. Mr Webb had clearly not been at enormous pains to find a fitting uniform; Verity's white coat was the longest ever seen. Although the shoulders were pinched and tight so that the epaulettes wrinkled under Verity's ears, and although the sleeves ended in wide cuffs just below the elbows, the coat itself extended like a white wigwam to within six inches of the floor. Here, almost precisely on a level with the termination of blue serge trousers, it ended. Verity looked mournfully down as if to apologise for the half inch of white calf that neither his socks, coat, nor trousers could conceal. Father introduced us. He would have shown Mr Verity round the Block himself he said, but things were a bit hectic. He explained this to the middle button in Verity's white coat because he could not crane his neck up further. Howard was not excessively short, but he lost six inches from his height by being permanently angled forward from the waist. This fixed running posture was the outcome of his habitual darting movements. He never walked, and was always about to move or to peer closely into something at roughly keyhole height, so he had lost the knack of upright posture.

The physical difficulties of face-to-face discussion between Father and Nurse Verity explained Howard's anxiety to have me show the new recruit round. For "Tiny" Verity, as he obviously became, was a Staff Nurse, and merited the guidance of a person of at least equal status. However, it was I who introduced Tiny to the people and functions of the Block, and I did not forget to show him the staff lavatory and to outline its timetable.

Tiny had not worked in a psychiatric unit before and, sensing some of the weirdness that must be assailing him now, I took him metaphorically under my wing. For a year had now passed since I first came here. By any standards, I was an old hand, a permanent fixture. Some patients were known to me from previous admissions and six or seven staff had come and gone. In making Tiny Verity familiar with the Block I momentarily captured for myself an illusion of its rightness and appropriateness.

By his softly sardonic good temper and lugubrious appraisal of the oddities of St Francis's, Tiny recommended himself to me. In the year ahead, his company was to lighten the creeping depression of many shifts, and cheered several off duty hours when we had coffee in my rooms or at his home with wife and children. He had studied for and obtained a diploma at an art school before taking up nursing. Painting was a hobby for him, not to be spoilt by the necessity of its earning money. Nursing provided the living and had, he felt, nothing to do with art so did not interfere with it. Tiny's wife re-tailored his uniform

**

The atmosphere in Ward I was oppressive. The slits below the window sashes raised to the maximum filtered in the smell of hot macadam from the yard. Inner smells of urine and floor polish mingled to hang heavily on the air.

Sandy Wilson sat patiently cutting toe nails, long curved discoloured talons, belonging to a skeletal form in one of the beds.

'They keep catching in the sheets,' he explained, 'and Mr Miles hasn't got the strength to shake them free.'

Mr Miles, the skeleton, lay mute on his bed. He was tall and horribly emaciated. There was barely an ounce of flesh on him. Each rib and wrist bone was a promontory; the orbits of his eyes craters with small dull puddle eyes at the bottom; the leg across Sandy's lap a bent twig loosely clad in white skin. I asked Howard what was the matter with old Mr Miles.

'He's not old,' said Howard. 'He's thirty, I think. See in the register.'

I looked in the register. Thirty he was; but he had the shiny, white hairless skin of an old man.

'He won't eat,' said Howard. 'They don't know what is wrong with him.'

'How long is it since he gave up eating?' I asked, as the register was as bare of information as Mr Miles was of flesh.

'Nobody knows. He won't talk. Perhaps he thinks he's being poisoned,' Howard whispered confidentially to me behind a violet hand.

'Or perhaps he's trying to kill himself,' I said.

'Yes, it could be religious mania.' Non categorised puzzles Howard was wont to put down to religion of one sort or another. But his chance to expand on this theme now was ruined by Potter, a bus driver, who declared continuously in song that he was forever blowing bubbles.

Mr Potter was as lively and florid as Mr Miles was deathly and pale. He sat on his bed in a nightshirt and bus driver's uniform trousers. For some weeks he had sung . . .

'I'm forever blowing bubbles,
Blowing bubbles in the air.
Oh see them fly,
Right up in the sky;
I'm forever blowing bubbles . . .'

….pausing only for lungsful of air and mouthfuls of food. He had cheerfully agreed with Father, who chatted pleasantly to him, that in exchange for his trousers he would sing less. I had gone to the "Shrine" to get them. This was a brick box with roof, window and green door, which stood in a yard behind the padded cells and was connected to the Admission Ward by a pair of lagged central heating pipes. Patients' clothes were shelved in bags in this hothouse, and brought out when required. Mr Potter's collarless pin-striped shirt was torn to ribbons, and his black socks were toeless. So I brought only his trousers, which seemed to be the most important part of the bargain.

They were olive green with deeper green braid down the legs.

Unhappily, even the return of such dignified vestments could not persuade Mr Potter to keep his side of the pact with Howard.

'Tone it down a bit do, else I'll have your trousers back.'

'I'm forever blowing bubbles. . .'

'Oh God, it's a madhouse', muttered Howard and left the ward. Shortly he came back.

'I think we'll have all the children who are dressed out in the yard,' he said. Provided no admissions were booked, this was an irregular routine on a few hot, dry summer mornings. Howard sent Riddle to shut and lock the high spiked gates of the courtyard, and sent me to fetch down Tiny Verity and his flock from the Recreation Ward. Mr Potter stopped singing for a while to see if he could qualify for the yard. Howard told him not for the moment, because he should really have been in bed anyway as a recent unobserved admission. Mr Potter started singing again.

Billie was first out into the sunshine. He appeared from the dispensary with a tubular steel and canvas chair as soon as he heard the great gates clang to. He sat against the wall under the office window.

'You want to be careful where you sit in this place my lad,' he cautioned as he composed himself. 'Too bloomin' easy to get a bed pan chucked over you, I'm telling you.' He smoothed his hair down as if it owed its sleekness to natural beauty, not to the fertilising effect of bed pan pourings. He sat contentedly in the heat. Gradually the Vaseline he had smeared round his nostrils to soften up the blackheads melted and glistened. He drowsed. He loosened his clothes and puffed them out like a hen taking a dust bath. He dosed.

Riddle leaned against the wall beneath the kitchen window where, by turning his head, he could see the green stomachs of Lucy and Mrs Scott who were sloshing dishes in the sink. Lucy was disconsolate because Corrigan was on holiday. Mrs Scott was disconsolate because her husband found the weather even more thirst inducing than usual.

163

I sat on a bench in the shade of the narrow laurel tree border that hid the high iron railings and the corrugated tin backs of cycle sheds beyond. To the left, the gates blocked all view above ankle height. To the right, a grey pebbledash wall belonging to some other property spread in vast dullness from the Unit to the railings behind me. Opposite, twenty feet away, the Unit itself stewed its red walls and yellow windows in the heat.

Verity sat on the bench next to me contemplating the patients at exercise.

A distraught and spotty man paced round and round the small macadam square gesticulating and muttering, talking and answering, casting glances to the sky and to the spaces immediately in front of his nose, but oblivious of everyone.

Ponderously, with eyes cast down for dog-ends, one of Y Blocks regular homeless visitors – "professional malingerers" Wilson called them – made his way over to the laurel border. Here he parted the dust-laden leaves; with ceremonial gravity he drew a sheet of folded newspaper from his pocket and laid it on the dry grey earth. He sat down, heels denting the asphalt in front of him, dark green leaves accepting his back and head as far as the ears, in a dry, dusty embrace. Watching the progress of Verity's cigarette towards discardable size, he sorted his meagre gleanings of the morning.

A quiet, aristocratic young man sat on the opposite side of the front steps to Billie. Pin-stripe trousers and black shoes covered his lower half; black jacket over a woollen vest bearing the red cotton letters "St Francis" completed his dress. He filed his nails with a woman's sandpaper stick, which Billie had given to him. He filed them diligently, buffing them on the lapels of his jacket.

'They say it's repressed homosexuality,' he said, eyeing me along his aquiline nose as I passed

up the steps to see about a cup of tea.

'Oh yes? Who are *they*?'

'Freud and all that lot.'

'Well, I shouldn't worry too much about that if I were you.'

'I don't.' He sniggered and lapsed into silence.

While pausing on the steps I noticed that cups of tea were being lined up on the window sill of the kitchen. Riddle was drinking his. Billie somnolently declined a cup. The homeless lounger in the laurels, on his feet now to retrieve Verity's dog-end, hovered across towards the kitchen in case he could have the spare cup of tea. Riddle drank it. A hand sparkling with soap suds came out of the window and flung some crusts down for the sparrows. The homeless visitor retrieved two and pocketed them. I took Verity's teacup and mine back to the bench.

An alcoholic sat sweating on the steps.

'I'm forever blowing bubbles. . .' rocked through from the Admission Ward in far from dulcet tones.

A pair of fat ankles in black stockings passed the gates.

Billie dosed.

Covered with barbed wire and netting, the rusty black iron steps of a fire escape rose against the front wall of the Block to end at an iron barred door in the wall of Ward III. Its bottom two open-work treads were included in the recreational facilities of the yard. Above them a gate prevented access to the upper steps. A blue-suited youth sat in melancholy pose on the bottom tread. Knees up almost to his ears, he let his hands hang limply down towards the ground. Each wrist bore a neat white bandage. He gazed silently at those insignia of misery. There was barely ever a time at St Francis's when there was no one to be seen with bandaged wrists. He, Barton, looked at them as he meant others to look at them – with pity, with question.

However he had been categorised – schizoid, depressed, hysterical – his problem and the problem of many similar persons seemed to be the same. He was unloving and unloved. Boredom and isolation exaggerated his drifting impersonality. Quick flicked razor cuts across his wrists temporarily changed the dull tempo of things, inviting interest, sympathy, a change of scene from drab flat to a brightly lit hospital casualty ward. Perhaps on visiting day relatives would come to see him here. He would show them the bandages on his wrists. We gave him clean bandages almost as often as he asked for them until he was discharged or went to one of the big hospitals "for a rest". By this time the cuts were long since healed and their stitches removed. Barton did not want to die. Least of all did he want to kill himself, or he would have chosen a more serious method. He wished perhaps to pain himself into living, or to being lived with for a while.

The homeless visitor rescued another dog-end from Verity.

An alcoholic sweated across to the kitchen window slit and begged for work to earn a cup of tea. Mrs Scott said 'No!' Lucy smuggled one through the gap while her superior went off to inspect the staff lavatory.

A taciturn and curly-headed young man loitered by the gates. He had prowled around the yard and peered into all the laurel shrubs. Now, as though disinterested and resigned, he lay down on the dusty, tar-specked macadam below the gates. He rolled over and stuck his face into the outside road.

'Help!' he cried at the top of his voice, rolling immediately away and scrambling to his feet.

Riddle walked over to him.

'What are you shouting for? You'll wake all the babies in East Dulwich.' The shouter did not answer. No help came. Riddle encouraged him by the scruff of the neck to the front door.

'Here, Father,' he said, unlocking the front door and pushing the lad through,' this young fellow wants help. Do you think you can help him a bit in here?'

'Ho, ho. Got a naughty boy here have we?' asked Howard. 'All right, come on in. I'll look after him Nurse, thank you.' Howard ushered him in to sit on a locker in the Admission Ward. He called 'Help!'

167

once or twice in the intervals between Mr Potter's bubble blowing song, then lapsed into silence.

Riddle ambled back to lean against the wall, his great polar bear grimace suggesting the frustration he felt in missing the opportunity to sit down, and to sit down on a nice soft patient, just because he happened to be in the yard.

The alcoholic sweated on the steps.

Billie dosed.

The homeless visitor sorted, opened and emptied his last dog-end.

Barton watched the blue veins swelling on the backs of his hands.

The distraught and spotty man paced round and round.

The aristocratic young man filed and buffed another finger nail.

Mr Potter blew more bubbles in the air.

Curly head cried, 'Help!'

A grey haired senile gentleman pretended to listen to an alcoholic gentleman, who was pretending to talk to him so that he could talk and hear a sensible voice. A coloured gentleman seated himself on the bench between them and interrupted both by declaring that the Lord was high and mighty and Judgement Day was at hand. 'Yes Ssah! Judgement Day is surely a comin'. Is you prepared?' Neither were nor weren't, so they nodded and examined their several toes.

Billie dosed.

Y BLOCK

Tiny Verity and I talked quietly in short slow sentences and long silences about the Block, the patients, the staff.

***

'They say,' said Verity, looking sadly over his glasses at the hot patients with us in the yard, 'about ten percent of the population seek mental treatment during their lives.'

'It's a hell of a lot,' I said, 'but I think that is a rather miserable statistic.'

Statistics of that sort are miserable. A gathering of friends and relatives becomes an unhappy affair if one starts counting them off and wondering which person in every ten will be carried off to the mad house. The incidence of mental distress is large. There are undoubtedly many uncounted who do not seek or get carted away for treatment. Just as many suffer physical strain and do not find their way to a hospital, so do others crack under psychological pressures, but remain outside asylums. A few commit suicide and perhaps are not counted. More find in time a faith or a love which acts as an anchor for them. Yet others pass from sickness to health without knowing that parallel changes in their body chemistry have occurred.

Ten percent of the population seek mental treatment. The statistic itself is nowhere near to being a fact. For included in the returns are individuals who seek treatment many times. Through the doors of the Block alone, approximately half were passing for the second time at least. Several were regular customers.

Yet each time one of these patients went on to an asylum, he became a new statistic. And when he was discharged he became another statistic – a "cured" statistic.

The real danger of such numerical statements lies not in their inaccuracy, though the inaccuracy is seldom obvious. They are frequently produced with the honest intent of raising concern in the size of a problem, but fail to do so. They fail because a number excites little human feeling. A number is stored without emotion in the profit and loss account of memory. There is ten percent about which we can do nothing. There is ten percent of a problem. There is ten percent loss this year. It is a figure that can be juggled with. And while figures are being added, their mean square values taken, graphed and interpreted mathematically, attention is withdrawn from what the figures mean. The intelligence, effort and money spent on displays of statistical expertise might in part be better applied to the study of human function and behaviour; to an increased endeavour to find out the several causes of many individual miseries. This impersonality of numbers may inspire and motivate some people, but it seems only to create enthusiasm for more numbers – figures rather than people.

In the heat of the yard, the powerless pity engendered by the observation of our fellows moved me to a dissertation on the shackles of statistics, whereas Tiny Verity was absorbed with colour. Colour to him was a fact. The range of shades achieved by different surfaces and blends of dye were marvellous. The choice of colour for a particular mood was something to be carefully sensed.

'But,' he said, 'what are those jokers trying to get at with their insistence on "the psychological significance of colour"?'

'I don't know,' I replied, 'except that blue, for example, is often considered a depressing colour or its use a symptom of madness. One even speaks of "having the blues".'

'Yes, of course, that's obvious. But one or two psychologists try to identify the choice of a particular colour as symptomatic of a particular type of disturbance.'

I knew what he meant, for Little Tom and Semple held forth about colour on occasions. Semple was concerned only with red. People who wore a lot of red, who had red cars, curtains or even biros were, he said, 'definitely hysterical.' Little Tom with equal persistence and no great originality classed lovers of greens as being homosexual, lovers of browns as having anal fixations. White indicated a guilt complex and pastel shades an effeminate personality.

Verity appreciated the poetry in such colour symbolism, but was occasionally niggled by the almost clinical seriousness with which the parlour game of colour analysis was applied. Players did not look at a picture for the picture's own sake, but to have an opinion about the artist. Persons were not judged by what they did and said and felt, but by the colour of their clothes and carpets. Clearly, Tiny had been annoyed by some abuses of the language of colour directed against him. And anyone who is slightly introspective is niggled by specious catch phrases and snap diagnoses that by their very simplicity are memorable.

I assured him that many of his colleague nurses here were amateur psychologists; that he must not let himself be disturbed by their diagnoses of his conditions. He was already no doubt categorised as the schizoid type (or the "sexual") because he was tall and thin. Should he at any time be observed to have a change of mood, Billie would at once exclaim, 'That Verity is as cyclothymic as a see-saw. I bet his bowels need seeing to.' Most surely of all, if Tiny made a pun – or even a clever joke, or expressed himself with alliterative emphasis at any time – then the staff would mark him as a full-blown schizophrenic. It meant nothing, I tried to console him in advance. It was merely that the possession of a faculty such as imagination, amongst a staff where that gift was rare, marked the owner out as an exception. An exception is little better than to be a witch. Altogether unconsciously, here in Y Block where the security of a leaden, balanced mind was a rare thing, and something for the staff to prize, it was a case of scratch or be scratched. Since it was not a twentieth century custom to burn a witch, the more subtle separation from the offence was achieved by tagging it with a label. For "possessed" read "schizoid", for "moody" read "cyclothymic". The staff talked of each other in the language of their profession, and stretched the language to cover diverse conditions with a few words. That these words were catch phrases was, as in all parts of communication, the greatest curse. For a catch phrase appears to hold in essence the whole and satisfactory truth. Repetition only is necessary for belief to be established. Enquiry beyond the pleasing catch phrase is not encouraged.

Even the pin-striped aristocrat baking in the sun was afflicted or minutely irritated by a catch phrase. He had heard or read somewhere that excessive attention to the nails was "repressed homosexuality". With the hallucinations and delusions he bore, such an additional and trivial accusation was perhaps insignificant. But when his brain did have a temporary glimpse of order, and followed for a while sane tracks, it was a shame that such an unprovable and glib hypothesis was stuck in the way.

***

Howard appeared at the front door and beckoned his children in. They entered with the same gladness or lack of gladness with which they had exited. It was as if each one felt that there was nothing significantly hopeful either side of the lock for him.

CHAPTER 15: Fools' Errands

In the after lunch line-up for escort parties Riddle and I sat on either side of a skeletal and silent patient, propping him up in his red dressing gown. We waited on the pew by the front door clutching transfer papers and the patient's green bag of belongings. Escort duty made a break from the claustrophobia of Y Block for us. Our patient would give no trouble because he was barely strong enough to raise a finger. Yet all the same, this, as every other similar occasion, was sad. On morning shift in the late autumn and early winter one might expect two or three trips delivering patients to one of the catchment area hospitals, which had more vacancies after the heavy spring assignments were over.

No patients arrived at St Francis's unescorted, or on foot. Either ambulances or police cars brought them – with varying degrees of reluctance – accompanied or ushered by a DAO or police, or occasionally both. Few patients left us alone or on foot. Rarely, gentlemen in unusual and frenzied drunkenness were admitted at night. Morning in Y Block brought an equivalently sudden sobriety to such drinkers. Credit is due to the duty doctors who spotted their causes and effects and discharged them immediately – never in my experience to return. One visit had provided a memorable hangover for them.

All others left us either as certified or as voluntary patients. The sadness for us lay in the coercion of the certified and the faithless promise of hope for the voluntary. The Johnnies and the Morses, the homeless and the regular alcoholics were no problem. But the acutely psychotic young men filled me with impotent pity.

To the north and south of London stand the great asylums. Bedlams, Workhouses, Lunatic Asylums, "Bins" or Hospitals – only their colloquial titles have changed. Red and dark bricked, these grim-faced architectural mixes of Victorian factory and gothic styles frown over the countryside. Blunt water towers and chimneys dominate the sweeping lawns and sad macadam drives. Each turreted institution block in the green-belt trees stands as a mute reminder to the homeward bound commuter that he is provided for if he goes mad. His neat and proper semi, however far strung along the road away from the asylum, lies within its pervasive gloom.

The faces of its long-term patients have taken on the impassive sadness of the asylum. The skin hangs on their faces like old wallpaper on a damp wall. Their clothes seem as inappropriate to housing bodies as the asylum is to housing and curing the mentally afflicted. But the asylum draws the patients back, possibly because it offers security. And within its confines effort and love battle half blindly on in a struggle to treat and cure. Doctors and nurses – dedicated, resigned, optimistic – work with pitiful official resources at their disposal. From the national and public endeavour one would think that the problems of mental disorder were insignificant. Or that all was known about it and all was known to be hopeless.

There *are* new hospitals. There *is* some research going on. But these bright spots have one ill effect: their demonstration minimises further questions and fundamental attacks on the problems. It is difficult for the public to be critical about what is not being done, when its eye is caught by the glittering signs of progress. Seen in perhaps slightly pessimistic proportion, what actually is being done to understand and cure mental maladies is akin to an attempt to resuscitate a drowned man by manicuring his fingernails while he lies in his coffin.

The coffin asylum draws its walking corpses back. The institutionalised hundreds have no hope, but they have here some sort of home away from the mad world. Those that leave, as our regular patients often told us, obtain a certificate which says in effect that they are sane. We do not have such vouchers of our own sanity. Nor should we deserve one while priorities of public money and concern allow even one single such asylum to stand as an ugly monument to madness?

It may be well imagined that it was not the loveliness of the destinations that encouraged the staff of Y Block to do as many escort duties as each individual could. A more persuasive draw was the possibility that the trip could be stretched out beyond three-thirty, when we would earn extra hours off duty in lieu of pay. In autumn too, rides through the country with a quiet patient could be pleasant, and some of the hospitals had large orchards whose windfalls helped to eke out the cheese diets of night duty. Cricket matches glimpsed through the jolting ambulance windows . . . transport café tea on the return journey . . . girls sauntering through the bright streets of Croydon – all small joys, a world away from the Psychiatric Observation Unit, lured us out very willingly.

***

I went to the front door to greet our ambulance. But the one that drew up was not ours. It brought another patient in.

He was a big fellow and he had been punishing the Meths & Tizer. His delirium was wonderful to see; but better seen through the porthole of a padded cell.

If Riddle and I had had any luck we would have been away already on our escort duty. This might not have been as well for the rest, however, because there would have been little strength on the staff. Strength was always a thing Howard had to calculate meticulously. It was not good having a shift or an escort made up entirely of weedy men. There must be always a nucleus of strong or at least agile young men. Only occasionally could two fit and capable men be sent on escort duty.

Today the Admission Ward at that hour was short of heavies. Billie was called over to look after the outgoing patient. Riddle, Howard and I were left to deal with the incoming dragon. Dragon might have been right. I was sure that a match to his nostrils would have produced jets of clear blue flame. His breath was powerful.

After a chase around the ward we got hold of the Dragon. Or rather, we got *a* hold. He swung the three of us about for a while, then Howard caught him round the neck and we pitched him onto a bed. Fortunately, an empty bed. I clambered onto the Dragon's chest and pinned down his arms while Riddle sat on his legs. My legs, meanwhile, were stretched down between and under Riddle's knees.

We had him.

But we were all in a pretty ridiculous position and could not move to do anything else.

Every now and again the Dragon erupted. His heaving raised everyone up a few inches and a leg shot out of control and kicked one of us with a big nailed shoe.

Impasse.

Then Sandy Wilson came in. Sandy Wilson – not Big Wilson the sadist who had his arm broken. Sandy was a mild, small, soft man with a lot of grey black hair and a nearly purple complexion. He wore thicklensed spectacles and coughed frequently.

He bore a tray of tea.

'Tea up dears.'

'What do you mean, tea up? Can't you see we've got bloody work on?' Howard was losing a lot of his gentian violet round the patient's neck and getting very annoyed.

'Oh,' Sandy peered and coughed, 'who's that you've got underneath you?'

'It's the Matron; come and help!'

Sandy trotted across to the desk with the teas and then joined us.

'I didn't hear anybody come in.'

'Good God, he's deaf as well,' said Riddle.

'What do you want *me* to do then, dears?' Sandy always pretended to be queer.

Perhaps he was, but he was equally civil and pleasant with both sexes. All except for Whale. But then Whale was not definitely either sex, and maybe that made it hard for Sandy.

'Help us get this bugger undressed,' said Howard.

'Get his ruddy shoes off,' I called. 'He's got me twice on the shins already.'

'All right dears.' Sandy bent down and looked into the mess of limbs at Riddle's end.

We could feel deft movements from Sandy's fingers. A double jerk at that end.

'Not *my* bloody shoes, Sandy,' I cried. Both feet were shoeless and cold and, before I could speak again, my socks too were dragged away.

'I am sorry, there are so many feet down here, I couldn't quite see.'

'Well, just put my socks on anyway.' I felt terribly vulnerable in bare feet.

'Now start again Sandy. And when you start on the trousers don't for God's sake take Riddle's off. We'll be here all night shovelling his belly back in.'

Riddle laughed. He was proud of his belly. He heaved it into his local every night, flopped it onto the bar and called, 'Fill that up please.' Nearly always

179

there was somebody who had not heard it before. So he got his laugh and repeated his performance the next evening.

Gradually, the correct shoes came off. Then the trousers. Then the shirt. At last the Dragon was naked. And his power dissipated. There is nothing more strengthening to a man than his clothes. If Sampson's hair was so long that it covered him, it is not surprising that shorn and naked he was weak.

After a good hypo the Dragon was lifted into the padded cell. His calm demeanour looked altogether to be preceding another storm, and he alone should have the benefit of the next one.

'I'm sorry about your shoes Nurse Lynch'

'Oh, don't worry Sandy. Only don't call me Nurse Lynch. It makes me wonder if my slip's showing. It was funny really,' I said, tying my laces.

Riddle and I adjusted our clothing and collected the outgoing patient from Billie.

'I shouldn't trust him too far if I were you,' said Billie as the ambulance drew up. 'He's very quiet and I mistrust them when they're quiet. It means they're brooding and plotting something.'

'He's asleep Billie.'

'Oh! That's it then. I told you.'

Riddle and I laughed and left in the blue coach for the country.

A fast though bumpy drive down. The patient admitted and receipt obtained for him. Always a receipt required. This was the final indignity for the patient. He was exchanged for a slip of paper. One or two who saw the transaction on the Admission Ward must have felt that they were being sold into bondage.

Sometimes a patient was not willing to go to another hospital. This was not usually out of a strong liking for us and St Francis, but an obsessive fear of the unknown.

Mr Lines was an office manager. He had been discovered interfering with small boys. It was not the crime that brought him in. The crime was just a symptom of his distress. A well-dressed, well-spoken and, one would have thought, a mild man, he was completely shattered.

All adulthood appeared to have been stripped from him. All self-confidence was gone. His pink and pleasant face wore an anxious frown. The miserable cloud that appeared to separate him from reality was unbelievably thick.

'What is that?' he would ask as you struck a match. 'Why do you do that?' He was labelled paranoid, and it seemed as though all his senses had become heightened. He noticed everything. But everything. A lot of things we do and say are odd. Look at them long enough and hard enough and they lose any realistic significance at all. Why pull that face? Why say that? Why make that pile of matchsticks on your desk?

There is no significance. These are just fidgets inside the brain; internal irritations that have broken into spots of action. There is no significance for us who are in sound and careless objectivity of mind.

But an introspective, frightened person lacking in self-confidence does not easily shrug things off as having no significance. He investigates. Ordinary everyday things do not bear very close enquiry. There are no obvious answers about them and the invented answers are prickly. Mr Lines was concerned about himself, so the answers he found were about himself. Minute observations about irrelevant actions were recorded by him and built into his plan of what was happening. The pattern of life had always been the rest versus Lines. Now he, Lines, was making mental note of the great conspiracy against him. Every detail was observed and recorded. Every action confirmed his suspicions about those around him. It was all part of the plot. There was obviously a plot and the plot was obvious. They were out to get him. He felt it. In every acid nerve end of his body he felt it. Now he was hot and fidgety, anxious with his questions: probe, probe, probe with the questions. But don't let them see that you are on to them. Keep cool. Put a bland smile on your face and walk about observing.

Mr Lines was over the border now. His questions had continued. Prowling the Recreation Ward and stairs, Lines had a question for every nurse and patient. Although it was October, the day was grey and November in every minute of it. Occasionally a lash of nearly frozen rain patterned the small windows. Why those streaks across the glass, nurse? Why have all the patients got green covers on their beds?

Lines paced up and down, now flushed and urgent, now calm and collected. After four days the consultant psychiatrist decided he would like to have Lines transferred to the new psychiatric wing of the teaching hospital. Help and treatment were offered him. It was all the same to Lines. It was all part of the plot. He knew. But no one should know he knew. Not now. He would go along with them so far and then make his getaway.

Billie and I were assigned to escort duty for Mr Lines. The journey was only a couple of miles and the patient was bland courtesy itself. He even stretched a hand out to help Billie up the ambulance steps. The ambulance swung down the long hill towards the river.

'What's the time?' Lines asked.

We looked at our watches.

Bang. Lines rushed to the back of the ambulance, grabbed the big door handle and flung the doors wide as the step folded down. Still gripping a handle, Lines teetered over the blurred grey of the road. As we accelerated down the straight stretch at the bottom of the hill, he gathered himself to leap out onto the road.

I fell across the floor, hooking the toes of my black shoes around the wheel arches and grabbed Lines by his jacket, hauling it in until I could grip him round the waist.

Billie yelled, 'Driver, sound the bell!' The driver did, 'And slow down!' The muscles round Lines' waist tensed again as he prepared to impel us both under the nose of a red bus. The driver applied the brakes and the lurch helped me pull Lines back in. Billie applied extra weight by pulling on my coat collar before leaping up, slamming the doors to, locking them and transferring his weight to the handle.

'Move on driver. Keep the bell going.' In sweat and clamour we arrived at the hospital. The driver and two attendants from within helped us to drag Mr Lines to his treatment. It must have been easier, I thought, to drag a bull to slaughter than to get Mr Lines in there.

It was wasted effort. Within a few days Mr Lines was delivered, with an escort of four attendants, back to St Francis's. The case notes indicated that he would have to wait for a vacancy at one of the southern asylums where the particular treatment (unstated) that he needed was available. It was also indicated that Lines had proved too volatile a patient to serve as teaching material. The list of his offences read like a charge sheet. He had locked himself in a cupboard. He had threatened to throw a doctor out of an upstairs window, and had actually thrown himself out of one on the ground floor. He blackened the eye of a female nurse and, despite his refusal of all food, grew more restive and violent each day. So he came back to us.

As Billie put it, 'We risked our lives on a fool's errand.' In many ways all out escorts were fools' errands, and sad.

CHAPTER 16: Sandy

The short stay in Y Block would have been even sadder for many patients had it not been for Sandy Wilson. Sandy, the complete opposite of his namesake, Big Wilson, was not an important person. At least, in his view he was not important. He preferred to be anonymous and was even self-effacing. By the staff he was generally accepted at the value he appeared to put on himself. But the patients occasionally saw into Sandy and found the kindness there; they were perhaps momentarily healed, and for a second were brought by his kindness into the world where other people live. Sandy did the dirty jobs and did not complain too loudly. Sandy would give his last cigarette to a patient and if you called him a fool he would agree with you, but he would remonstrate mildly and find an excuse for his sacrifice.

However much Sandy was ridiculed, or more likely just ignored, some of his unselfishness rubbed off onto other nurses. A small exercise of charity towards a patient was often Sandy-inspired. Without any more understanding of mental sickness than others, he was able to be an observer and guardian of the sick in mind without losing the capacity to care for people difficult to love. And since concern for others – despite the fact that Y Block's "others" were reminders of what we ourselves might have been but for the grace of God – concern is a rare commodity and Sandy merits more than passing mention.

Sandy Wilson was born in Wales. His father, a miner, was killed in a pit accident when Sandy was eleven. So before there was a hair upon his chest, and before the merry games of youth had toughened his muscles, he became the head of the family. Two small sisters grew large mouths to feed. And, like some small sisters everywhere, were ungrateful.

Sandy worked for a lens grinder and watch repairer. Bent over a green baize table six days a week to keep the family improperly fed and clothed, his chest became constricted and his eyes strained.

Years of this left their mark upon his face. The skin, untouched by any sun, grew white and loose where no smiles flexed up the muscles. Then his lungs, creased and soaked with cold, damp air, gave back to his heart blood that was not properly cleaned. The heart pumped this dutifully seventy beats a minute, year in, year out, to every limb. But soon the capillaries at his ear lobes and in his nose became cyanotic. This aged Sandy prematurely: with a purple wax face and slender, feeble hands, he was not a handsome man.

The young girls, even his sisters, called him other things but Sandy. "Owl eyes" would do if his glasses flashed in the lamp light. "Sampson" when he looked pathetically weak. No woman would think about actually marry Sandy.

'Why, he's nice enough I suppose.'

'And harmless.'

'But he's such a creep. He wouldn't say boo to a goose.'

Y BLOCK

No woman fell in love with Sandy. And, after his sisters, he would have been suspicious of any woman.

Only his mother he loved; with a loyalty and tenderness that never left him. She died and Sandy never forgot her.

There were no meals waiting for him when he got home now. He prepared his own and his young sisters' meal. He was keeping them at school as he promised his mother. They were going to be teachers.

His years of sacrifice were wasted when one gave up the idea of teaching, got married and left the district; and the other sister died. This cloud hid a silver lining perhaps? Not for Sandy.

He packed up his old job and moved to a new firm: a go-ahead career selling clocks, watches and acceptable wedding gifts by the hundred. Now he could work just five and a half days a week and be comfortably off.

Then came the depression. Whether it was the Big Depression or a local slump Sandy was always vague about it. It was too close to him to be of anything but personal significance. He lost his job. The chances were that he would never have taken it if his sister had not married. Going to find a suitable wedding present for her he had seen a vacancy advertised in the shop's window. On an impulse (a novel sensation for Sandy) he applied and got the job. His old firm, who would never have sacked him, were quite upset; they appreciated he had wanted to make a break, but he could not go back to them when this new firm failed: job ended.

Sandy found a job as a labourer with the town council's direct labour force. He fainted twice on the first day. The second day they made him a clerk in the foreman's office. The third day an accountant sought that job and Sandy was fired.

In desolation he sold, or mostly gave away the household goods to his mother's friends. He had none of his own. He left for London.

He did not expect to find the streets paved with gold. Nor were they. But at least he found an inside job. For a year or two he worked on the geriatric wards of St Francis's. Then Y Block offered him the price of an extra packet of cigarettes on his wages.

Sandy was full of tenderness. He was as gentle with old men as if they were his babies. They snored in the night and Sandy turned them. They spat, dribbled and were fountainheads of phlegm and nasal discharge; Sandy wiped them clean. Three times in a row they soiled the clean sheets and their shirts with excreta and urine; Sandy remade the beds and bathed them. His hands were never sudden or rough. I saw his face peed into while he was hardening bed sores with surgical spirit. He swore, of course, but softly and away from the patient.

He would never let Big Wilson or Riddle near an old man in case they hurt him.

He lived by himself in a single room near Peckham Rye. Occasionally, I saw him eat a slice of white bread and butter, but apart from this his diet was slim.

Perhaps he was afraid to put on weight that his heart could not sufficiently supply. Perhaps he wanted to keep himself light so that in old age he too could be lifted tenderly and nursed to the grave when his brain had turned to chalk.

Sandy made the tea for others. Sandy cleaned the padded cell. Sandy worked on Christmas Day and Boxing Day, and August Bank Holiday and Easter and Whitsun. For his annual holiday he stayed in his one-roomed flat apart from two days in Wales. Here he visited his mother's grave, placed flowers on it, paid and arranged for it to be kept for another year.

He was never thanked. The Sandys of this world very rarely are.

'Why do you do it, Sandy?'

'I'd like to be treated this way.' He never was.

Through the long nights he would take on extra duty so that a man could be with his wife. He would sit on the stairs, two steps up, so that he could watch the needs of both Wards I and II. His yellow fingers caressed a cigarette and he drank his tea.

'That's all I want,' he said, 'a fag and a cup of tea.'

Sandy apparently did not have any imagination. If he had he could not have been what he was. There was just unselfishness in him.

The last time I saw Sandy was when I went off for a week during my second winter on the Block. He was clearing up someone's mess. Two days after my return I noticed his name had been crossed off the shift list.

'Where's Sandy?' I asked. 'Has he left?'

'Oh. Sandy. He's dead. He died last week.'

Even Howard, who could work up a bit of volubility at times, had nothing more to say.

Sandy had felt a bit poorly on the Monday. Just his chest again he said. No need to get anybody back on duty on his account. He'd be OK in the afternoon. After lunch the upstairs dormitory was locked to patients and Sandy went in to have a lie down for a while.

Dobey, wanting to speed the passing of the morning shift, went in to that dormitory for one hundred and forty winks as well. He thought Sandy was quiet, but dozing until…

'Is that you Dobey? Can you help me? I feel a bit ill.'

Sandy rarely complained. He just stated facts. Dobey crossed to him.

'Good God,' he said, 'you're a bad colour.' 'I can't really breathe,' Sandy choked.

'I'll get a doctor.'

Dobey went, and doctor and stretcher arrived together. Sandy was wheeled over to the main hospital.

At half past three he died. Oxygen could not puff life back into his poor frame.

There was a collection for a wreath. His sister got his savings. He was forgotten by the world.

Sandy would never have hoped to have been put on record. Would have thought there were more important things to be done. But Sandys always think like this. Yet were it not for the constant hand they place on the world's wheel, it would not go round so smoothly nor for so long for so many patients.

CHAPTER 17: Homeless Men

The year's efforts to supply London with any sort of lengthy summer failed and the year became depressed. It gave up the struggle to retreat gracefully through autumn, and plunged us into winter immediately. Now on the narrow approach road to St Francis's a wet wind plucked green leaves from the plane trees and slapped them on pavement and gatepost. The laurel leaves in the courtyard were washed clean. Gutters ran full, to drip and freeze until the Block looked like some lumbering tanker icebound in arctic waters.

Sandy was missed in the Unit then, at least by the underling attendants. For it was the long season of old and homeless men. It took a deal of Sandy-like patience to be charitable and useful towards them. Infestation, dirt and smell were constant presences on the admission bed.

Our regular and varied intake, with in winter additional numbers of homeless and senile men (and women in X Block we heard), were added to towards spring by the attempted suicides. All these were a heavy load. The first flock of homeless patients to enter the Block heralded winter here as surely as swallows herald spring in other places. They came at all times of day or night, always escorted by the police. They had no family or friends to call a Duly Authorised Officer to admit them so they became the responsibility of the law. Generally, they had to appeal for this attention, either by giving a demonstration of being a public nuisance drunk in a roadway, or a private nuisance curled up on a smart doorstep. If these methods failed them, obvious pilfering could be effective, particularly if reinforced by assaulting the police constable when he arrived. Should the hardships of life not become apparent to the vagrant until late at night, he usually found that the destructive luxury of throwing something through a plate-glass window brought 'help' immediately.

Some homeless men preferred prison, and hoped that their sentence would last through the bleak days of winter. Others had a leaning towards hospitals. The pretence of violent stomach pains occasionally secured a warm hour or two in the casualty department of a general hospital but very rarely earned a whole night's bed with pretty nurses in attendance.

How the homeless came to learn of places like St Francis's is not known. It may be assumed that they heard from itinerant ex-patients, meths drinkers and down-and-out alcoholics who shared occasional bench or embankment accommodation with them. There must have been some detailed information exchanged because they not only knew where to commit their nuisance to be admitted to a particular unit; they had a fair grasp of symptomatology too. Yet nearly always they chose to simulate the same gross psychosis.

'I hear voices in my head.'

'Do you now? Do you only hear them in a police station?'

'No, I've heard them all year. But they're getting worse.'

'What are they saying?'

'They're telling me I've got to kill someone.'

'Who?'

'I don't know yet. The voices are from outer space. They tell me someone's interfering with me with radio waves. That's why I hear buzzing in my head as well.'

Caution as well as concern encouraged the police to bring such vagrants to us. Perhaps they were right to do so. Punishment would not change them. Yet it was difficult to understand them. In the psychiatrist's case notes the brief assessments ranged from "work shy, malingerer" to "mildly aggressive psychopath, depressive condition"; or occasionally where the doctor had interviewed the patient after he had been cleaned up and was in full histrionic swing the assessment would be "schizoid; auditory hallucinations; disorientated".

Of diagnoses it would be foolish to disagree with "work shy". But "depressive condition" seemed nearer the truth. For each and every homeless patient was isolated and downcast. They were seldom talkative about themselves or indeed about anything. They gave the impression of having at some time in the past been beaten down and crushed so that resurrection on Earth was impossible. They had lost almost everything except the ability to walk from place to place. A few found some work in the fruit fields of Cambridgeshire or the Vale of Evesham during the summer. This, together with dustbin gleanings at other times, kept them going.

Some homeless patients did not like people. The burden of relationships with other people was shunned by them as surely as were the responsibilities of un-portable property or permanent work. Even the onus of a long conversation was shirked. A homeless patient might go through the tale of his delusions for the police and the duty doctor, but then leave the office or turn over on the bed and say no more. He had come to roost for winter and hoped not to be disturbed.

**

I sniffed as I beat and blew the first sharp frost out of my fingers and walked into the Admission Ward. Green screens round the admission bed. I sniffed again. 'Vagrant in, already bathed,' my senses told me. The sickly reek of an oily disinfectant poured over all the hairy parts of admitted vagrants indicated that bugs, body lice and fleas had been admitted as well, and were being dealt with.

Verity's head was visible above the screens.

'Been sharing your Brylcreem around then?' I asked him.

'Cheeky bugger. Come and help me get a few more of these bugs out will you.'

I stepped through to where a patient named Paddy lay docile on a blanket. His creased and weather-beaten face was inscrutable between the tangled sticky messes of hair and beard. More of the white oil anointed his chest, armpits and pubic hair.

'We've bathed and scrubbed him. Then Billie poured a whole can of this stuff over him but still the bloody lice crawl out,' Tiny said. 'It's my belief they like the smell.'

'They're the only ones that do,' I said, combing out a further armour-clad parasite. 'The amount of stuff Billie's poured on, they must be strong swimmers as well.'

Verity had found a pair of tweezers with which he patiently sorted through one of Paddy's armpits. From the dispensary came noises of disgust as Billie washed his hands. Big Wilson stood by the property book in which he had been able to itemise the clothing but nothing else. The clothing was sent off for fumigation, but it might as well have been burned. Outer rags were damp and mouldy; inner rags were lousy.

Paddy was moved into a bed next to one of our regular homeless patients admitted the night before. They looked at each other with disdain. Each affected to despise the condition of the other. The regular patient had threepence-halfpenny noted on his property list. Paddy had nothing. His fingernails were long, black and unbroken. The regular patient's fingernails were assorted. On each hand the thumb nails were bitten down to pink skin, which colour existed nowhere else; the nails of his first three fingers were cracked, split and filthy; but the nails on the little fingers were long and hooked and comparatively clean. They were so obviously cared for that they excited the attention of the examining doctor. He hoped to unmask perhaps some crucial fetish but O'Leary explained that they were for cleaning out his ears. O'Leary was blunt but accurate.

After lunch the police delivered a third homeless patient to us. He was paralytic drunk and we wondered whose generosity or folly had made this state possible. Verity and I undressed him while Billie stood by. The top layer of black and khaki coats came off fairly easily. Then we struggled to get the tight woollen jumpers – three of them – away. Beneath these, protecting a collarless shirt, and keeping it in its original creases, was a good supply of newspapers. After these were removed there was not a great deal of the patient underneath. Only his legs were fat. Billie now stepped forward to help unwrap the swaddling bands that made up the bulk of the patient's legs. On and on the uncoiling continued until admission bed and floor were draped in dirty bandages. Then, towards the skin of each leg, pound notes and fivers began to flutter free. Billie counted out loud and stacked the notes in two piles – one for each leg – on the bedside locker. When the last tenshilling note came away from the patient's left ankle he was known to be worth eighty-three pounds a leg.

Verity and I had not seen so much money before. Billie was most concerned to get his additions right, then was quite amazed to find that he was right and there was an equal exact amount in each leg. With the patient sonorous in drunken sleep it would be foolish to pretend that we did not momentarily grieve that some of this wealth was ours. Big Wilson had already gone off duty and it was Dobey who recorded the amount and sealed the notes away with the patient's property.

'It's only fair, said Dobey. 'Some who do the property think this sort of thing is a windfall. No names, no pack drill,' he said, 'but Wilson isn't always above taking a bit.' It was typical of poor Dobey that his demonstrations of admirable moral qualities were spoiled by simultaneous demonstrations of incredible thickness. If he were asked now if he thought Wilson was a thief he would shake his head and smile and say, 'No names, no pack drill,' and believe he had never mentioned Wilson's name at all.

I checked back in my mind to remember if Wilson had been on duty when my pay packet disappeared. He hadn't been, so that mystery was not cleared up.

We gathered together the newspapers brought in by the latest addition to the ward. Unfolded, they revealed no further savings accounts and were destroyed. We could be certain that whatever value newspapers had for our homeless patients, they would soon gather more. When they were on their feet again, the search for dog-ends took second place only to the collection of newspapers. Outside, these had a practical value: sheets of the larger newspapers provided good body insulation worn under a shirt; small papers were folded for shoe lining; thin papers yielded the wherewithal to roll dog-ends into new cigarettes. Occasionally, a vagrant might be seen reading a newspaper. If he could not read, at least he liked to be seen looking at one. There is magic in newsprint for those who have trouble in the attic. In waiting rooms and libraries all over London the local "barmy" is to be seen drooling and snoozing over the daily paper. And if he has half a chance he will take it away with him.

We had to clean out the lockers of our "no-fixedaboders" at least once a day for they are great hoarders of things. Bits of string, odd buttons, tin lid ashtrays, empty match boxes – anything that takes their fancy – are lifted away to a pocket or are stuffed into bulging trousers. Knives had to be most thoroughly counted when homeless patients were in. Like glum magpies they wandered around securing small possessions for themselves.

When encouraged to sit in the Recreation Ward they were the sorrow of Miss Hall on Thursday afternoons. Miss Hall was the occupational therapist, petite, dark haired and bright eyed. The sight of her well-shaped figure hurrying along the corridor was of full therapeutic value for us and her smile was good to see in Y Block. She worked hard in the geriatric wards on other days, teaching weaving and basket making. Her skill and patience helped to make cramped old fingers nimble, and her mere presence lightened the old folks' dull, bed-ridden days. But in Y Block there was little she could do.

Even a sound mind is unlikely to do more than whet the mind's appetite by two hours spent trying to sort out the complexities of a raffia-seated stool. Put a shaky mind to this task, particularly when the shaky mind will not see that stool again, and the result is exasperation for the patient and frustration for Miss Hall. Even so, a few of our patients tried to be cooperative. But not the no-fixed-aboders. If they saw her coming they feigned such engrossing madness as to be excused her attentions. Only Paddy, when he gained the freedom of the Recreation Ward, lacked the experience of our more regular visitors and was caught off-balance.

Miss Hall descended on him like a nest-building sparrow with bits of wicker, raffia and (luxury) brightly coloured string. Paddy recovered his mental imbalance and smiled cheerfully. He took all the gifts she had to offer. He listened benevolently with many sagacious nods to the complex instructions and let her go confidently away to attend to others. Paddy's face took on a determined air.

The wicker should have been cut to eleven and a half inches.

He cut it to eleven.

The raffia he shredded until it was all in pieces as thin as a spider's cord.

The brightly coloured string he knotted. Then he knotted it again and again and again, and departed to the lavatory after dropping it all into the lap of the regular vagrant. This patient was so deep in his performance of lunacy that I had to recover the materials from him. Miss Hall felt that he might do some permanent damage if he actually ate the wicker, and performing a hair cut on his neighbour was hardly to be considered therapy for either of them.

Miss Hall was not to be blamed for spending more of her allotted Thursday hours tidying the upstairs bathroom cupboard where her occupational stock in trade was kept. She had no more success with our homeless patients than did Miss Tracey, the Psychiatric Social Worker.

CHAPTER 18: Miss Tracey and Odd Cases

Miss Tracey worked the whole year round, and appeared to work every daylight hour. She was the only Psychiatric Social Worker for the Unit, making quick visits to see patients and then rushing off to sort out the problems they had left behind. She worked on her own, remembering names of regular admittances, and introducing herself with a smile to new faces in the recreation ward.

Miss Tracey was not more than thirty-five, and her physical attractiveness was not marred by a slightly stocky build. Large and gentle, her brown eyes glowed with understanding and tenderness. Short, almost straight, brown hair curled under at the nape of her neck and at her forehead. Streaks of grey in the rich brown of her hair, together with tiny crows' feet about her eyes, lent a mature seriousness that was balanced by her mobile, smiling mouth.

A small army of Miss Traceys could have worked miracles amongst the hundreds of patients passing through the Block each year. A small army of clerks and typists could have enabled her to spend more time actually in the Block where her contact was invaluable, and in visiting relatives to whom she was liaison officer and ambassadress. But some bureaucracy had deemed that Miss Tracy should be saddled with a mass of paper work: insurance cards to be stamped, sickness benefits to be claimed, employers to write to, families to contact, financial matters to arrange – whatever the job there was always a duplicity of forms to go with it. Her hands were always full of papers and cards which claimed the bulk of attention during her conversations with our inmates - which was a pity since few seemed as able as Miss Tracey to make the morose talk, and the rambling perhaps coherent for a moment or two. The clerical demands of her job lessened the time given to the psychiatric and rehabilitation benefits she offered.

When Miss Tracey came into the Recreation Ward a new homeless patient would rise from his chair and drift over to her. While she paused, scanning the room to match a face to a form in her hand, he would hint gruffly that he was prepared to accept benefits. Despite urgent shuffling through her sheaves of paper, Miss Tracey found that she could not help him with more than a smile and a kind word. Homeless people have no addresses. They have no official identity. Despite their living presence, bureaucratically they were not considered real people at all. Miss Tracey could not spend more than a moment or two with them.

There were all the regulars for her to see. Winter brought its crop of old men. She knew that spring shortly would bring pathetic pieces of humanity who had tried and failed to kill themselves. Desperately she hoped that she was able to help them a little. But the homeless patients were beyond help. There was no time. The Psychiatric Observation Unit was full and, in addition to the typical range of sufferers, each week brought its "odd cases".

Amongst the medley of individualists who made up the Unit's clientele it may seem perverse to isolate any as being particularly odd. Each person with a shattered "schizoid" mind; each maniac, depressive and alcoholic was idiosyncratic. Yet, however much the analysts spoke or wrote, one couldn't help questioning whether in every one of these separate mental conditions there were parallel physical events: the blocking and reversing of chemical processes in the brain cells of the schizophrenic; an acid overspill on nerve cells and the motor tracks of voice and limb in the euphoric maniac; toxins in the cells of the depressed; metabolic gaps in the alcoholic make-up that stimulated a craving for strong drink.

Whatever are the causes, effects or symptoms of these men, however little is known of their sicknesses, and however individual their manifestations, they are alas commonplace.

Others, who took a great deal of Miss Tracey's time this winter were less prone to categorisation and defied one even to imagine what their sicknesses might be. Each one stood out like a harlequin in a funeral procession.

***

Mr Coiles was neither highly coloured nor interesting in appearance. He was a tall, lean country boy with pale off-white spotty skin. His complexion spoke of dim-lit offices rather than the market gardens where he worked. Pottering about between greenhouses or plucking thistles from the garden beds, he would have excited no attention. He was not very bright as far as could be judged. Even so, now at the age of twenty-one he had decided that the market garden was too small, too dull to keep so rare a flower as he.

He stuffed his pockets with all the wages and savings that he could draw on and packed a few rough-cut sandwiches alongside. Like a moth magnetised by lamp light he made towards London. Here his best Sunday suit was sufficient with the money it contained to impress the commissionaire and receptionist of a smart West End hotel. His bored expression and negligent dealing out of pound notes put an aura of aristocracy about him that secured a fine suite of rooms for his holiday. Here he stayed, glutting himself with unaccustomed service. He took all meals in his rooms but declined to let the cleaners in. The management's suspicion of his eccentricity was roused when he slipped out after dinner and returned with fish and chips and hot dogs. The management enquired discreetly if Coiles enjoyed the food the hotel supplied? Manifestly he did, because it was all eaten. The kitchens were surprised to see burnt chips and fish bones returned with pages from a month-old Mirror, when they had sent up creamed potatoes, steak and that day's Evening News. The upstairs maid expected some sauciness from young gentlemen on her floor, nor was she alarmed that Coiles did not wear pyjamas. However, an explicit Anglo-Saxon invitation to sexual intercourse from a youth, naked except for black boots, did cause her to talk about Room 231 to her equals and betters.

So, with a discretion that was the better part of business acumen, the management presented Coiles his account daily. After four nights he was unable to pay. His pockets yielded nothing but the crumbs of his rough-cut sandwiches. But Coiles declined to leave. While other persons were about their afternoon idleness, the police were called and took Coiles away. He had nothing to say.

No charges were preferred and since Coiles had committed no public nuisance the police were at a loss to know what to do with him. On an inspiration, they brought him to us. Three policemen honoured Coiles with their company in a fast squad car. They gave jovial accounts of his behaviour while in London, which accounts, even if they did not justify Coiles admission to us, explained the policemen's reluctance to keep him "pending enquiries".

It was all too much and too strange for the country boy. The excitement of forced and unexplained progression from luxury hotel to police station to emergency mental unit set him trembling at the knees. As the duty doctor was on the premises when Mr Coiles was admitted, he decided to interview him as soon as he was bathed. Within ten minutes, Coiles was standing in slippers and night shirt waiting for the psychiatric summons. Whether fright turned his bladder muscles suddenly to jelly, or whether he had not been able to find the hotel lavatory, Raggle did not know. Yet as Raggle stood by Coiles and placed a guiding hand upon his shoulder, Coiles relieved himself mightily. Slippers and Raggle's feet were soaked in the un-staunched flow. Rivulets coursed across the tiled flooring and threatened to seep under the office door.

We cleaned up the floor and Coiles. Raggle, with exemplary patience, confined himself to a fervent wish that next time Coiles would hold his urine until he was being interviewed. Raggle felt it might be of more clinical use, he said, if the doctor had the benefit of such dramatic micturition.

Next day Coiles was in the Recreation Ward. Miss Tracey chatted with him and, consulting the case notes to see the official instructions, arranged for his brothers to collect him. The thoughtfulness in her suggestion may not have been apparent to Coiles' family, but that way they and Coiles were saved the embarrassment of his return with an escort of two lunatic attendants.

***

Ronald Wildash was not a once-only visitor to Y Block as Coiles had been. In fact, though his total residence was brief, this was his seventeenth appearance in three years. Although the common theme to his malady was one of self-violence, he was never very serious about it. He showed a caution which belied his overt attempts at dying. Once admitted to our care he seemed anxious to get out of it again, and rarely howled for sympathy. As far as Miss Tracey could discover, there was no particular incident or person that triggered off his attempts upon himself. He was not certifiable and scorned the whole idea of voluntary treatment. That in itself was quite rational since there was no agreed treatment for him. For our part, we assumed that the Unit had some horrible fascination for Mr Wildash, and that it was both his disease and perhaps the cure of it.

Be those things as they may, he possessed a long list of varied crimes against himself. By this seventeenth bout of Wildash versus Wildash, he had run through a whole gamut of grievous bodily harm. Perhaps he was so well known in East London that the police brought him in on sight. He had previously been picked up jumping, or threatening to jump, from places more public than dangerous. He had taken he said doses from bottles where labels were cautionary, but which contained little or none of the poisonous sanitary fluid they advertised. He had on separate occasions cut minor veins in his wrists and ankles. His Adam's apple was scratched by numerous blunt knives. Perhaps the sixteenth occasion in a relative's gas oven had gone on too long and softened his brain, for attempt seventeen had taxed Mr Wildash's imagination to the limit. With a double-edged razor blade, which also nicked his fingertips, he slashed a criss-cross of cuts into his scalp. The top of his head was a mess of cut hair and blood. Though Wildash pulled his tie tightly about his neck to diminish the flow of blood, one small artery right at the top of his skull sent a four inch jet of blood regularly into the air. Delivered to us, he sat patiently on the edge of the bed while the red fountain throbbed away.

It took an hour's hard work before he was cleaned up. The duty doctor, a pleasant young woman who really was more interested in those parts not exposed by the razor cuts – his brains – carefully cut Wildash's hair away and sewed up the wounds. Verity and I meanwhile staunched the flow of blood by twisting towels about Wildash's head, releasing them at intervals so that the severed vessels could be found. Wildash acknowledged our efforts with thanks.

When Miss Tracey came across him later in the Recreation Ward she disguised her despair at seeing him again. Although it involved considerable telephoning, letter writing and a dozen forms to be filled, she arranged for Ronald Wildash to spend some time at a hostel. This at least spaced out his visits to us, and he came only once more (cut wrists again) in the next six months.

***

Smith, Gentle and Beddington were unusual amongst our patients because they all had gross physical abnormalities. Generally speaking, the bodies of Y Block's inmates were outwardly average and normal. Complexions varied from the florid to the pasty dry-white that so frequently appeared in young schizophrenics, but the collection of bodies to be seen on bath days was much as might be expected anywhere.

Mr Smith was normal to look at. He was twentyeight and well built. As Riddle and I bathed him on admission and recorded his scars, there was a noticeable profusion of them on his palms, elbows, knees and buttocks. Old burn marks indicated a carelessness or maliciousness that was hard to understand. Smith's feet and toes were scarred and blistered too and Riddle noticed that the nail on the large toe of the right foot was bleeding. He asked Smith how he had done it. Smith looked down and plucked the broken section of nail from the skin to which it was attached.

'He don't feel a bloody thing,' said Riddle, and pinched the skin on Smith's back to confirm this impression. There was no response from Smith. Together we checked over his body for areas of sensation, but found none.

'God's truth,' exclaimed Riddle, 'I envy that bugger.'

'I don't know,' I replied. 'It must be inconvenient and possibly dangerous not to know when you are damaging yourself. He could sit on a fire and not know until he had caught alight.'

'Looks as though he might have done that too,' Riddle said, pointing to a brown-red weal across his buttocks. But Riddle appeared to be still unconvinced that such insensitivity could be a disadvantage. Perhaps the idea of being able to sit down violently absolutely anywhere appealed to him. He sat down now upon the bath edge. Smith joined in the conversation.

'I can't feel anything on my skin at all,' he said flatly. 'It's neuro-something or other.'

'What do you do for a living?' I asked.

'Nothing at the moment. I have done all sorts of things - Labouring, kitchen work, but it's always the same story. I get hurt or I break something; or somebody gets upset because they think it's queer not to be able to feel. I'm a bloody nuisance at home. Don't know what to do. I had a blackout and kicked up a shindig in a pub. Knocked a bloke down. That's why I'm here.' He spoke without sorrow in bald statement of fact. The "blackout" explanation was typical jargon to describe a loss of temper when actions were taken that later the person regretted.

Smith was a trifle edgy while he was with us. His anger against himself was quickly turned against others – and particularly other patients – which was in itself unusual.

If Smith appeared to speak without sadness, Mr Gentle was another extreme. His abnormality was an undeveloped arm. He was fiftyish, of short stature, dark haired and tubby. Small watery blue eyes glistened behind thick-lensed spectacles. His face was puckered like a baby's. Red skin and blue shaved beard combined to give his face a purple hue. A fat crease in the centre of his chin was lined with bristles inaccessible to razors. A dark blue suit hung on him in perpetual crumples to match those of his face. His whole body cringed when he was approached, and he tried to hide his immature left arm. This was an entire arm, but belonged by rights to a child of five. It was soft and white. Pink dimples backed the knuckles. As though to exaggerate the arm's smallness, Gentle held it with the elbow crooked into his waist and the hand bent in against the forearm. The diminutive fist clutched the cuff of his sleeve to hide the whole limb.

Gentle cringed and Gentle whined. He made no reference to his arm and yet one felt that it was his whole life. He had the arm of a five year-old boy so he behaved like a five year-old boy. I wondered what he would do if this offending, excusing arm were lopped off one night while he slept.

'Why *don't* you have it off?' I asked him in a kindly man-to-man sort of way. 'Surely that's best if it's a nuisance to you?' Gentle whimpered and more tears appeared in his eyes as he burrowed further down into his bed. He had no answer other than a pout and a petulant gesture with his good hand. He spoke to no one.

Mr Beddington spoke to everyone about his affliction. He was paralysed from the waist down. 'An accident,' he never tired of saying. 'I'll tell you the whole story but you won't believe it.'

Whether we believed it or not we heard the story again and again. He wheeled himself across the Recreation Ward to each patient in turn to recount his story. No reaction was necessary from his listeners, only their silence and the appearance of looking at him, or preferably at his legs.

'You won't believe it, but I was married. We lived in South Africa for six years. But my wife was a tart. I had a good job and got a good screw from it.

Technical Manager I was, and out there with that sort of money you live all right – servants and the lot. But that wasn't good enough for her. Wanted to live the life of a real lady and have good times *all* the time. So she picked up with this fellow who didn't have to work. They were out to cocktail parties and running round with the smart set day and night. Clubs and race courses then back to our place.

'I didn't know he was knocking her off. He was an oldish bloke, all grey haired and respectable.'

'Come along with us, do,' he said when I had a couple of weeks off.

'I can't afford all that sort of thing,' I said. 'I don't want to go to your bloody night clubs.'

'You're a miserable git,' my wife said. Every day she went on: 'Why don't you live a little? See how real people live. I think it's nice of Ronny to ask you along. He can get into these clubs and parties and things. He's a real man.'

'So I got dragged along. I don't know why that old ponce wanted me with them. She was a tart and liked having men round her. But if he was knocking her off I don't know why he wanted me around.

'We went swimming. None of your hanging about on public beaches. Ronny had friends with a posh private swimming pool. She was a tart showing off her body to everyone.'

'Isn't Ronny super?' she asked. 'What a lovely brown body. You wouldn't think he was nearly sixty would you?'

213

'He looks more like bloody seventy,' I said, 'the great ponce.'

'Well at least he's fit,' she said. 'See him diving in?'

'He was doing belly flops off the side then swanking down to the bar to bring her back more "drinkies". He brought me back a few. Oh yes. He was a proper gentleman.

'I can dive,' I said. She didn't try and stop me. There was a big diving board and I went in off the top step. He didn't tell me there was only about four feet of water. That's when I did this.'

Beddington gestured towards his legs.

'I hurt my head too. They dragged me out unconscious. I was in and out of hospital and gradually my legs went. Paralysed. Stuck in a bloody wheel chair. I reckon they did it on purpose. Now the doctors say I've got personality defects. All because of that bitch. Of course, she and him are getting on like a house on fire now. I wish she was in a wheel chair. He wouldn't be knocking her off then. And the doctors can't find out what's wrong with my legs either. I'm well shot of those two people and I'm not going back to South Africa. But I want compensation. Don't you reckon he should pay compensation? He can bloody well afford it.'

Beddington enlarged on his desire for compensation. He had consulted lawyers and received little to encourage his hope. He had written to newspapers without success.

214

Y BLOCK

Although he was not paranoid, at the very least he carried an enormous chip on his shoulder. He had been wronged and wanted compensation. His story was verbal evidence of the wrong that had been done to him: his paralysis visible proof. It was an obvious thought that his mental condition produced the bodily one; that if the symptoms of paralysis were removed he would develop other symptoms to replace them. He urged us to believe that before the accident he was a gay, cheerful man and a good fellow, whereas now he was short-tempered and miserable. His deliberate disagreeableness to people once they had heard his story was designed to reinforce this impression. But possibly it was not all deliberate.

Because he had not slept well since the accident two and a half years ago, his various doctors had given him sleeping tablets. One of Beddington's complaints was that he had to take phenobarbs to get a wink of sleep. Frequently in Y Block we saw the results of barbiturate poisoning. The chaotic effects of an overdose were only more alarming than the insidious effects of regular dosage. Patients known to us from many readmissions – labelled neurotics and psychopaths or misfits – deteriorated in mental condition after years on barbiturates. It was not by any means clear just what irritability, selfishness and general unpleasantness was due to the progress of their ordinary characters and diseases. Yet over and above the changes we expected were changes often concurrent with the patients' use of phenobarbitone. The evidence was not statistical, and did not lend itself to analysis. But it was not from fear of addiction alone that made the staff avoid taking barbiturate pills if they themselves had trouble sleeping. They sensed or feared that such aids were unpredictable and could be stealthily evil.

So the total picture of Mr Beddington was not a happy one. Since there was no one in this country who wanted to bother with him, he went with protest to an asylum for a spell as a voluntary patient. Miss Tracey achieved this by promising him the hope that there he might receive some help in obtaining compensation.

Miss Tracey could do little more in the cases of Smith and Gentle. These were bucks that had to be passed on. Smith also went as a voluntary patient. Miss Tracey contacted Gentle's married sister, and the single sister with whom he lived. They came down and persuaded Gentle to "go away for a bit". Whoever lived in optimism it was not these three patients and, if we were honest, neither did we have hope for them.

CHAPTER 19: Work and Dr Tindall

Even now, at the height of the busy season, it could not be said that we worked very hard in Y Block at St. Francis Hospital. Our main efforts, apart from perpetual stock-taking, were those of endurance, tolerance and the long tedium of "observation". Heavy work was carried out by O'Leary if he was on duty, or by patients if he was not. Any shift may require the use of some brute strength: a patient to be restrained in bed; a violent or delirious man to be coerced to the padded cell; a homeless patient to be removed from the lavatory where he had set up camp. But these incidents lasted only a short time. Their effect was adrenalin to the system and, since few apart from Big Wilson were addicted to adrenalin, where possible Howard, Raggle and Semple counselled passive methods of preserving order. Riddle loomed large at hand when these failed.

Riddle and I went to the padded cells to fetch a young man named Grant who had spent the night there. He was stark, staring raving mad. He sang and shouted and waved his arms about. The previous evening it had been discovered two hours after the nightly medicine round that his sedation tablets were still under his tongue. He had lain in foxy stillness since they had been given to him. Such restraint proving too arduous for the vigour of his lunacy, he spat them out and gave way to a solo concert. It being impossible to persuade him to take more tablets, the

217

night shift deprived him of his night shirt, gave him an injection and settled him in the pads.

We eyed him through the porthole before releasing the spring bolts on the door. As part of the "settling" process Little Tom had turned the central heating up. Now I turned it down until the dial behind the big brass handle showed a temperature slightly below subtropical. Grant's big, pink, athletic figure lay sprawling over the cream coloured rubber floor. He was wide awake, playing with himself and sweating.

'Give him his breakfast in there,' Howard called, 'then if he's OK we can give him another injection and let him go back to bed.'

Leaving a cardboard plate of porridge and a plastic beaker of lukewarm coffee balanced on a radiator outside, we shot the bolts and walked in. Grant stood up in the attitude of some handsome all-in wrestler then started mimicking the stance of Riddle, who walked like a bipedal polar bear. As Grant glowered ferociously at us I expected him to launch an attack at any second. I would rather he had. Instead he snorted raucously and dragged his snort to the back of his mouth to roll it there with gathered phlegm. Glassy eyed, he peeked round Riddle and smiled at me. Then he spat his mouth of phlegm full into my face and sat down. Laughing, he rolled over to avoid Riddle's boot.

Howard trotted in with a hypodermic syringe. Although I could barely see where to aim, as my eyes were gummed up with the mess from Grant's mouth and nose, I gave a hearty thwack to Grant's left

buttock while Howard plunged the needle into his
right. This standard procedure to keep turbulent
posteriors level during injections gave vent to my
anger.

'Hee hee,' chortled Father in his wheezy fashion.
'Young Raggle gets peed on and you walk into a
dollop of spit. You want to be careful where you are
standing.'

'Oi'd plaster the porridge all over his face if he'd
spat at me,' said Riddle. I felt like doing so. But Grant
was now sitting eating it, singing loudly to give
evidence of his good spirits, so we withdrew and I
consoled my pride with a thorough wash.

***

'Are you staying up here widge me?' Allan called
from the Recreation Ward as I let myself out of the
staff lavatory-cum-washroom. Doddery liked to be
released from any permanent station when possible
so that he could wander around looking owl-eyed and
sage. He fancied a chat with Lucy and Mrs Scott
while they were in the Block, and then wanted to be
seen standing importantly by the admission desk
when Madam came to do her round. 'We have got a
lot of work in,' he would tell her if he found the
chance. 'We seem to have more to do each day.' Then
he would look cheerful as though to indicate that
despite his white-haired old age he was still man
enough to tackle alone all the work that might be put
his way.

'No,' I said. 'Sorry, I can't stay up here; Father
wants me downstairs. There are lots of specimens to

get.' I was glad not to have to stand in for that old hypocrite while he went on "walk-about". And in any case, it was true. There was an unusual amount of work to be done.

This had come about partly because of Dr Tindall, partly because of Mr Mahouk, a French Algerian epileptic patient and partly because of another younger man who had died of meningitis a few weeks before. Dr Tindall was ending his three months stint as the day-time duty doctor on Y Block, which was part of his psychiatric training. He had started out with an abundance of theories and firm principles we supposed gleaned from textbooks, lectures and other sources of the schools of thought which have free range we were told in psychiatric medicine. Dr Tindall was a pleasant man and sincere. He turned up on time and was extremely civil and shy.

His qualities were of no avail in breaking down the barriers between our staff and psychiatrists. Not even Billie was lured into confidences by the tall, dark and bespectacled good looks of Dr Tindall. However amiable, psychiatrists were not liked. Even less liked were the lofty theoreticians, the professors, who came down from the teaching hospital to see their pupils and patients. Undoubtedly the backs of St Francis's nurses were stiffened by jealousy. The doctors' status and pay, hard earned though it was, created envy. But these were not the main causes separating us from them. Mental nurses had no faith in what was being done about mental illness. It was agreed that a great deal of brain power was expended by some of the doctors involved: that they were intelligent people. The grouse was that intellectual energy was spent polishing up theories, arguing about them, and then regurgitating them for others. In the Unit our complaint was expressed in clichés: "the quacks have their heads in the air", "when it comes down to it they don't know their arses from their elbows". All this was unkind and inaccurate. But a grain of truth was there. The amount of knowledge about the insane is scant, yet there is no shortage of pontification by some of psychiatry's high priests. The sincere, capable mental nurse who is anxious to see real progress made, is a rare bird: he is as rare as an active practical, working Christian amongst a disputation of theologians. Similarly, the mental nurse dislikes the exaltation of theory above facts.

Like his predecessors and followers, Dr Tindall had no easy passage. He was not welcomed as a fellow worker. He tried to institute a meeting each week at which even the least qualified assistant nurse could report his observations about patients before the patients were categorised and sent out to the asylums. Howard and Semple squashed these meetings. It was not entirely pig-headedness on their part. Verity was asked if he had been talking about one patient behind that patient's back. Verity was niggled and replied sarcastically that he had, and what was more that he was actually the voice that other patients heard; and he alone was responsible for the interplanetary radiation that yet another man claimed was interfering with him. My solitary contribution was to draw attention to one particular patient. He was in his twenties and had a long history of minor disturbance. Bathing him on admission I noticed that his prepuce was distended and tight so that it was doubtful whether it had ever been retracted. I was quite aware that his penis was not directly attached to his cerebral lobes, but thought that the condition merited attention. Nothing was done about it.

Howard, Semple and Raggle went back to being the sole reporters of staff observations. To Dr Tindall they explained that the Unit was short-handed and we were needed at our posts. To us, Semple shrugged his shoulders and said, 'It's no bleeding good. Unless these witch doctors do time nursing, actually being on the Block and in the wards day after day, they will never learn. You can't tell them anything.'

Perhaps Dr Tindall was luckier than others in that he did learn something. Howard helped him. Dr Tindall came into Ward I to do the routine check on a newly admitted patient. Riddle and Dobey were sitting on the man's legs. If Dobey was pinning a patient down it was fair indication that the man needed pinning down, for Dobey was a gentle person despite his gorilla build. As his wont, Dr Tindall asked the nurses to leave him alone with the patient. They demurred, Dobey grinning toothily and Riddle fidgeting into a more comfortable position. Dr Tindall asked Howard if the nurses could step outside the screens for a while. Howard advised against such complete removal of restraint, but then, commenting to himself about the necessity for people to learn, peered through the screens and beckoned his attendants away.

Almost immediately there was a scuffle and Tindall found himself dragged into bed with the patient. In resisting this nuptial embrace, his glasses fell off and he was tipped out onto the floor. Here a roly-poly took place with a deal of grunting and kicking. At the table, Howard and his henchmen pretended to be occupied and to talk about other things. Dobey did make as if to intervene in the peculiar examination going on behind the screens. Howard stopped him. Eventually, Dr Tindall called out to the patient, 'Oh, come back here please!' The patient, adjusting his night shirt, appeared from behind the screens and walked over to the desk. Howard and Riddle took him back to the admission bed again.

'Have you finished your examination now, doctor?' Howard enquired with a straight face.

Tindall was sitting on the floor replacing his glasses and rubbing his lower abdomen.

'Er, not quite . . . perhaps I'll do it later, then I can make notes at the same time.'

Dr Tindall was a voluminous note maker. He filled pages for each patient, and marvellous were the questions he asked. Sometimes their apparent irrelevance was equalled only by the answers he received, but at least now he would carry on his lengthy interview with an attendant lurking nearby.

Tindall was absorbed by notes and theories, but it was sheer bad luck that affected him with Mahouk and Timothy. Mr Mahouk stayed with us longer than

223

any other patient. He spoke only a few words of English and, because of the gross confusion that followed his frequent seizures, not much sense could be made of his French. He had been admitted a short time before Dr Tindall began his spell of duty. There was no agreement about where Mahouk should be sent. In addition to his epilepsy he was feverish and excitable, then lax and ill. For six weeks he occupied one of the side rooms off the Admission Ward. Lengthy and laborious interviews by Dr Tindall proved fruitless. Then it was rediscovered that Mahouk had tuberculosis. That information had been uncovered before in routine checks, but escaped later notice. This galloping consumption was too far gone to do anything about and before Mr Mahouk could be sent away he died. Tindall was undoubtedly upset. He was a good doctor and positively concerned for the patients, and he might have thought it unreasonable that any should suffer from diseases which he was not at this moment intent on assessing.

Mr Timothy was perhaps more of a success for Dr Tindall. He was very ill on arrival. Trainee psychiatrists were brought to see him, and professors. He was diagnosed severally as a schizophrenic with pneumonia; a hysteric with 'flu . . . other more elaborate theories were of even less value. Dr Tindall was not satisfied and arranged for a consultant physician to be brought in immediately. He diagnosed meningitis, but only hours later Timothy died in the padded cell. He was there to prevent him receiving further injuries when in back-arched spasms he threw himself out of bed.

Dr Tindall's experiences with Mahouk and Timothy put more work on us. That pleased me because it was a welcome change from the long, sad round of watching, with only intermittent breaks to clean up a mess or make a bed. Dr Tindall wanted specimens of every possible sort from all patients: sputum, urine, faecal matter and blood. No one was exempt. As befitted my humble station – there were no blue pips of rank on my epaulettes – I was trusted with the collection only of the sputum and faecal matter. Corrigan, with suitable accompaniment of grunts, oaths and sweat, did the labelling. It was remarkable that he had let himself be drawn into such hard work, but he could not spend the whole day skulking in the staff lavatory.

Sputum was rapidly collected: everyone could be persuaded to hawk and spit, although the degrees of accuracy in projecting it into minute cardboard canisters varied. Grant should have been around to give them all lessons in phlegm throwing, but he was detained in the pads.

The acquisition of faecal samples was largely a matter of hanging around until the subject obliged into a bed pan. A wooden spatula then removed a small quantity for analysis.

Many of the very old men had swollen prostate glands and had to be catheterised twice daily. Billie liked to break off from drawing blood to do this. He was good at it. He carefully oiled the thin rubber tube before inserting it in the patient's urethra; he was very fussy and apologetic if blood came away when the end of the catheter pushed through to the bladder. Whale did not consider the job successful until he had wriggled and poked with the tube until blood did appear. Both of them allowed me to hold the pan into which the urine was drawn. Whale considered it an honour for me. Billie let me hold the outlet end of the catheter too. Such frustrations encouraged me to work with Tiny Verity when possible and we took turn and turn-about with the operative part of the procedure.

Dr Tindall himself carried out the collection of cerebro-spinal fluid samples, since this was a minor operation. It amazed me how even the most deluded, crazed and restless patients remained still for this procedure. The preparatory ritual may have been therapeutic, or possibly frightening. Even Grant behaved himself. Raggle arranged him on a bed with soothing assurances that something was being done to help him. Rarely did the maddest person not believe that something could be done to benefit him even if he was convinced that there was nothing wrong with him. The more magical and serious the "help" appeared to be, the more agreeable he was about it. So Grant was quiet while Raggle laid him on his side, supported his hips with pillows and drew his knees up to his chin. Dr Tindall and Semple rigged up a paraphernalia of glass and rubber pipes and a finely graduated manometer. Scrubbing up, sterilisation of the lumbar area and a local anaesthetic impressed Grant even more. Raggle carefully blocked his view of the enormous needle used to make the puncture. Half a glimpse of the doctor's gloved hands working that needle into the vertebral canal would have ended all therapeutics for the day. Luckily, Grant did not see, and he continued to lie quietly while the line was connected up, pressures taken, sample withdrawn and the business finished.

All specimens were gathered together on an enamel tray in the dispensary, to be taken over to the main hospital pathology department. I asked hopefully after each of these Tindall-inspired sessions whether anything had come to light. Ordinary ailments did but nothing that had any new bearing on the range of psychoses in Y Block.

As far as mental sickness is concerned, there is still much work to be done. There is no field in which tenacity and imagination are more needed.

CHAPTER 20: Testing Times for All

Dr Tindall's spell of duty had ended. Although there was some remission from the slight labours of specimen collecting, the series of temporary trainee psychiatrists who worked for a week each until the spring, resurrected the intelligence tests. As I was suspected to have had an education, the administration of these was assigned to me. It was Howard's idea.

'Nurse Lynch can take the patients and do those,' he said as Semple came away from the office muttering.

'As if we haven't got a bleedin' nuff to do,' Semple moaned, and slung the sheaf of question pads on a bed. The senile occupant began with trembling fingers to examine them upside down.

'Here,' said Howard, 'give me those. I don't think the quack wants to know what your IQ is. Mr Lynch, I should get started by taking Mr Lancer into Ward II. Lock yourselves in and see that he does the test properly.'

'Yeah. Fat lot of good that'll do Lancer or the quack,' said Semple. 'He's got an MD (mentally deficient) patient down to be done as well. Perhaps he's trying to make quite sure these blokes've got brains at all. Don't want to waste 'is time trying to cure heads what've got nuffink in 'em. Don't matter about our bleedin' time.' Semple sat down cackling with the Racing Mirror. I collected Lancer and locked us in, and the polishing O'Leary out, of Ward II. Mr Lancer consented to be seated in front of his intelligence papers spread out on the trestle-type dining table.

Frank Lancer was living proof that money cannot buy a sound mind. His father was rich; a very successful tycoon in the toys and fancy goods business. Lancer Jr spoke with a broken German accent but that might have been an act which he chose to keep up. He was an only child and money had not been denied him. He was twenty-nine. His father had until very recently encouraged him to take part in the business. Frank was well educated and he had travelled with his father in Europe and the Far East. He had a pilot's licence and his mother had persuaded her husband to give Frank a "little plane of his own". By all accounts, that had been her most recent act of marital persuasion, and possibly her last. She was now abroad on an extended cruise accompanied, Frank was sure, by a family friend who had almost as much money but no restrictive business ties.

Frank had begun to do outrageous things at business meetings. Then, authority reported, he began to do silly things in his aeroplane. It was not clear to our non-aeronautical minds exactly what those things were, but it was understood that being abusive to control towers figured in the complaints. Frank had great good humour and, though wearying to be with for long, was amusing in short doses.

He had long and plentiful curly brown hair. When admitted, he was accompanied by a DAO and a

General Practitioner. The display of wealth and influence was reinforced by his dress. He wore a blue suit and waistcoat (hand stitched so Billie said), gold and precious stone cuff links, gold bracelet and nametag on his right hand, gold wristwatch on his left. Pearl tie pin and an extravagant signet ring completed his jewellery. His shirt and socks were so dirty that even Frank himself lowered his protruding eyes in disdain when he peeled them off. Evidently, he offered the admitting nurses money from a bulging wallet – "Just to see to ze laundrie unt everytink" – but he was not discreet enough about it for them to be able to accept.

Mr Lancer Snr was, as always, heavily occupied with business. With Christmas at hand he also was abroad making arrangements for trade with which to enrich the next Christmas. Frank settled down with us, talking freely in his guttural, accented tones both to people present and others not present. He appeared glad to be away from his executive round during the Christmas season. His mother sent him a telegram:

FRANKY: SO SORRY YOU IN HOSPITAL AGAIN STOP

SO SORRY CANNOT MAKE IT BACK TO SEE YOU STOP

HAVING A SUPER TIME STOP

GET WELL SOON DARLING STOP MUMMY

Franky recalled this telegram now when I tried to draw his attention to the intelligence test. He chatted to the light bulb. He consulted crumbs under the peeling green linoleum of the table top. With intention stiffened by a pair of horn-rimmed spectacles he had found in his pocket, he stared briefly at question number one and put an arbitrary tick in one of the boxes alongside. Ten minutes more of sporadic attention to the similarities or inequalities of the diagrams in question number one resulted in ticks for all the boxes alongside. Frank altered the five patterns in question number two until they all looked alike. Twelve minutes later he returned from a trip to the window and marked himself a generous ten out of ten for question ten without reading it. He signed a staccato sigh.

'Just now ven I'm needink her. My muzzer is avey wiz her fancimann. Vy could she not comink to help me do ziss? Blutty test. Ziss eez a blutty test. I am tellink you.'

'Now Mr Lancer,' I said in my best conciliatory tones, 'it's not as bad as all that. Let's go through the instructions and start again. It's only got to last an hour.'

'An hour test? No. I cannot an hour test do vizout my muzzer. Blutty not.'

Despite his assurances that further efforts were not possible, I rubbed out his first transgressions, explained the instructions and started timing him again. Here and there he filled an answer box correctly. With lapses and mutterings the paper was finished.

'I done a blutty hour test,' he told Semple when I took him back to the Admission Ward, 'unt my muzzer's viz her fancimann.'

'You'd better do the MD after lunch,' Semple told me. 'You've been an hour and three quarters with Lancer. Have you marked it as well?'

'No, not yet,' I said. 'Had to give him a bit longer. He wouldn't have got any done in an hour.'

I took the mentally defective patient through the same intelligence test after lunch. He was truculent and bound up with a heavy cold. He did the test in bed while I sat beside him. Even with the distraction of the Admission Ward all around him he scored nearly twice as highly as Lancer.

Semple took the completed papers into the duty doctor. We hoped that they were manifestly useless as information. It was a time consuming and pointless exercise to give intelligence tests to our patients, even if you believed in the validity of such tests. Performance could at best only be an indication of the patient's level of disturbance. Assessment even of this relied on having either a normal reference point for the patient, or a standard one for everybody. There were no reference points. All that was learned was that a distracted mind may at a particular time do an intelligence test badly.

Lancer did not let the ordeal disturb him. In a few days he was to be taken to the clinic at the teaching hospital; meanwhile, he wandered around gazing at other patients. His sorrow and concern for them was voluble.

'Zay are qvite mad you know,' he told whoever was at hand. 'Peety somesink can't be done. My muzzer might do somesink. She's wiz her fancimann. My ole man, he don't vant to know.'

The case records showed that Mr Lancer Senior had spent a considerable amount of money trying to buy Frank a new mind. "Treatment" in London and Zurich had been unavailing. Perhaps that was why he did not now "vant to know".

***

Howard and Semple expressed regret that Lancer was removed so soon. They would have liked for him to be present for the Annual Management Committee Visit. Frank Lancer had money; he was therefore taken to be a representative of privilege and power. Few such patients came to us because their families and friends, in greater number and with more *savoirfaire*, had them taken care of privately. Howard and Semple were not articulate about the reasons why they would have liked Lancer on display at the Committee's visit. But the reason, I think, was clear: Lancer was one of "them". He showed that might and authority were brought low by lunacy, even to as low as the very humble poor. They did wish to show the Committee how tolerant they were in attending the crippled and rejected offspring of the rich. Through Frank's presence they wished to emphasise that madness was not the curse of only the obedient servants of the community; that they, the masters, the Management Committee, could not afford to look superior. However lofty their station and however far above the common herd, they should not smile and wash their hands. 'See,' Howard would have said if he had been able, 'we have one of your people. He's bourgeois, or aristocratic, or a holder of power. Now will you do something about it? Now, just from this one hospital will you make some sort of stand or some gesture to the outside world? Will you stop frittering your time away deciding about the colour of paint in the nurses' quarters? Get out and raise your voices. Think! Ask for money, men, ideas, research. Love. Because if we can't expect you to love one of the humble poor sufficiently, you must love one of your own.'

Howard and Semple did not have the gift of persuasive speech, nor did their honest brains turn lucidly upon a problem. Frank Lancer was already transferred to another place. This was the umpteenth year with its ordained management visit. Howard and Semple, Raggle and others who might at one time conceivably have risen an inch or two above the cramped sad rut of Lunatic Attendant, were cautioned by the habit of years to think of other things. There were promptings from the office and Mr Webb.

Mr Webb wanted another stock check. I was sure he dreaded that the Committee would discover the loss of the straight jacket. Everything must be present and correct and Mr Webb must be able to face the Committee knowing that it was so. It was one thing for people to get old or go mad or anything inevitable like that; but it was quite a different kettle of fish if canvas straight- jackets, bed pans, rubber sheets and white overalls went missing. That would not do.

234

On her rounds Sister hinted, ever so kindly, that one member of the committee was quite a martinet, always feeling for dust on radiators.

'And your radiators are a weeny bit dusty, I've noticed.'

'Oh yes. Thank you Sister,' said the Charge Nurse on duty.

'Don't forget the lavatories will you? Mr Pollitt always looks in there. He has connections in wholesale plumbing and sanitary ware you know. I must say your floors are very clean. They don't get such a nice shine in the geriatric wards.'

'Yes Sister. No Sister.'

'Mr Howard *will* make sure all the staff have clean white coats, won't he?'

Three bags full Sister.

'Check the stock.'

'Dust all radiators.'

'Clean, double clean, flush out and for heaven's sake don't let a patient use a lavatory before two o'clock when the Visit is timed.'

'Keep the floors like a skating rink. Is O'Leary on this morning? Fine! Make sure he keeps the polish off the walls.'

'Ask Nurse Corrigan to let Lucy clean all the door knobs on both sides of every lock.'

'White coats all round and remake all the beds.'

'Nurse Verity be extra especially careful to do the drugs round before They come. And couldn't you lower your trousers a bit? They're very fancy socks you've got on.'

'No I couldn't. They'd fall down and then the Committee would see my arse, and I'm not letting O'Leary go over that with the Squeegee just to please them.'

A crescendo of last minute instructions issued forth from Howard, glowing with a fresh layer of gentian violet:

'Billie and you, Mr Verity, downstairs in the Admission Ward. Where is Billie?'

'In the dispensary putting his make-up on.'

'Where's Corrigan?'

'He was here just now.'

'Oh Lord. He's always missing when he's wanted.'

'Mr Lynch, you go upstairs and look after the Rec. I'll send Corrigan up to help you when he turns up.'

Since any patient thought likely to untidy his bed had been roused, dressed and shoved upstairs, leaving only three patients downstairs, it seemed fair to have a couple of white coats on duty upstairs in the Recreation Ward.

'Mr Lakhani. You stay on the landing upstairs. You can unlock any doors They want to see behind.'

'Very good.'

'Please don't let Matron catch you rolling up menthol cigarettes like she did last year.'

'I find they're better for my throat. Always rolled my own since I was a medical "stoodent".'

'That's not the point. We're not supposed to smoke on duty!'

'Oh, I passed it to a patient. She thought I was rolling it for him. She never saw . . .' Lakhani drawled

236

on as he waddled slowly upstairs. He was unperturbed. He explained to me how nonchalantly he had continued rolling his cigarette, put the tin away in his pocket, then popped the cigarette into the mouth of a senile patient. He did not seem to think that his subterfuge and great presence of mind had been laid bare when the patient ate the cigarette. Matron was just being snooty when she told Howard about it. Lakhani should not have taken it as a personal criticism. Matrons were always like that. When he was a medical "stoodent" he'd known a Matron . . .

Two o'clock came and went. Half-past two dragged by dryly, with Semple racking his brains to think of a way to get a cup of tea. At three o'clock *They* came. Door banging, voices, the tramp and trip of feet passing along the downstairs corridor into the Admission Ward. A silent head-craning spell of inspection; a loud voice calling out then drowned by a flurry of conversation. Feet and voices travelling upstairs. The Committee trooped along to the Recreation Ward. The men looked at the patients. The women looked at the furniture. Matron looked at my white coat and smiled a glazed smile of recognition. She had either seen it before or had counted the buttons and found none missing. It wasn't me she recognized, I was sure.

About turn and file off downstairs. Mr Pollitt in the rear, bald-headed, black-coated, plump.

'Ah nurse, can you let me see in here?' He pointed to the Ward III dormitory door. Lakhani opened it and Pollitt stuck his head round to see that it was a dormitory. 'And here?' Pollitt laid his hand upon the outer door of the staff lavatory. Lakhani unlocked it in silence. Pollitt sidled in.

'I'm in here,' Corrigan bellowed from behind the lavatory door at the top of the steps.

'Oh!' Pollitt paused to examine the sink, glanced at the sky light, nodded to Lakhani and scurried off to catch up with the main party, which was just being let out.

Corrigan descended from his throne.

'What a bloody time they've been.'

'Oh, they've only been here three minutes,' said Lakhani.

'I know. But *I've* been in there since ten to two.' Corrigan's face was red and angry.

'It's not my fault,' said Lakhani.

'No, but you needn't have let them see in here,' Corrigan said.

He went down to get a cup of tea as Billie came panting upstairs to the Recreation Ward and flopped down in the one vacant chair.

'Well, thank goodness that's over,' he puffed. 'What a palaver. I've never been so embarrassed. It wouldn't have gone off too badly really. Oh dear.'

'What's the matter Billie?' Clearly he was in a tizzy, like a mother who has caught her debutante daughter in flagrante at the Season's Best Ball.

'It was all very nice and Matron all sugar,' said Billie, 'then your friend Grant, the one who gobbed at you, disgraced himself. Filthy beast. Didn't know where to put my face.'

'I thought he was quite quiet in bed today,' I said.

'He was. Good as gold. Then all of a sudden, just as soon as the Committee had come through to the Admission Ward, "Shit!" he cries, and "Shit!" again. Right out loud. None of the other patients made a sound but him. Sat up in bed, stared at them and cried out, "Shit!"' Billie imitated Grant's posture and an expansive declamatory gesture of his hands. 'Yes. "Shit!" he cried.'

Billie was quite carried away and overcome. Patients were eyeing him askance. I suggested he go downstairs and have a cup of tea.

'Bloomin'-well *need* one, I can tell you,' he said and left.

What with Pollitt, Corrigan, Grant and Billie, it seemed this day was to be remembered for its rearend theme. Perhaps the Management Committee were persuaded how important vital functions are to mental health. We hoped some good came of their visit. From the expressions on their faces one imagined that to them the important thing was to be seen to be concerned. They did remark how good a match for the walls were the new green curtains in Ward II. Nothing further was reported of their visit.

CHAPTER 21: Another Christmas and New Year

Johnny, the cheerful, high-grade mentally defective patient who greeted me on my first day at St Francis's, was back for Christmas. For the boon of paraldehyde or chlorpromazine as his nightly medication, he laid up tables and carried dirty linen to the sluice room. His hairless but smiling face lent a little seasonal happiness and sanity to the Block, which it otherwise lacked. Below the surface it always lacked it. Except possibly for a maniac in full euphoric outpourings, the mentally afflicted are not happy. Tension, sadness, distraction so deep that they are beyond comprehension, grip them from morning rise to drugged sleep. The gloom they generate within themselves spreads and pervades the very bricks that confine them.

As I looked down the register to see who we had in for my Christmas spell of late shifts, I hoped that some families might have a happier time now that their loved, heart-breaking or despised relatives were removed to us. In the Recreation Ward some familiar faces stared at the television screen. In the Admission Ward a couple of beds were fitted with cot sides to take the perennial old men. Youth and age were represented by extremes.

'Pop' was ninety-eight when admitted and ninetynine when he left. He was still strong, solid and over six feet tall with a mass of neat crew-cut white hair.

He wandered a little. His arteries were like clay pipes. He was deaf. This was no foxy deafness, the pretence of old age. He was absolutely solid stone deaf. Now and again his silent world became unbearable and he broke out in anger. His rage was terrible to see. He had been brought to us in a rage in the small hours of the morning. He had had a terrible row with his wife (ninety-four) and left the house after breaking up the crockery. A Christmas and a birthday in Y Block were to be sobering experiences for him. His wife and he had not been parted for either celebration since the Boer War, and might not now have been had they still lived in their old terraced house in Chiswick. Here neighbours living in similar confined intimacy knew Pop. They knew he and his wife did not always get on. In short, they rowed. Pop had brought both Silver and Golden Wedding anniversaries to noisy climaxes. He told us his wife was an old fool and "past it". Whatever "it" was, Pop had a periodic rage and avoided it. The neighbours, glad of an active part today in tomorrow's gossip, took Pop in and fed him. Others sneaked around to Mrs Pop and gave her a square meal. But on this occasion when Pop stumped out on his wife he had nowhere to go. For the convenience of such elderly folk, he and his wife had been removed by the council to a new flat. The labour-saving gadgets and the crockery were just as fragile and vulnerable to Pop's deaf rages; but when he left his flat and wandered a mile away back to

Bridge Road, only the crumbled foundations and a mess of builders' boards stood where familiar backto-backs had huddled in unsanitary friendliness. He was brought to us by the tireless police.

A sympathetic doctor added vitamin pills and beer to his diet. Pop recovered his wits and was only angry then that he could not "get back to the old dear" for Christmas. There was transport in, but no transport out.

***

Beyond the fact that Isaiah belonged to a small West Indian family, and had been assaulting women, the referring officer could tell us little about him except that he was absolutely beyond parental control. To be sure, the DAO enquired diligently about his parent's hint that part of his sickness was in the sexual assault of women, but nothing specific came to light. Isaiah was eleven years old. He reached barely as high as a woman's armpit and it was difficult to imagine what form his assault might take. Billie supposed that Isaiah kicked their shins and shouted obscenities that he was too young to know the meaning of.

'Poor dear,' he said. 'It's a shame. It's not his fault, I'll be bound. Peter, that *nice* DAO, said Isaiah's parents couldn't control a glove puppet. I'm sure he was right. Isaiah's not mad.' Billie chucked the effervescent little terror under the chin and cooed and small-talked to him. Despite the fact that Isaiah responded with vigorous and noisy misbehaviour, Billie continued to spoil him, insisting that he was not mad. Raggle declared that both of them were, and that the sooner one or the other was taken into care the better.

Raggle, as ever, moved quietly and undemonstratively about his work. He volunteered to take the shift on Christmas Day, so that Semple, whose heart was beginning to give trouble, could spend the time with his wife and teenaged son. Raggle was also a family man with three small children to support, but he regarded himself as young and fit. However young he was, it was not apparent on his face. Its paleness was broken by wrinkles and lines about and between the eyes. Large, clear-framed spectacles appeared to weigh his head down. Thin straight brown hair started above the furrows of his forehead and licked back to cover a wide bald patch on his head. He spoke softly, with a trace of a Welsh accent. He stooped as though carrying a load on his shoulders when he walked. The good temper and evenness of his manner could have been ascribed to resignation. He looked and talked as if he had given up all hope of seeing solid changes in mental nursing during his life. Yet he regarded the Block's unhappy patients as wayward children.

As an Assistant Chief Male Nurse Raggle was more than that to Father. He relieved him of every piece of nursing or administrative work he could. Semple, the other Assistant Chief, handled any figuring that had to be done; Raggle did the rest. Thus Howard was left to come and go and indulge in his mild obsessions as he wished. Raggle was presumed to hope that Father would retire and he would then take over. But inwardly Raggle preferred to be a second fiddle. He worried and did not like to take decisions, though there were few enough to take. I doubt if Father himself could remember when he last took a decision of any consequence.

Christmas Day was quiet. There was little to trouble Raggle apart from the tantrums of Isaiah. Pop spoke only when he wanted something, and then shouted in the hope of someone hearing what he was saying. Two old men and a Polish man were in the Admission Ward. The Pole had been to us the previous spring in a far livelier frame of mind. Then, he felt persecuted, now, he was convinced he was going to die. He lay in a bed nearest the desk, hands still upon the counterpane, eyes averted to heaven. Before the morning shift came on, he persuaded Whale that he was going to die. Could he please have the Last Rites and Holy Sacrament, he asked. Whale liked to be known as a good Catholic; on Friday mornings when the Priest came to Y Block, Whale pointed out the Believers to him. The Priest was as faithful in his visits as he was indiscriminate in deciding to whom he should speak. He might have known that he was the only representative of any denomination to come to Y Block. He spoke kindly to the Catholics and listened patiently to any others who caught his cassock and babbled at him. He looked pained and helpless for the hour he stayed, but came nevertheless the following week.

The Pole pleaded with Raggle to fetch the Priest.

'You had him here yesterday,' said Raggle.

'I'm going to die.' A tear glistened in the corner of the Pole's eye. 'I must have the Priest.'

'But the Father came yesterday, and you had Communion then,' Raggle said with finality. The Pole was mute in his misery.

But Whale had gone straight from night duty to Christmas Morning Mass. He told the Father that he was wanted in the Block. In the afternoon the Father came, smiling as he rang on the door to be let in; glad to be of practical use. Raggle was mystified. How good of the Father to come, particularly on Christmas afternoon. Was there anyone he had especially come to see? The Priest explained that he had been asked to call. There was a sick Polish patient on the point of death.

'Oh Lord,' said Raggle with more exasperation than piety. 'This way.'

Raggle led the Priest into the ward, catching hold of green screens as he passed. He set them up around the Pole's bed and pushed a chair in. The Priest hid his surprise that his subject for the Last Rites was the same as yesterday.

'*Is* he dying?' he asked.

'Not as far as we know,' said Raggle, 'but you never know.'

Raggle didn't look forward to the idea of three hours denying the Pole's religious request. So the Priest went ahead. Low and sacred murmurings followed from behind the screens. The patient took the Sacrament. The Father slipped away. The patient closed his eyes and waited in transparent peace for death to come. Death logically follows after the Final Sacrament. The Pole waited, lying very still in imitation of death. Perhaps it would come now if he waited patiently.

It did not come. But the Pole slept like a coffin nail until Boxing Day when it was sadly revealed to him that he was not in Heaven.

Raggle removed the screens. I served out tea to Pop and the old men. The Pole slept. The others, served by O'Leary, had their tea in Ward II and returned to the Recreation Ward to be mesmerised by television. Little Tom and I accompanied them.

'Give Hoover! Give Hoover!' a commercial jingle sang out its message for the season.

'Oh for God's sake do give "'oover" said a homeless patient. Two minutes later a slow smile broke out on the face of a long-haired young man in red corduroy dressing gown and slippers.

'Oh, "give over",' he laughed. 'That's a good one.' His face remained open from the laugh; saliva trickled down his chin unheeded. His thin shins were brown from burns.

'Why are Tony's shins scorched?' I asked Little Tom.

'Scorificated. That's the word,' he replied didactically. 'You see Tony is a Vegetative Schiz. You must have seen him here before. He was here a year or so ago anyway.'

'Perhaps I missed him. By why are his legs "scorificated" then?'

'You see, when he's at home he just sits. He's probably been sitting since he came out of Cane Hill last time. He sits right in front of the gas fire all day and doesn't move. His legs get hot and burnt. Tony won't do anything for himself now.' Little Tom turned away from Tony, lowering the nightshirt which he had raised to show the brown scorches running from ankle to knee. 'That's why his legs are burnt. And that's probably why his family had him brought in for Christmas. *They* want to get near the fire themselves for a bit.'

Little Tom jaunted off downstairs. A young nurse from the geriatric wards had promised to call and see him at half past seven. She hailed from the same part of Ireland as Little Tom and, meeting him in the pay queue a week before, had promised to bring a "little drop of hooch" to celebrate Christmas and the propinquity of their births. They settled down in a padded cell to drink and chat the shift away.

Raggle doled out medicines.

Rain fell. Patients were put to bed.

The night shift came on.

I went back to my brown room for puffed wheat and bed.

***

Fog was freezing on the glass behind the limp muslin curtains when I woke. Across the hall in a room identical to mine I could hear the shuffling and muttering of Kitty as she arranged her antimacassars and faded photographs. Kitty was an old spinster to whom Mrs Baron had given the room at a modest rent. She was slight and bent; hair yellow-white like old paper. Her hands, arthritically clawed, stopped a jangle of cheap bracelets falling off either matchstick wrist. She wandered from her room softly calling in a high pitched whine:

'Freddy! Freddy! Are you there?'

From the billows of her bed Mrs Baron shouted for Kitty to go back to her room. She knew from short experience that as soon as Kitty failed to get an answer from Freddy, she would wander into the back kitchen and turn on the taps. Water taps and gas taps were the obsessions of Kitty's failing mind. Whereas other people might spend their declining weeks checking constantly to see that taps were off, Kitty checked to see that they were full on. Mrs Baron followed her with screeched admonitions.

Kitty's last rational act three weeks before had been to find a room here where she was not alone. For the last twenty years at least she had been convinced Freddy would come home. The photograph of him in a silvered frame showed a young moustached man in tunic and puttees, cap under his arm, belts and eyes shining in the glossy pride of the moment. Every day since 1918 Freddy's photograph had been dusted and arranged. Freddy was killed on the Somme. Kitty said he had been killed. In her next breath she said she knew Freddy would come home. With a burst of sympathy springing out of her withered breast, Mrs Baron took Kitty in and cared for her. There was nothing to gain. At the same time and with the same inexplicable spontaneity, Mrs Baron bought me an ironing board, with attached seat.

'It's for you and Paula,' she said, 'you'll need it when you're married.'

I laid up my breakfast on it and pondered the significance of Mrs Baron's acts. They were as out of character as new green shoots on a long dead tree.

I warmed my feet at the gas fire. Boxing Day. Should I just sit here and scorch? What would they do if I stayed here in front of the fire like a rotting, helpless vegetable and did nothing for myself? They'd send me first to St Francis's, that's what they'd do. God forbid. What a thought. The very idea of being sent to the Psychiatric Observation Unit lent speed to my legs – even so carrying me there in the way of duty.

Fog froze on eyebrows and hair while I trotted through the grey mid-day stillness to the Block. No one waited behind the door to let me in. I rang the bell. Johnny pressed his narrow forehead against the wired glass of the door and grinned, turning to tell Semple that it was Nurse Lynch coming on duty. 'You're bleedin' five minutes early,' admonished Semple.

'Sorry,' I said.

Semple turned away. His dark eyebrows were fused into one by an angry frown.

'There's been one dead, one in and one out,' laughed Johnny. He stuck four fat fingers in the air by way of additional explanation. Neither Howard, glowering at the desk nor Semple, rushing in and out of the office to answer the phone seemed disposed to pass the time of day. Doddery Allan from the Recreation Ward doorway gave me a cursory nod as I let myself into the linen room. Corrigan was in there putting buttons in his white coat and tee-heeing to himself.

'Did you hear what happened?' he asked. 'One dead, one in and one out?'

So that's where Johnny picked up the summary riddle.

'No, I didn't. The staff aren't very chatty this afternoon. And there aren't any escorts today anyway.'

'No, there aren't. Don't need to be, either. Tee hee! It's like this: I'll tell you what happened. Whale was on night duty last night. One of the old men in Ward I died just before he came off. Knowing Whale he probably kept him going on Coramin until seven so as he wouldn't have to lay him out. Then one was booked in just as the morning shift were due on. He's no trouble. Hasn't got a name either, so he says; lying in bed 4 downstairs. The casualty department of the Northern Hospital sent him in 'cos he's an amnesiac. Looks an ugly customer to me – I don't know about amnesiac. Now where was I?'

'Early shift on, busy laying out the old man and admitting a new one at the same time.'

'Ah, yes. Well you can imagine. Father was doing his nut running hither and thither while Semple and O'Leary did the work. Doddery came in late and watched all the dressed patients having breakfast in

Ward II. Then he was told to look after them in the Rec. You know Skinner?'

'Yes. He's the lad with the freckles who walks around with his head on one side, smiling. Doesn't say much.'

'That's the one. Well, he took a knife while he was at breakfast. He could have taken the whole bloody table and Allan wouldn't have noticed. Semple and O'Leary were in and out of the sluice room getting hot water and getting rid of sheets from the corpse's bed. Father locked the door when they'd finished. Tee hee! Oh dear, what a laugh . . .'

Corrigan spluttered and reddened with the amusement of it all. His eyes closed in momentary ecstasy . . . 'Skinner had slipped away from Doddery's party as they went upstairs and hid in the sluice room. Howard locked him in. So he unscrewed the window stops with the knife, lifted up the sash and climbed out. That was about nine o'clock.

'At half-past eleven Johnny asks Allan how many for lunch. Allan calls down, 'Tirteen!' Semple hears him and says, 'Count again. There should be fourteen!' Father went round in circles counting everybody. He made it fourteen then realised he had counted Doddery in with the patients. 'Skinner's gone!' Doddery cried and darted off to the sluice room. 'Here's a knife. He's made off through the window. . . Of course, these knives are just right for screw-drivers: blunt ended, they're no use as knives at all.' Corrigan wiped his eyes.

'There's been such a ding-dong down there. Nobody will speak to anybody. Howard's blaming Semple and Semple's blaming Allan. O'Leary is screwing the window stops back. Talk about shutting the stable door after the horse has bolted. They'll never catch Skinner now.'

Corrigan went to the Recreation Ward to tease Allan. I went downstairs.

For two or three days Howard redoubled his zeal for checking locks, then unlocking to check behind them and locking again. On New Year's Eve Semple was still answering periodic phone calls from the main hospital offices.

'If that's the bleedin' Assistant Matron ringing up to find out if there's any news of Skinner yet, I'll rip the phone out and stuff it up . . .'

'It's the outside phone, I think,' Raggle interjected.

Semple answered the phone.

'Yes it was. Good job. I've told her Skinner will have gone back to his granny in Brighton ages ago,' Semple continued as he came out of the office. 'Here a minute, Ragg.' Raggle and Semple held a low consultation in the foyer. Raggle returned to the Admission Ward and stood between beds 4 and 5.

'Here, Butler,' he said suddenly to no one in particular. The "amnesiac" in bed four sat bolt upright. Then lay down again slowly. Raggle walked out and made a phone call.

'Should I relieve Lakhani upstairs?' I asked Semple. There had been practically nothing to do all afternoon and evening in the Admission Ward.

'No. Leave it for a bit.' He beckoned me outside. 'The police are coming in a moment to arrest the bloke in bed 4. That's what the phone calling has been about. His name's Butler they think. Wanted for theft and grievous bodily harm in Liverpool. They nearly had him there but he threw his landlady downstairs and got away. He's tried this "amnesiac" stunt before. They'll have to arrest him in the ward 'cos they've got to get a look at him first to make sure. There might be trouble so stay down for a bit.' In a louder voice Semple said, 'Look Nurse Lynch I've put you down for night duty again tomorrow, if you don't mind. A lot of the blokes have got 'flu.' Semple himself sniffed to prove it was an undiscriminating malady. 'Dobey's wife is ill so he wants to go on early shift. Wilson's down with it and Riddle's just getting over a heavy cold. Do you mind?' I assured him, with an exploratory sniff to test my own state of health that I did not mind.

I stayed downstairs while Butler was arrested. There was no trouble. Handcuffs were snapped on his wrists and he looked downcast. A policeman threw a blanket round his shoulders and took Butler's green property bag in his hand. Butler was led away. The Polish patient who had so earnestly required the Last Rites on Christmas Day lay seeing but not attending the scene enacted before him.

I felt chilled by the metallic finality in the click of handcuffs and went upstairs to let Lakhani go early.

New Year's Eve.

The medley of patients appeared glad when it was half-past eight and bed time. I ushered them along to Ward III, collected teeth and spectacles, helped the old men into bed. Corrigan came round with the tray of sleeping draughts and left. With just the desk light pulled low, I waited for Riddle to relieve me.

This ward, like the others below, was quiet.

'I hope the New Year is a lot happier for you,' I said to the beds of sad faces as I left. 'May it bring some peace you haven't known before.'

Just for an instant it seemed that a common feeling spread through the dormitory. A head or two rose above the pillows and said, 'Thank you Nurse. Thank you.' A thin voice from an end bed said, 'Same to you.' I nodded and left.

Back home to my dreary room. Mrs Baron nursed Kitty, who spluttered away with bronchitis and 'flu. She died a dozen pairs of wet sheets and six days later.

Mrs Baron paid for the funeral.

CHAPTER 22: London's Winter Toll

Fog and frost and influenza did not stop Londoners celebrating the New Year – publicly and privately. Y Block had nothing itself to celebrate and was excluded from joining in with outsiders. We continued to welcome damaged and distorted minds to be categorised then forwarded to the hospitals considered most suitable and that also had a bed. Day and night the patients came.

Chalky had found double reason to celebrate. On the first day of the New Year he was married. No doubt January 1st was a sensible choice of wedding date if he were ever likely to forget anniversaries - because he was unlikely to forget this one. His Scottish pleasure in economy perhaps played a part in the naming of this one day for the two celebrations. But if Chalky had two good reasons to celebrate, he had two equally good reasons for not celebrating in the way he did. For Chalky was very severely epileptic and he was an alcoholic. The fact that alcohol was disastrous to his physical and mental condition did not deter him. With his bride and a few friends he returned after the wedding to the in-law's flat, which was to be the couple's home.

Here a long bout of double whiskies marked the double event, until Chalky, at a point when his drinking companions had reached the stage of merriment, had a violent seizure. His wife appeared anxious then that the reception should end and the honeymoon begin. Black coffee and neglected anticonvulsant pills were brought to Chalky. His friends were on the point of leaving and Mrs Chalky had almost got her husband into bed. But then, for some strange reason, his confusion temporarily cleared. The friends must on no account leave, he insisted, when the party had only just begun. More drinks were served until everybody was drunk, and Chalky the most drunk of all. He assaulted neighbours who came after midnight to complain about the noise. His wife, in a maudlin state of tears, remonstrated with Chalky as he blackened her eye. A young inhabitant of the same block of flats tried to intervene and was kicked where he had particular masculine reasons for wishing not to be kicked.

Eventually, in the small hours of the morning, the police brought Chalky to us. The DAO, who had suffered a great deal of abuse and some scratches while in the back of the police van, filled out the papers and gave the background details to the duty doctor. Chalky's wife stayed outside in the fog on Little Tom's advice; the excuse for this was that she would have to stay with a member of staff if she were inside, and no one could be spared. She cupped her face against the glass of the door, watching to see what happened.

For all that it was three o'clock in the morning, and he wore only pyjama jacket, trousers and shoes, the duty doctor wanted to be as thorough as he could be. While we restrained Chalky on the admission bed, Dr Foote heard the DAO's account and let him and the police go, taking the sobbing woman with them. 'Right,' said Dr Foote, 'I'll see Mr White in my office now.'

It was really the Block's office and not Dr Foote's, so Little Tom was not too pleased. And it was crazy to try to interview the patient in his present state. 'He's confused and violent, you know. Wouldn't Mr White be better in bed?' Little Tom suggested.

With a smile that showed Foote had only the best motives, he said, 'No that will be all right. I'd like to have a talk with him straight away. I'll call you if I need you.' Quite plainly, Dr Foote wished to let Chalky unburden himself, and to reassure him that he would be comfortable here for the night. Chalky was beyond consolation now. He was so explosive and edgy, steering him off the bed and into the office was like rolling a barrel of nitro-glycerine.

Two minutes later there was a thud and a shout for help. O'Leary, that solid one-and-a-half-eared Irish worker, ran out of the ward towards the office. He was met by the patient coming through the door like a bullet. He had no time to dodge and caught a fullfisted slam on the jaw that felled him like a shuttle.

Little Tom and I dragged Chalky to a padded cell and left him there. Dr Foote hopped from one similarly named member to the other. Although he had received a hard blow on the chest before Chalky shot out of the office, he was now more concerned for the patient's welfare. O'Leary felt his chin and rubbed the back of his head where it had struck a radiator tap as he fell. In barely coherent tones he joined Little Tom in persuading Foote to leave Chalky where he was and return to bed.

'Tomorrow's another day,' he said softly.

It was also the third day of another year, the twentyfourth year that O'Leary had been in mental nursing. He did not take kindly to having his progress as a Lunatic Attendant marked by scars and bruises. It was all very well if it was unavoidable, but here was a case when, if notice had been taken of "them as know", O'Leary would be less dented.

***

Long after the hectic twelve days of Christmas were over, and when we were on duty in the Unit, whether we thought we had 'flu or not, the giddy night life of London went on. Chalky was away on a solitary honeymoon at a sanatorium. More old men and mildly mental sufferers found their faculties dimmed or tilted by the pervasive poisons of influenza and bronchitis and fog were admitted. Wally Beer suffered no physical disease as far as could be seen, but he chose a nearby concert hall to stage his collapse. The collapse was so obviously of nervous origin that he was persuaded reluctantly to come to us. Wally was a popular musician of national fame. He thumped out rhythms on the double bass and lent his voice to others in the group, whooping and grunting to several orgasms a night. The fans screamed. Wally Beer and the Boys performed. But however natural and basic their talent appeared to be, it was a strain for Wally. Tubby, barely over five feet tall, he sweated and nodded his clean crew-cut head night after night. And after each multiple climactic performance he felt that he could not repeat it; he was washed out. So he started taking pep-pills. They, and the alcohol which was so necessary to work up the mood, combined to great effect in Wally. He was not only able to keep up the ecstatic performance on stage, but could carry on afterwards. Eccentric behaviour set to music and applause is acceptable to managers, stage-hands and the hangers-on of the great. But when it is continued in the dressing rooms, and then on the stage in the middle of someone else's act, even show business people who are renowned for their tolerance became concerned. The papers next day were brief in their report: Wally Beer collapses during show. Doctors advise rest.

He did not "rest" with us. His manager came in with him carrying a large suitcase of clean clothes, talcum powder, aftershave lotion and a stack of glossy magazines. The DAO explained that this was the only way they had been able to persuade Wally to come for observation.

'This is a bloody nut house,' Wally muttered when I led him into the Admission Ward. 'I'm not effing well staying here.'

'You'll have to, for the night anyway,' I said.

Wally's entourage had left, and Wally did not like what he saw. Nor did he feel fit to face it alone.

'I can't stay here. I'm not mad.'

'That's what we are goin' to foind out,' Riddle told him. 'And how dare you suggest that the poor souls in here are mad? These are your public. Oi never hoped to hear a performer such as yourself say a thing loik that.' Riddle was not consistent with his brogue. He only laid it on thickly when he was pleased with himself or teasing someone. Wally could not appreciate in his present state that he was being teased. He felt that he was being goaded. That in itself was not an unreasonable thought. Riddle was sore because he had so much property to count and list. Beer was loaded up with stimulant drugs, sweating and panicking. Riddle had shown him the keys and let Wally check for himself that all the doors were locked and he would have to stay in the Unit overnight. We had managed to make Wally undress and now he was standing naked on fat, unsteady legs, calling for his own pyjamas. They were duck egg blue silk with W B monogrammed on the breast pocket. Regulations were absolutely inflexible: no patient could wear his own night attire. Wally was incensed and began to shout and rave in his famous husky voice. He staggered around the ward waking an audience for himself. He cried about "persecution" and volunteered there and then to lead an attack against the tyranny imprisoning them all.

'You'll ruin my voice,' he said as Riddle pushed him back into bed, one hand on his chest and the other on his neck.

'You'll ruin it yourself,' said Riddle, 'shouting about like that. Oi thought you said just now these men were all mad? And now you want to be the leader of them all? Oi think it's you who's mad.'

Beer raised both tubby hands and made to scratch Riddle's eyes. I caught his fingers and bent them back.

'Don't do that,' he yelled, 'I won't be able to play my bass.'

Suddenly he was remembering all his professional assets. I let the sticky fingers slip from mine.

'Right,' I said, 'try and put up with it for tonight. Get some sleep Mr Beer.'

Eventually he did. One of the Block's favourite female duty doctors, Dr Julia, gave him a quick physical while he lay in his own bed. She was at least the favourite of Tiny Verity and myself. She was quick and deferential to whichever nurse was in charge of the night shift. Recently, the Unit had acquired for nights only the company of a small black cat. When our Dr Julia entered, the cat ran up to greet her and to rub itself against the sheer nylon delight of her legs. Then Dr Julia would crouch down on her haunches to stroke the cat, revealing shapely knees and pleasant curve of thigh to those attendants who sat at the desk and took an interest in such unusual beauty in the Block. It was perhaps a small pleasure, but a welcome one in the long, ugly necessities of the night. Riddle was not the least of those ugly necessities. His very presence precluded tact or diplomacy, or even common sense in pacifying a patient.

Wally Beer slept fitfully. Next day his release was permitted. It is not possible to tell if that was a good thing. Not long afterwards he graduated to hard drugs. Then he did not come to us but to the police, for his decline was no longer his private problem, but part of an organised mess of crime.

***

Smog and London took their toll as winter dragged on. More and more old men became erratic, unpredictable nuisances in their families' houses. Blood ran slowly and coldly in their arteries, which hardened and seemingly bound up the muscles and the brain. They were brought in to us, very often one felt, in the hope that they would die. Sometimes with antibiotics and vitamins they recovered a little. If they then were going back to their families, they were pathetically grateful. They stared at us with eyes all bearing the ivory crescent or full ring of senility between pupil and iris, and thanked us. If they were being sent away to one of the big repositories for senile patients, they thanked no one.

Most often they died. They died in their own good time. Tiny Verity might very lightly press his hand upon the chest of an old man; rhythmically he would work his stiffened rib cage for him for a while. When Tiny stopped the patient would settle into his own laborious wheeze and cough once more.

'What's the point?' Tiny asked. 'They had better die in their own good time. There is no point in oxygen tents or constant nursing to keep such sad old folk alive.'

I disagreed. I liked to see even an old and battered frame come to life again; to enjoy a feeder full of tea in the morning. But I agreed that the chances of recovery were slight, and the rewards for each one doubtful. Only on those occasions when there happened to be a spontaneous resurrection from a senile patient's physical decline, together with a recovery of his wits, did it seem worthwhile. But these cases were impossible to predict. Though it was flattering to think otherwise, these rare improvements appeared to owe little to our nursing, but rather to be arbitrary miracles.

So we sat in the night and listened to our old men, and listened to the approach of death. Sometimes for three hours or more the breathing would become shallower and slower. Dry throats whistled and scraped. We could lay bets but never guarantee which man would go first. We would prop up their chests to aid breathing and it made little difference. Slowly they wound down and their springs uncoiled. They slept, and peace worked from the outside in, until they were silent. Then another breath . . . and silence . . . then the last.

The watcher is a child again in innocence. Here is a figure, the semblance of a man. All ages show upon the face, yet none. The life is gone. Perhaps it is stopped. It is just a clock that has stopped ticking, a brew that has stopped fermenting: and yet the body looks as though some elements have been resolved and taken from it.

His soul (what's that?) has gone to Heaven (where's that?). The living, acting, thinking, sharing thing has stopped. Heaven is what this man has left behind of beauty. We have his Heaven or his Hell on Earth. A thing so graceful in itself as death does not need fancy tales of Heaven woven round it.

Always in the night there is a moment for musings. In the first minutes of death no one breaks the silence. Work would begin soon enough. Let mystery claim attention for a while.

Then it's off with the bedclothes and fetch the tray of things from the dispensary. Bandages, cotton wool, scissors, Elastoplast, Biro, soap and water, towel and flannel, and the shroud. The man has gone and we must close up his house for him. No need for hesitant fingers. Do this quickly while it is easy. Let his face still be soft as he goes out.

Thoroughly, the body is washed all over then dried. Hard work this can be when the body has neither warmth nor movement to help the task. Gently, the jaw is tied up and eyelids are laid down. Care must be taken not to bruise or mark the delicate skin. The anus is blocked up with cotton wool, the penis tied off with a bandage. Now the nostrils are packed and it is almost done. The previous occupant's name of this house is put on Elastoplast; a tag for the arm and a tag for the leg. Then we help him into a long, white shroud. This is always long, with ruffs at the neck and wrists. Within twenty minutes his body is gone from the ward.

Had he left the ward on his feet, behind him there would only be a slight memory. Death reinforces the memory. We think more of someone who is dead, not just absent; if they make us think about him at all.

CHAPTER 23: Spring

If human beings hibernated from November until February, spring might not be such a contrary season. Love, foliage, song and hope are supposed to blossom and the year to be born anew. But the mental and physical deprivations of a London winter depress many systems. In New York they say that the advent of a fresh financial year raises the suicide rate significantly. At St Francis's we did not often see the results of such rational attempts at self-destruction. Our patients were beyond the considerations of tax returns, honour or business failure. They, in their own very private worlds were at a low ebb.

To judge by the patients in Y Block who gave Miss Tracey such heartache, suicide is not a simple matter. All the year round we admitted the results of attempts, but many more arrived in spring. The reasons for seeking or seeming to seek the peace of death were as varied as the sicknesses we admitted. Profoundly depressed patients, generally with long histories of voluntary and certified stays in mental hospitals, groped for their bottles of barbiturates, or sealed themselves into the womb-like privacy of their kitchen stove and turned on the gas taps. Some were rescued and taken to a hospital, then transferred to us. Drug effects largely wore off. The cellular damage done by gas did not. Men who were withdrawn from their gas or motor exhaust pipes, escaping only just before death, were in worse mental shape afterwards.

A few became half-brained psychotics; more recovered only as far as a state of permanent confusion and dull delirium. They went away from us for a life of premature senility.

People with shattered minds who had suffered a few years of their complaint found the agony insupportable. When they heard voices and saw visions, the reality of hallucination gripped them. When the malady left temporarily, relief was obliterated by the trembling anticipation of its return. Then, while they were still young, many sought to break up and destroy the bodies that housed such disordered, unhappy minds. They were violent to themselves, as if in the destruction of their bodies they would punish and kill the disease for all time; make it impossible for the demons to follow beyond the grave; gain victory, immortality and sanity in one last violent battle.

The determination of such sufferers may have been so great that they were successful. We frustrated the intentions of a few. Certain beds in the Admission Ward, next to and in full view of the desk, were reserved for potentially repeating suicidal patients. They were never free from observation.

Stan had been admitted to a general hospital after an overdose of rat poison. The dose that he took might have been too great for a rat but not enough for Stan, who was a big man. They pumped him clean of the poison and nursed him back into consciousness. He appeared grateful. He smiled. He leapt from his bed and hurled himself through a window, fracturing legs, arms, ribs and skull on the asphalt below. Even so, he survived and some weeks later, strapped onto a stretcher, he was carried into Y Block. He frequently gained and lost consciousness or slept intermittently. On waking, he eyed the attendant nurses from behind the yawning chasm of his despair. He took his medicine and injections without complaint. Three days after his admission, Stanley smiled at Verity when he handed him his medicine. His head fell back on the pillow and he died.

'Oh Christ,' cried Verity. 'He's gone.'

'That's what he wanted, wasn't it?' Big Wilson roared from behind his mug of tea. 'If they want to do it let them do it. If it was up to me I'd give them a gun and let them do it properly.'

'You bastard,' said Verity. 'How do you know Stan still wanted to die?'

'Don't call *me* a bastard, Verity. His like are the scum o' the earth.' Big Wilson swept out pointing at Stan.

Verity lifted up the still, white hand of Stan and let it fall; pulled down his eyelids and left to call the doctor.

***

For every Stan who died eventually by his own hand, there were half-a-dozen others who did not really want to die. Men who wanted help signalled their distress by teetering on the parapet of a Thames bridge, or by shallowly cutting their wrists. They complained of "trouble with the wife" or "things being in a mess". Some had treatment for what it was worth; Miss Tracey tried to help them all and sort out their domestic problems.

No one could help Johnny St Clair. Had he been rich, he would have given all his money for a means to his own death. Though he came in after Stan, and did not know his end, he would have liked a clot to block one of his life-giving arteries. He would have swopped any death for his. Johnny St Clair was dying in a way that made him weep in fear and horror. He could not be classified by any means as insane, but the balance of his mind was tilted against those who denied him the right to die as he wished.

Johnny St Clair's life had not been a roaring success. If we are honest, only a few lives are. Yet he had some fulfilments; and until recently had found pleasure in his work and in a game of badminton with the lads from his office. Billie, looking and muttering through his records when Johnny first came in, described him as a "prune". That was Billie's joke: a prune is his name for a black-coated worker. Billie took prunes to work his bowels; a black-coated worker is "someone who works in the city". Billie laboured over and repeated his joke whenever he had the opportunity. The fact that Johnny St Claire was a bed-bound tragedy did not deter him. For Billie found life good: therefore he presumed without question that anyone who did not was mad.

Mr St Clair had dry gangrene. He was dying and he knew it. He had no family to deceive him. Each day he saw that more of his dead feet had flaked away.

He was not a hero and found no consolation in the special attention the doctors paid to him. They stuck needles into his legs, each day higher without sensation.

'For God's sake go away and let me die,' he begged. He wept and wept for a bottle of pills, an injection, anything. Once he had been in the Guards, and he regretted now that he had not seen active service then, ten years ago, and been killed rather than now having to watch his body crumbling away to death. Twice before admission he had attempted suicide. His landlady foiled his first effort by gas. On the second occasion he procured a revolver but was seen with it in Richmond Park.

He pleaded with us separately and together. It was his death he said, why should he not decide when and how to have it? We could not argue. We were not arbiters of death; our task was to restrain St Clair and others in life; hold them on their narrow twisted tracks in the hope that they might straighten and lead to a cure. Billie tried to jolly St Clair out of his mood:

'Hush now. You're going to be made better, you silly boy.'

'Don't talk like a bloody old woman. I'm dying.'

'Oo, what nonsense! Drink your medicine and be a good boy.'

Johnny dashed the draught from Billie's hand and turned to sob into the sheets.

'We'll be glad when you go to another hospital, I can tell you,' Billie said petulantly. 'It's upsetting to the other patients.' A few of these who were in

possession of sufficient faculties were aware of an
atmosphere of distress, and became more fidgety in
their turn. But Billie was the most disturbed. He hated
an exhibition of what he regarded as cowardice. He
was selfishly glad when St Clair was taken to another
long-term care institution. St Clair died there later as
his disease - not he dictated.

***

It was useless to complain, either in Billie-style or
with the ravings of Big Wilson, about patients living
or dead. The months of January and February had not
yet done their worst. If there were no other
emergency psychiatric units in the country, St
Francis's Y Block received enough cases to satiate
the curiosity of the most morbidly interested. With
none of the passion for death that St Clair showed, I
still wished from time to time that I was doing a
normal National Service – even if it involved armed
combat. 'The first six months will be the worst,'
Howard assured me when I started, 'then you won't
bother.' He was wrong on both counts. For sheer
misery in the spectacle of human tragedy, this spring
was the worst. It wasn't lessened by being perceived
with senses dulled by a heavy cold that lingered until
Easter. Nor did I find it easy "not to bother". The very
fact that there was nothing that I could do, other than
modify my reactions and act always with as much
careful tenderness as I could muster, increased the
sense of frustrated concern. It was impossible to be
totally detached in observation. Our subjects were not

odd creatures from another planet. They were me or you.

Coincidences in the spring admission of suicides, alcoholics and addicts emphasised links of similarity among them. The wards were never without at least one alcoholic sufferer, and usually it was not his first admission. Individual histories repeated themselves. The young alcoholics, quiet and often unselfish, were relatively popular with the staff after sobering up. Though their whisky-induced deliria caused violent rough-houses on admission, they were passive thereafter. They left us with their good intentions to be cured at one of the hospitals catering for their needs. Too often, however, they were readmitted at a later date.

Reasons for failure varied. Listening to any of those given, it was easy to dismiss the alcoholics as having fundamentally "weak" characters. They were "weak" in respect to drink. But in no cases was it selfindulgence in something enjoyable. Even the compulsion they felt, seemed barely a thing of the mind. It was a physiological craving. The kick of alcohol in the bloodstream demanded further kicks. When money could not buy these kicks in respectable bottle form, further methods were found. First methylated spirits were mixed with cider, then with cheap lemonade. Bottle-bought delirium tremens was mild compared to the rotting hysteria that followed the intake of meths. When that was unavailable, alcoholics' bodies still craved drink. If they possessed a room, some distilled boot polish until there was sufficient to produce oblivion; others passed the tubes of their gas rings into milk. The resultant brew sent them into a screaming abyss from which their brains could not completely recover. Though they knew the depths to which the drink would take them, their trembling hands still made its poisons available.

'It's not until my body is sodden with it, and I'm unconscious, that I can stop,' Lawrence told me while I monitored his pre-transfer bath. 'The first taste is enough. But I never feel at the time that the first taste will do anything at all. I've always been like it.'

'What drives you to it?'

'I'm not driven. I haven't had any great tragedies. No women have upset me too much. My family was OK. But I can't stop at the first drink. Once that's passed my throat I've got to go on.'

'But you've seen in here what some of the old blokes with your trouble are like. You know you'll end up dead – and twenty or thirty years sooner than you need to. If you know that first drink is going to kill you, why have it?

Lawrence explained the difficulties of refusing; the lonely embarrassment of declaring his weakness to others; the shame of having to belong to Alcoholics Anonymous when other people belonged to normal clubs. He had struck unlucky with AA too. In his words, they were "extroverts and ponces"; an opinion no less firmly held because it was based on one isolated contact. Since a universal pill to kill the craving seems unlikely, perhaps alcoholics should bear a small brand upon their foreheads. The brand would indicate to everyone that the man suffered a complaint; that nothing need be done, but he must not be given drink; to give this man just one small shandy is tantamount to murder. When someone cannot look after himself, the onus is on others to help him.

Observing and musing: alcoholism is a compulsive form of suicide. The risk is taken despite the consequences. Other addictions are more nearly experiments with death. Benzedrine and marijuana are to many people what shandies are to the alcoholic. They are the first step. The physical addiction comes with heroin and the "hard" drugs, and is preceded by the suicidal intent to find another world. That world may be one of hallucinations, euphoria or merely a heightened sense of *being*, but it is always an escape, always an experiment with death. The addicts who came to Y Block were well along the paths of their explorations. Each dose they had taken put them further out of touch. Some lingered and teased themselves before arriving at death; others started towards it and barely cast a look back over their shoulders. Unlike the alcoholics, drug addicts were interested in their journeys. Unlike the determined suicides, the means of travel were important.

Y Block was kept reasonably well informed of the immediate fate of most patients who left us. Referring Officers, ambulance drivers, regular patients and our own staff's reports after escort duty brought news of patients recently transferred. But Van Greet, a South African, went away to a "sanatorium" in Cornwall and we did not know what happened to him. It is doubtful whether many of the Unit's lunatic attendants asked after him anyway. For reasons that were not obvious, they did not like Van Greet.

He was a doctor. Large and well-built with an impressive aquiline nose below a wide forehead, he was a dirty, trembling mess when admitted. He had been experimenting with death by Benzedrine, later (it was suspected) mixing in other addictive drugs and then morphine. He clutched a sheaf of papers all covered in sprawling handwriting. Page one began sensibly: "*Some aspects of Schizophrenia*". Three lines and a few pills later the writing was uncontrolled. Generously and drunkenly the words careered up and tip-tilted across the page. Then the subject matter became gibberish. On every page or so half a line stood out, ordered in its writing and syntax, before lapsing to even worse scrawl. On page ten there was one final effort at meaningful communication: "*The pound note test:* One reliable test for the schizoid condition is to offer the person a pound note in the left hand. If he tears it with the left hand right hand half . . ." Before the point of this clinical technique was reached, Dr Van Greet's fountain pen proved inadequate. Pencil took up the scribble and became so wild that not even a single letter was formed thereafter. Page after page of unequally wavy lines were all that the doctor achieved; sixty more pages of drug-aided lunacy.

Similarly, his efforts at living were now childish. Though the wastage of his years of qualifying twisted me into agonies of hope that he would improve, he did not. He rushed about babbling infantile remarks to those present, then lapsed into silence. He broke it for brief intervals to accost a nurse intent on some task, crying, 'I'm a doctor, I'm a doctor,' only to stand paralysed and trembling before the task he had interrupted. Perhaps it was the general staff bias against doctors that caused their dislike of Van Greet. Or perhaps it was the fear and loathing of the addiction which he represented. For the attendants, even if they had no qualms about their own sanity, they feared the curious perversion to drugs. They knew they themselves were not prone to alcoholism. They did not know if they could ever half-knowingly be lured into the suicidal state of other addictions. It seemed to happen so simply. It could happen to anyone. It appeared scarcely possible that a few grains of a white powder could control a man. Yet heroin does. It is the master in every relationship.

When the gay round of London's season ended, Peter, a young photographer from Chelsea, was brought in. He did not recognise Tiny Verity, but Tiny knew him. Peter had been for a time at the same art school. Then he took up photography with help from his family. Newly established in the right area for financial rewards he was doing well; twenty-three and life before him, then someone introduced Peter to heroin. This "friend" was one of that smart and knowledgeable set who disguise their lack of individuality and mental poverty in the current coffee house uniform; people who know nothing and are going nowhere but always find someone in London to advise. The "friend" of course never had it himself. But he was proud to air the knowledge that he knew someone who did – and could secure introductions. For a moment in the "queers' corner" of the coffee bar he was a big fellow. He was a small, stupid fellow, and a murderer. Certainly he did not jab the syringe into Peter's arm. He did not buy the poison for him. But he lied ignorantly about its harmlessness. He boasted stupidly of the value of knowing and sharing such experiences with eccentric and individual people. Possibly, if Peter had not been slightly homosexual it would not have mattered. But the "friend's" words had their effect. He borrowed a shot. Within six months he was brought into us in a state of terrible deprivation.

Tiny Verity was on duty when Peter was admitted, as he was when Peter died. Tiny came back from escort duty at about three in the afternoon. He poked his head round the Admission Ward door and wandered reluctantly across to the desk to return a receipt for the transferred patient to Semple. He gazed down his nose at the ward and asked mockingly because of his own great height if anything was happening down below. We assured him that nothing was. Semple looked up from the Financial Times wherein he was frequently immersed since his son had gone to work in the city.

'I think Billie's on heat. He's spent the whole bleedin' afternoon upstairs with Allan.'

'Oh.' Verity twisted up his moustache with a finger to show the smile underneath. 'Peter
       Corling's quiet.'

'He was out for a leak just now,' I said.

Verity wandered over to look at Corling.

'He's very quiet,' said Verity, putting the back of his hand against Corling's cheek, 'and cold.'

'They often are,' said Semple. 'It's a cold job for an addict going without his fix.' 'He's dead,' said Verity.

Semple folded his paper and, grunting about the nonsense of stocks and shares or Verity's diagnosis, walked across to the bed where Peter lay.

'He bleedin' is.'

Verity looked sick. He didn't answer Semple's questioning look. It was not easy to be certain, but I thought a sort of sob was choked behind Tiny's blank expression. His eyes shone through his spectacles and the moustache trembled. Semple saw Verity was affected.

'Cor. Don't take it too bleedin' hard mate.' He laid his three-fingered hand kindly on the small of Verity's back. 'It does get you though, sometimes, don't it?' He turned towards me. 'I remember when I first went into nursing. A lad from my street came in. Only nineteen. "Be sure to take good care of 'im," 'is muvver said, "now you're a nurse an all". Of course, I said I would. I didn't know 'e was going to bleedin' die. But 'e did. In my arms.' Semple readjusted his false teeth. 'He'd 'ad some belly ache but we thought he was laying it on. 'Pendicitis. They didn't operate

277

in a hurry in those days. If it was peritonitis, which it was, they was gone before you knew it. I sat 'im up in bed and gave him a drink and 'e just died. I was bloody shocked and miserable for weeks.'

The depth of Semple's emotion recalling the incident even after many years, was emphasised by his offer of a "bloody" instead of a "bleedin'". Semple had to be very roused to make that exchange. He talked, not so much to entertain me, but to allow Tiny to compose himself or cry unobserved if he wished. There was only half-an-hour to go of Verity's shift, so Semple sent him off. I went with him and listened to the account of Peter Corling's last few years. The sadness occasioned in Verity was not just on account of the death. Given the patient's shocked and dehydrated system, shattered by the few months of abuse the heroin had given it, it was not surprising Peter's light went out. What upset Tiny was the fact that it was so unnecessary and had such a small beginning; that it could have happened to him; that it could happen to anyone; that he knew Peter and therefore knew that he was not a separate class of person, particularly liable to addiction.

CHAPTER 24: Subjects for Concern

The atmosphere in the Unit swung erratically from morgue to madhouse. Deaths came in batches leaving their impressions, which faded and gave way to the surfeits of present behaviour. Shifts blurred. Time itself had no sense. People, scenes, incidents clicked into view and out again. The smells of urine, polish and disinfectant had long since become such permanent nasal occupants that they were only appreciated on returning after a couple of days off. The Block's noises lingered in the head long after a shift ended.

'How far is it to Catford? How far is it to Catford? I've left the gas on. How far is it to Catford? Please tell me how far it is to Catford.'

'Oh, Mr Raymond, please have a rest. It's about five miles to Catford. I've told you. Other nurses have told you. The gas has been put off. There is nothing to worry about.'

Mr Raymond heard no reassurances. His brain had two or three grooves in which to run. It would scrape away in them until the brittle wax of his nervous system was hot and melted and ran into a mindless, shapeless mass.

'How far is it to Catford? How far is it to there?'

Little Tom brought tablets for the patient. Mr Stephen Raymond, height five-feet ten, weight eight stones, age twenty-six, took the tablets into his scrawny hand and gulped them back as if they could answer his question. He paced up and down the Recreation Ward with dressing gown flapping open. Continually he asked his question.

Little Tom eyed him firmly. 'What does the doctor say is wrong with you then, Mr Raymond?'

'I'm suffering from schizophrenia with paranoia, obsessions, auditory and visual hallucinations,' he recited, 'but please tell me how far is it to Catford?' Nothing had meaning for Stephen. There was no answer to his question. Exact measurement on a map gave the mileage Stephen spoke of wanting. But he paid no heed to the answer. He was lost in the confusion of his own illness. His question really was, "Please can you help me?"

Across the ward an older man of similar build took no notice of Stephen. If he had been able, he could have told more clearly than anyone just what Stephen suffered. Once he had felt the same agonies of shattered, unreasoned obsession. Voices had mocked him. He too had been a little boy lost in the years of manhood. A job as a cinema projectionist fell through when he was nineteen, when he could no longer both do the work and listen to his malady. Now at each temple were the slim twin scars that showed he had had "treatment". Prefrontal leucotomy was a psychiatric panacea at the time. It did do something. As one previously depressed patient who had had the operation said, 'It is a bit easier now. I see things distantly – like through the wrong end of a telescope.' Then he sniggered and rose to micturate in a corner. There was a rumour that Stephen might have the operation. It would have been as well to cut off a broken leg instead of finding where the fracture was and healing it. For the older man opposite was now a mindless vegetable. Perhaps the severance of the lobes had been too complete in his case and, truthfully, Y Block only saw the failures of any treatment. But there were so many of them in proportion to the patients we admitted, that scepticism, even hopelessness were natural reactions amongst the lunatic attendants.

Few of our patients had missed earlier treatment. Their domestic conditions were not all so insupportable that relapse was unavoidable. They had not been cured. Empiric treatments according to the hospital or the fashion were carried out. The worst that could be said of these was that they were sometimes dangerous and sometimes useless; that they occupied skilled time and intelligence to the exclusion of research. The extremes of treatment emphasised the dark groping in psychiatric knowledge: analysis at one end and physical applications at the other. Honest doctors did not hold rigorously to the theories as to how the treatments might work. But being no less human than others, they wished to do something, and to be known to be doing something.

Insulin and electric shock therapy seem to be the machine age variations on the hot and cold bath routines of earlier years. From the evidence available in Y Block, they were no more effective; and it was impossible to say whether any improvement in the patient's condition was a result of the rest and attention given to him rather than the treatment.

Even Little Tom, who loved categorising and predicting what treatment would be prescribed for a particular complaint, had few illusions. He was not complacent, but like many others, was so bound up in the business of giving labels to patients that labelling became an end in itself. It was restful to look around the wards and dole out labels.

Drugs were to be the answer in the future. Already many different brands had their advocates. Seeing the effects that organic and chemical disorders had on the minds of our men – poisons changing personalities, addictions producing hallucinations, diseases causing depression – it is reasonable to try opposite chemicals to produce opposite effects. The answer will come this way. But it cannot be hoped that the magic bottle of mind medicine will be easily and experimentally found. Firstly, the insane patient is an unhappy person who would not wish to have more experimental unhappiness heaped upon him. Secondly, it is hardly better than a waste of time to pour new oils into an engine that is improperly understood. The primary and laborious task that can and should take, for example, all of this country's present expenditure on military defence, is to find out in detail how the human being works. It seems to me that Britain could not make a nobler offering to the rest of the world, nor to Britain herself, than to banish the curses of gross insanity for ever. Apart from the addition to human happiness which every politician aspires to make, this would not be without its economic advantages.

That is what I suggested to Little Tom. But Little Tom spoke of military strength bringing peace and of nuclear deterrents; of the need this island has for strength – not of mind but of defence – and found a label for me. And he stared expressionless around the Recreation Ward. These people were others. Little Tom was himself and mightily defended; but not defended from the things we saw by anything more permanent than his own attitudes.

***

Little Tom continued his medicine round. I was left to guard and observe the discord of the Recreation Ward. Two alcoholics jerked away at the ping-pong table until one of them stood on the ball and crushed it. At the piano a Maltese gentleman, who had drifted from asylum to asylum collecting symptoms as he went, sat as though attendant on inspiration. His wrists were bound with the white insignia of attempted suicide; his face was puckered with the deadpan creases shared by institutionalised patients; he was depressed and aggressive, isolated in his own miserable company. Suddenly, with bloodshot eyes lifted to the ceiling, he began to play. He could not play, but his hands thumped the keys while his body swayed in a dislocated rhythm of its own. The mangled sounds rose to a crescendo that put the Maltese patient into a state of ecstasy demanding further climax. Hands and elbows could not wring from the piano all the passion he felt and, standing now, he assaulted black notes and white with his forearms before crashing the lid down in a maestro's gesture of a performance completed.

Meanwhile, upon the cushions of a bench, Mr Solomon Lobisha stretched his tall, angular body. Head on one arm, he eyed nothing with bloodhound serenity. Dressed in identical nightshirt and red corduroy dressing gown, a fat Polish patient approached him. Silently, and with movements in parody of a slow motion film, the Pole lay down beside Lobisha. He lifted his dressing gown and with an air of total disinterest went through a shadow performance of a crural sexual act. Lobisha rolled his eyes and, seemingly with great effort, summoned an expression of polite acceptance. His face bore the look of one who expects strange things, and merely hopes mildly that some good may come of them. No dutiful spouse tolerated marital advances with more resignation than Lobisha while the Pole gently continued his pornographic pantomime.

Eventually, as if he were taking his leave of an esteemed visitor, Lobisha rose and shook the Pole solemnly by the hand.

'I also am a British subject,' he said, and bowed and shook hands again. 'We are all British subjects.'

Solomon Lobisha was as conscious of his status as many of our coloured patients were. Two or three a year were brought to us from places of public importance. Sometimes they carried knives; once a gun was concealed in the man's clothing. Practically always they carried an uncompleted letter written in their own hand and addressed to a person of rank. They sought the solution to their own mental discontent, in supplication or in an attack directed to a pinnacle of authority. The vigilant police brought such patients in various states of confusion or aggression from the House of Commons, Downing Street or the doorstep of someone that week in the news. They came to us firmly convinced of their sanity and the ability of A Great Person to solve their problems.

Mr Lobisha was apprehended scaling the walls of Buckingham Palace. 'I am a British subject,' he shouted. 'I must see the Queen. The Queen will want to see me. I am a British subject.' His letter commencing "Dear Queen . . ." continued more in the same vein. Lobisha was not armed or violent, but one realised that, obsessed as he was with the idea that the Queen was responsible for his happiness, he could easily have become the cat's paw for others with less honourable intentions. Newspapers have magic for those who have trouble in the attic, and so also do the names that appear in them. Lobisha knew that things were not right with him; he felt that if he could share the limelight with a public figure, some attention might be drawn to his unhappy condition.

I waited for Doddery to relieve me, then went below to report to Raggle.

'Your Polish friend is copulating with Lobisha,' I said. 'I didn't break it up 'cos it was all very decorous and quiet.'

'No. Quite right,' said Raggle. 'There is nothing you can do about it except make a note. They are both as mad as hatters. I'm surprised at Mr Lobisha though,' Raggle continued after some thought, 'I understood he fancied Princess Margaret.'

'No, that was the last African we had in – the one found with a knife in Kensington Palace. This one was after the Queen. I think he thought the Pole's attentions were all part of the service here.'

'Yes. Well the service here isn't quite as good as that.'

Billie tripped into the ward wiping traces of egg custard away from the corner of his mouth, and a little more which had dribbled into one of the channels between his three chins.

'I suppose we could put Billie in a crown and send him upstairs,' Raggle said, turning to laugh. 'What do you think about that Billie?'

'I think you're too bloomin' saucy,' said Billie. He had not heard a word but did not wish it to be realised that he did not appreciate a joke.

'Am I out on escort this afternoon Nurse Raggle?' Billie asked to turn the conversation to a serious note. Raggle assured him that he was, and named the hospital.

'O goody-goody-gumdrops,' said Billie. 'I shall be able to get some more bay leaves. D'you know I'm right out?' We did not know that Billie was right out of bay leaves, but we did know that Billie loved to go to this particular hospital. Outside Henry Porter Ward there grew a large bay tree that Billie fleeced of young green leaves for his spice cupboard.

'You're down for escort with Billie,' Raggle told me as he and Billie left the Admission Ward to get Solomon's papers in order for transfer.

I glanced through the register to memorise the names of newly admitted patients, then walked from bed to bed with the bed board list of occupants. I was due to go on night duty the following weekend and, as there would be no more patients going out until then, I followed my usual practice of knowing as much as possible about our guests. To be forewarned made for quiet nights. Just to address a sleepless patient by his name sometimes had a settling effect.

In bed 2 Mr Plessey moaned and wriggled in a semiconscious state. He was young, well built and looked fit enough. There was disagreement about why he was here at all. He had crashed his motorcycle some four weeks before, fracturing his left thigh, which was now fixed by a femur pin. At the same time he had damaged his brain, which was not so easy to fix. He was often delirious and needed frequent restraint. Since we could do nothing else for him, it seemed likely that others had decided that nothing could be done to cure him either.

Bed 3 contained a man of unknown age or name. His face was finely boned and pale. Large blue eyes gazed with interest upon the ward, and his hair, thinning on top, was neatly combed. "No Name" was recorded on the bed board. He was sensible and pleasant, but knew nothing further of himself other than the fact that he had arrived in London – he thought by train – the day before. He realised, he said, that he was suffering from amnesia and he thought it had happened before. He spoke with a slight Yorkshire accent and so the staff called him "Yorky" as that was easier than "Mr Unknown Man". Yorky was listed in the register as suffering from an "hysterical fugue". That meant that shortly he would be denied the privacy of his amnesia. In the afternoon a dapper and darkly smooth psychiatrist arrived from the teaching hospital and had Yorky put to bed in the empty upstairs dormitory. Here he hypnotised Yorky and discovered his name and address as well as some of the domestic background which had precipitated the fugue. Yorky did not seem to share O'Leary's delight in this treatment, but then Yorky found life without a past very much easier. O'Leary rejoiced in the magic of hypnotism, nearly always contriving to be at hand when the psychiatrist did his stuff and followed every move and revelation as though at Divine Service. The hypnotist who treated a patient with O'Leary nearby, had the bonus success of practically hypnotising O'Leary too. Not that he recalled (as far as we could tell) hitherto unknown secrets of his past, but he was impressed beyond measure by the therapeutic powers of the hypnotist. He would collar Father after such a session and ask if all the patients in the Block could not be similarly treated. Father was conciliatory and explained gently that not everyone was accessible to hypnotism.

O'Leary was disappointed and waited impatiently for the next "No Name" to appear on the bed board.

Beds 4 and 5 were occupied by old men. Bed 6 contained one of our regular patients. Mr Miles, like so many other young men who came for psychiatric observation, suffered the various agonies that were listed under schizophrenia. Though his eyes were open and his ears unblocked, what he saw and heard bore little relation to his immediate environment. It was as though a nightmare with voice and vision had descended on him while he slept, and refused to go away when he awoke.

His neighbour was getting dressed. He was a thin, angry, red-haired young man with the palest of pale blue eyes. He was an art student and his behaviour had proved more erratic and untoward than his companions in their various poses of eccentricity could tolerate. He called now for his sketch book and pencil, which Raggle provided and then sent him upstairs to draw under the tutorial eye of Allan. Within ten minutes Allan came down to tell Raggle that the art student was a bit of a nuisance because he kept scribbling and swearing.

'Couldn't you keep him down here for a while?' As evidence of the reasonableness of his request, Allan deposited a sheaf of crumpled sketch papers on the desk.

'Look,' he said, laying his small head over to one side in a gesture of pathetic martyrdom, 'he's half done about twenty drawings and then crossed them out. Seven of them are supposed to be me.' There was the rub. Either they should all have been of Doddery, or there should have been none at all. We cackled over the drawings and eventually Allan wandered back upstairs.

'He hasn't got my likeness at all, at all,' he muttered as he retreated.

Only one of the side rooms was occupied this morning. Whale had had Patrick Benton removed there. Whale did not like Benton, who was a research physicist at Oxford, and came to us every year or so. Now he was lying in the mess of the "loose box" in an attitude of crucifixion. His eyes were shut and his arms outstretched upon the parquet floor on either side of his mattress. Beneath the straggling brown hair of his moustache and beard, a thin fixed smile could be seen. He had lain thus the whole morning and was likely to stay in the same position as long as he was with us. He made no sound and acknowledged nothing that went on around him. I could not understand why Whale and Big Wilson disliked Benton so particularly. They both used every opportunity to talk at him while he lay mute and crucified on his mattress.

'You are a burden to us tax payers,' they said. 'Can you hear? *We* have paid for your education and now you lie there like a useless animal. Catatonic. Bloody crazy.'

Benton made no reply and, if he heard, made no sign of hearing. I left him, closing the door quietly behind Whale.

***

Y BLOCK

I joined the press of nursing attendants in the kitchen for lunch, then came back and sat at the Admission Ward desk waiting for the escort ambulance to arrive. From behind the closed door of the dispensary the raucous voice of Big Wilson rose above the slower, lower tones of Verity. To the dissatisfaction of both, Big Wilson had found himself put on late shift. He had been peremptory towards Verity – 'Och, you do the medicines, I'm drinking me tea' – and Verity had suggested that Wilson himself should do something to justify his pay packet. A stream of abuse followed, which Verity was inclined to ignore, but with swearing and roaring Big Wilson followed him from the dispensary to continue his tirade.

Billie, already buttoned and belted into his Macintosh, came fussing into the ward.

'Goodness me, aren't you ready yet Nurse Lynch? You'll have to look sharp you know my boy, the ambulance will be here any minute and Sister hasn't done her round yet.'

She timed it as the ambulance arrived. I had changed my white coat for the blue jacket and had only to surrender the key. This, for the sake of security, was threaded by a lace onto my belt; the belt, which was vital to the suspension of my trousers, had to be unbuckled. Now as I stood in the middle of the ward trying to hand Raggle my key, those bulky blue serge trousers collapsed in a heap around my ankles.

Sister swivelled round to eye me with amazement.

'What are you doing nurse?'

'Going to the lavatory,' I said too softly to be heard
. . . 'I'm handing over my key matron.'

'Where on earth do you keep it?' Loud laughter, led
by her, was drowned by Raggle and Billie as soon as
they took their cue. Raggle was glad of an excuse for
laughter to make Big Wilson's distant swearing
inaudible. Sister was very pleased. She did not realise
she had made such a funny joke, and then she had
been called "Matron", which added to her pleasure.
Her face was reddened with smiles when Raggle let
her out.

Billie was already settled in the ambulance, leaving
me to bring out the docile Solomon Lobisha. Billie
chatted about his new flat on the way down and tutted
me almost to sleep with accounts of how he could see
Windsor Castle on a clear day, and how the airing
cupboard had been built right next to the larder so that
all the butter ran and the milk went off. At the
hospital Billie obtained his receipt for Mr Lobisha
then bustled out to gather his bay leaves. I wandered
down the wide, dark corridors towards the kitchens
in search of a cup of tea and a chat with any pretty
nurses that might be around. The journey was
fruitless on both counts and I made my way back to
the ambulance through the recreation wards. A figure
sitting in a green chair in one of the large and sunless
wards triggered a chord of memory as I passed by. I
stopped and looked again. He looked at me without
recognition, pipe clenched in a broad, flat pugnacious

face. Steel grey, ball-bearing eyes fixed in the distance between us. Barrel chest and pigeon toes were motionless. 'Hello,' I said and smiled. I walked on trying to remember his name. He must have been through our hands. Suddenly, on an inspiration of its own, my mind's eye dressed the figure in a white coat.

'My God, it's Herring!' I said aloud to the empty corridor. 'It's Herring, Herring,' the tiled walls flung back. So that is where he got to. I felt remorse that I had not really missed him, or known what had become of him; and surprise that nobody in St Francis's had mentioned him. Through frequent trips to this hospital, and the efficient grapevine that linked the mental nurses around London, it must have been known. I told Billie on the ride back. He knew about Herring and knew that the talk of his son's electrical businesses was all delusion. His son was an out-ofwork layabout. That was all he had to say of his late colleague.

Billie did, however, expand at great length on all the recipes he knew that benefited from the addition of bay leaves.

CHAPTER 25: Mrs Baron Again

As Easter approached, I decided that Mrs Baron was certainly deranged. 'You can always tell them by their eyes,' Howard had said. 'The head cases always look funny in the eyes.' Perhaps he was right. The eyes did seem significant, which made me wonder why it was that we never had any blind persons in the Block. Was that chance? Or was it that blind people suffering from mental disorders were "observed" elsewhere? Or could it be that the inability to see was inconsistent with insanity? I did not know. Yet in our patients the eyes nearly always claimed attention. So now did Mrs Baron's.

She had nursed Kitty with care and tenderness, and though she found smiling to be against her nature she was not totally ungenerous towards me. The unexpected ironing board proved that. But the evidence of her eyes was bad; they were eyes that looked at you but never saw; eyes that turned in and did not like what they saw there either.

The oppression of the Unit was not relieved by finding Herring locked away, and the whole spring season had been macabre. Mrs Baron's gloomy digs did not cheer me in off-duty hours, and the cold I picked up at Christmas still loitered in my head. Paula was on holiday. I decided that as my shift of nights ended I would take a week's sick leave. I had not taken any so far and felt that perhaps some was due to me. Although I did not hold strong hopes of success, I intended to look about for other "humanitarian" work. The loneliness and helplessness of the job at St Francis's was at times intolerable.

Fortunately, I did have friends call occasionally to see me in my brown rooms. David, a Cambridge friend, and a girl named Ann came one Friday evening. We ate and chatted, and after another cup of coffee, I got up to go on the last night shift of the week. They had some time to wait for a train; the raw spring evening would have been dismal spent on a platform.

'Don't get up,' I said, as I prepared to leave. 'Stay here and finish your coffee in comfort.'

It was ten to nine. Carefully, I emptied out my pockets onto the mantelpiece. Since my pay packet had been stolen I now always removed temptation before going to work: keys went under the clock with my small change and the one pound note left in my back pocket I wedged under the clock too.

'Put the gas off and the light out when you go, won't you? Goodnight David. Goodnight Ann.' I left for work.

The morning saw me promptly back at my room ready to take my two days' rightful holiday and one week's unofficial leave. There was a note pinned to the door: "You can take a week's notice."

What the hell!! I knocked on Mrs Baron's door. As if she had been waiting for my arrival there was a clack of false teeth falling into position and the door opened.

I had not seen her in sleeping attire before. Voluminous nightdresses enveloped her. A massive frilly mob cap hid all but a few tangles of steel – one hoop to each hair by the look of it. She was getting balder. Teeth, not quite settled in, flashed and jiggled.

'What do you want then? Can't you read?'

'Yes I can Mrs Baron.'

'Well?' I hadn't really paused long enough to make that "well" necessary.

'What's it all about then?'

'What's what all about?'

Now then, I thought, don't let's drag this out by playing silly buggers. You know what I mean.

'The note on my door telling me I can take a week's notice.'

'So you can.'

'Why?'

'Because I don't like your dirty sort round here.' What on earth could she mean? It was over a year since my bladder technique of waking up had had consequences. To make my bladder wake me early I had drunk over a pint of milk as I lay down to sleep. Some of it had spilled on the floor and some on the eiderdown. The marks made were very slight. Anyway, she cannot have noticed them.

'What do you mean?'

'You know what I mean.' Oh for heaven's sake Mrs Baron, get to the point. I looked at my suit of serge and checked my hands. All very reasonable considering.

'Have I peed on the lavatory floor?' Perhaps shock might bring her to the point. In my innocence I could think of nothing worse than to pee on the landlady's floor.

'No. I would not worry about that. Accidents can happen to anyone.' It would not be an accident next time I did it.

'What then?'

'Running a BROTHEL, that's what.' I was too stunned to speak. What was the woman raving about? I would not know where to begin running a brothel. I know what goes on in them. As I told Paula, one reads about that sort of thing. But as for running one! For a start, I don't think I'm the pimp type that prostitutes might work for. I would be on my own in a brothel, and not come by much business that way.

I recovered my composure.

'What do you mean?'

'You. Running a brothel,' she repeated as if to get me used to the idea. She failed. 'I heard you last night.'

'I expect you did.'

'First you was in on your own. Then you was out. Then you come back with a girl and a fella.'

'Well?'

'I seen them both about these parts and they're no good. He might a been all right. But she's a bad 'un. I seen her hanging about on the corners round here.'

'Impossible.'

'What do yer mean, impossible?' Her grammar was disintegrating at every sentence.

'He lives and works in Sheffield. She is at college in Reading. They came up here for the day yesterday.'

'Oh you can lie. But you won't save yourself. I know what I know.'

'I'm not lying my dear good woman. I'm stating facts.' I liked that "dear good woman" touch. Real Victorian delicacy. And, as I expected, it infuriated the old woman.

'Don't you "dear good woman" me. I'm not your "dear good woman", don't bleeding worry.' She was salivating like a dog.

'How long's it been going on that's what I want to know. Right under my bloody nose,' she shrieked in martyred amazement.

'How long has what been going on?'

'You running a bloody brothel! In, out. Come back with a girl and a fella then out again leaving them to it.'

'They were friends. They must have left twenty minutes after me. They had a train to catch.'

'They did.'

'Well?'

'There was a POUND ON THE MANTELPIECE.' Payment. I was shaking with suppressed laughter. She could not believe it. She did. She thought I rented the room out for people to have intercourse; allowed twenty minutes and charged a pound. A terrific idea but I had missed out on the idea.

'If I charged my friends for twenty minutes on that shaky old bed of yours I'd be rich.' 'You probably are.'

Delusion upon delusion.

'That was my last pound. I empty my pockets before I go to work.'

'I don't believe you. How could I? You can't believe a fella who runs a brothel behind your back.'

I could not think of a less innocent front for a brothel than her back. She looked like the mother of all whores. And I think her last argument begged the question slightly. There was obviously no point in arguing. But I could not suffer the inconvenience of changing digs without giving her a run for my money.

'What do you think I was doing for the two hours before I went to work?'

'I don't know what dirtiness you was up to an' I don't care.' She now decided there was no point arguing. 'Look. You bin runnin' a brothel. You was in, out, back with a fella and a girl. You was out again. They went, and when I looked round the door there was a pound on the mantelpiece. Now you can pack your bags and get out and I don't want to see you again.'

She slammed the door.

I heard the bed creak as she got back into it.

Later, I found out that David hadn't even kissed his girl in my room, let alone romped about on the bed. This was not due to any lack of desire on his part but because he had heard Mrs Baron moving about. In fact, she had even stuck her head round the door, muttered 'sorry' and withdrew. Daft faggot, I thought. If she wanted the room why did she not just tell me the rent was to go up by five shillings? That would have finished me.

I slammed into my room and noisily packed my bags.

The front door banged behind me. I heard a voice in the inner recesses: 'Good riddance to bad rubbish. Running a brothel behind my back.'

She would have purchased only a little distilled comfort with all my legitimate earnings, and none with the other. In a fury at the idiocy and inconvenience of it all I consoled myself with the thought that she was mad. 'You've known it all along,' I told myself. 'You can tell by her eyes.'

CHAPTER 26: Back to the Block

A long train journey is soothing to the system. Barely had the ten o'clock train pulled out of Paddington than I felt the worst depressions of Y Block being rhythmically drawn off my mind. Mental images of old men dead, young men dying, lunatic attendants themselves attended, and the glazed eyes of the half-evil, half-angel Mrs Baron gave place to real sights and sounds. Children playing in the oneflower-two-veg gardens of the back-to-backs; sunlight glinting in the peacock puddles in station car parks; then the trim houses of the rich; then fields; then the still, cloud-reflecting waters of a canal; and woods greenly shadowing their bluebell mist. No cacophony of noises now, just the rattle-tum, rattletum of the train excitedly doubling in friendly tempo at the passing of a fellow train.

Before the green sanity of my village was reached I knew that I would make only half-hearted efforts to find another job. After a few square meals and long walks with the dog over the Easter-flowered downs, it did not seem worth changing the job at all for the months remaining. And anyway – I reasoned to hide my own obstinacy and reluctance to back out of a situation that was not congenial – there were advantages in being in London. I had to settle upon a career. There would be countless letters to write, interviews to attend, decisions to make. London was central. I could do more night duty to leave the days free for settling the future.

After a few days at home I packed my bags again and returned to East Dulwich. This time, ignoring the hand-scrawled advertisements in the newsagents' windows, I asked at the grocer's if they knew of digs near the hospital. Within an hour I was settled in at "Trelaw". This terraced house was only a hundred yards up the road from Mrs Baron's brown box, and it had the stucco Victorian dignity of three storeys. Mr and Mrs Couchgrass were an old and kindly couple spending their retirement contemplating a move to spend their remaining retirement in Wales. Eventually they would not go to Wales, perhaps because they knew reality could never match the quiet pictures of wet grey sheep on even wetter greyer mountains that filled each wall of their house.

They were glad to put two first floor rooms at my disposal (with unstinted use of the bathroom), and glad to have me watch television with them if I would, and glad that I liked a cup of tea brought up to me. He or she creaked or thumped up to my airy attic room, or the box room just below at the back where I could sleep during the daytime, with a cup of tea whenever I was heard waking. They made no complaint when my primitive cooking stank out the top floor. They welcomed Paula like a daughter when she returned for her last term. And Mrs Couchgrass insisted on washing a shirt for me before I went off for any interviews.

Y BLOCK

Walking up between the green-budded, lamp-lit plane trees and past the Porter's Lodge I counted my blessings: pleasant lodgings and only a few months to go; marriage at the end of the year and I was still (I hoped) of sound mind; the prospect of buying a cheap old car to rattle down to Brighton with Paula on my days off, there to bathe and eat quantitatively in her aunt's house; the decision made to establish a career in industry. I knew now that humanitarian work as a career needed, for me at any rate, to begin later in life. Some selfish achievement or success had to be won first. For these prizes were not to be had in careers loosely termed "vocational". Bitterness and tightness of mind and heart seemed to assail most of the men I knew who plunged permanently into social work during their youth. Compassion was squeezed out of them. Unless exceptional, they were moulded into the corsets of the system as it was. Privately, they had difficulty in disguising their feeling that they had given of themselves and now wanted to be given something more in return. They could not hope to shut their eyes to the public reaction that they were doing "vocational" work therefore need not be praised or paid above a minimum – because it was their choice. So it was the fleshpots of industry I contemplated. But for the present, more and more night shifts with their bonus days off.

Jauntily, I climbed the steps and rang the bell.

A ginger pink face, topped by scant colourless hair that curled in agony above petal soft ears as it lost its battle against a spreading bald patch, peered through the wired glass. I was let in immediately.

'You must be Anthony?' Wet blue eyes with ginger lashes gazed softly at me. 'Billie's told me about you.' The young man paused as if waiting for me to tell him some more. 'Yes, you *have* got *super* hair.'

I grunted. I did not want to speak because that meant taking a breath; a breath of soap and urine and floor polish.

'I'm Bob,' he said. His lips were loose and thin; they declined ever to set in any specific expression but stuck together like two pink serpents enjoying the contact of their own two bodies. When he said "I'm Bob" he managed to make both b's sound as though they were p's. They softened up his Yorkshire accent. He was thirty to thirty-five I judged.

'Yes. I'm Bob. I'm new here.' He adjusted the drooping ruffles of a navy blue silk handkerchief in the breast pocket of his white coat. 'They put me *straight* on nights. You see, I've done it all before.' He waved his hands towards the wards, then offered me one to shake. He gave mine a little squeeze with his fingertips as I loosened my grip.

'I'm Lynch,' I said, thinking that we had better get that straight. Don't want any of the "Tony" stuff or else it will be "ducky" next and invitations to a "little party at my place". If Billie was an old woman, this one was a practised flirt. I put decisive military masculinity into my step as I went upstairs. Bob Holroyd's eyes followed me until he heard another ring at the door. He hurried to peer through the glass and to open it.

'You must be Tiny Verity,' I heard him saying. 'Billie's told me about you. Gosh, *aren't* you tall? It must be *super* to be tall . . .'

I wished Big Wilson was coming on duty because I dearly wanted to know what Bob would say to him. But Wilson hardly ever did nights and I saw little of him in the remaining months. In any event, even Billie can only have had about ten minutes to gossip with Holroyd, and surely must have discussed only the principal features of a few of the staff. Or what Billie accepted as the principal features.

Holroyd was a very good tea maker, he said, and liked to make lots and lots of tea when he was on duty. He did, bringing each cup into the ward separately for each attendant. Then he stopped to chat. He liked to catch me when I was doing a rare stint alone in Ward III.

'I'll show you my photos,' he said.

'That's nice.' I thought perhaps he was an amateur photographer and might brighten the tedium with an exhibition of his work.

'This is a good one,' he said, offering me a signed portrait of Mr Universe. The muscles bulged and curved like a butcher's diagram of best cuts. I wanted to take a pen and number the parts.

'I wish *I* was a bit bigger,' Holroyd sighed. He was not short or skinny, but his mottled flesh hung on him and his chest could barely provide space for the ornate tie pins that he wore.

'Here's my favourite.' He slid a tattered photograph from behind the cellophane window of his wallet. A much-married male film star beamed at the camera with Hollywood's own mixture of rugged, loving, geniality. Scalp and loins were disguised as Red Indian, but the razor cut side-boards and symmetrically hairy bare chest were manifestly Pale Face.

'Him just take umpteenth squaw, yes?' I said, endeavouring to steer the conversation, or at least the mood, away from men's beautiful bodies.

'Yes.' Holroyd's voice dropped and he put the photographs away. 'What about that bastard downstairs?' he said to draw attention to the vices of a man who was not his hero.

'What bastard is that?'

'You know. The Guardsman. The one who has been interfering with *little girls*. Now *there* was a *real* vice his tone indicated. And Billie had lost no time in pointing it out to Holroyd.

'No. I don't know about him. I've been off for a few days.'

'He's like a lot of others. Not mad just bad and trying to hide it as an illness.'

'Well, it is evil of course. Yet the man's inability to control his badness is a sickness. I wouldn't mind if some sense was made of trying to cure the selfindulgence. There might be no harm in punishing the offence at the same time. At least that might keep both parts of public opinion happy. But, as it is, if an adult gives way to any antisocial urge, however biological and compulsive it may be, one lot want to lock him away forever and the other lot cluck and coo and dole out psychological sympathy . . .'

Bob stood with his pink serpent lips parted. He eyed me with a childish admiration.

'Oo, you are a talker, aren't you. Thought you were the strong silent type before. Still waters run deep, eh?' He gathered the empty teacups and walked away. There was a slight wiggle to his hips. His dove grey, worsted trousers were just too immaculately pressed and his small inward pointing toes rubbed their brogue suede tips together as he walked.

'I meant to say,' he said, turning round in the doorway, 'if anybody should ever ask about me – outside the hospital I mean – a stranger or anyone - don't let them know I'm here will you? There's one or two people *I* don't want to meet.' He winked with an air of familiar conspiracy and then glanced over his shoulder as if it wasn't really a winking matter. Then he sidled off.

He did not refer to his wish for anonymity again. I had the impression that he was not really on the run or avoiding any particular suitor, but rather trying to clothe himself in the extra glamour of a little mystery. He did what work was required of him without a great deal of fuss and was not difficult to get along with provided you forgot that he was not actually a teenage girl. Yet the Guardsman, who was universally abhorred by the Block, was pleasanter and more intelligent company. I talked with him before he was "seconded for treatment". The fact that he wore no special clothes, talked in no identifiable way and had no revealing expressions to declare his weakness to the public, meant that he was regarded as doubly unnatural. He was hated, avoided and feared as a snake in the grass. Whale, Billie and Holroyd made no bones of their disgust. Whale even ventured to tell Billie that the Guardsman was "a dirty creature". Billie, to his discredit did not disagree though he knew, and Whale knew he knew, about Whale.

In the winter before my two years began, Whale had been charged with importuning in a gentlemen's lavatory in Holborn. Howard, on an occasion that must have needed a preparatory pint or so of gentian violet, appeared for the defence. He appealed strongly for Whale who had, he said, been "overworking", and had never offended before despite years of opportunity. The violet presence of Father impressed the court more than Whale's recent purple past. He was discharged. Howard and Whale did not speak of this. In the long nights of summer Little Tom and Lakani told the tale. For already summer was descending hotly on the Unit and, where the press of winter had discouraged gossip, now in idle nights it flourished.

***

Not that it was all talk and no action. Though my spirits were buoyed by the short break, they were undefinably lowered when Holroyd admitted me to the Unit. It seemed that the Emergency Psychiatric

Unit could have done without yet one more unusual character unlocking the doors to this sanctuary of oddities. But something happened to lift my spirits again. On a May night when even the moon seemed to conspire with the central heating to fry us all before breakfast, Ginger was admitted. I played a part in "curing" Ginger. He was hysterical.

Ginger was five feet tall with spindly legs and arms. His body was almost as hairless as a baby forty years younger. Only a deep-vaulted barrel chest and large sexual organs gave us an indication of his age and maturity. Ginger's wife brought the DAO and him into us. The persuasion of her massive bulk held that officer in a fright almost as great as Ginger's. The staff of Y Block received whoever was brought in by the proper authorities. We could not select or decline a patient because we thought he was not mad. Ginger, I was certain, was not mad. Even his hysteria was well controlled and deliberate, and I felt that his escape into histrionics was well justified if it separated him from Mrs Ginger for a while. She was of a complexion similar to her husband's, but sported a considerable amount of additional body hair. Her flesh was firm and healthy, even the dimpled wrists and knees had a gloss of good health. Sixteen stones of good health.

Ginger, already in striped pyjamas, was in the throes of a great tantrum. He fell about and yelled; he squeezed himself into a ball and set himself earnestly to trembling. Though he had shrieked at his wife four hours ago to get him into a hospital, he had not bargained on being so quickly moved to a second. The casualty officer in the local hospital had not been able to keep pace with all the symptoms Ginger proffered. Nor could we. His wife departed crying, 'He's mad. Stark raving. But you'll see, he'll snap out of it when he finds out where he is.'

We told Ginger where he was, and he heard for himself what his wife thought he was. There was no abatement in his symptoms. He swung his head over the side of the bed as though to vomit; he lay prone and trembling; then supine while his limbs threatened to become disarticulated with their separate gesticulations; he clutched his knees and trembled; he lay motionless as if in a coma; then he heaved himself into the air and shook and flailed about in all directions, frothing at the mouth. Not once during this performance did he so much as bruise a finger against the bed or wall.

His examination took place in the brief intervals of stillness. There was no history of ill health, insanity, headaches or any form of trouble. There was no visual or auditory disturbance. But Ginger was a very good actor and extremely fit.

Sedation had little more effect than an aspirin on an ox. It was well into the larger of the small hours before Ginger took any sleep at all. Then as Billie made himself comfortable on two chairs, and while I composed myself on the admission bed, Ginger started up again.

'Water. Water,' he whispered.

'Shut up and go to sleep.'

'Water. I must have water. I'm parched.'

I fetched him water. He gulped it back and we settled ourselves once more.

'Water. Water. My throat's on fire.' Whimpering and tossing increased.

'Hold your noise man. I gave you water.'

'I'm thirsty. Oh, I'm thirsty.'

Billie said, 'You'd better get him a glass of water else he'll be on all night.'

'He'll be on all night anyway.'

I went. Just as I got back to Ginger's bed with Big Wilson's mug full of water, Ginger got into his biggest histrionic routine so far, letting out great yells for water as if his arse were on fire. I let him have it. I picked him up out of bed and shook him. I smacked his face. I poured the water slap and slosh right over him:

'If I get one squeak out of you before morning I'll flay the hide off you. I'll have your guts for garters and your tongue for a watch strap. So belt up.'

He licked his lips and lay quietly. In five minutes he was asleep.

'It's worked,' said Billie.

'Yes.'

Actually, I was ashamed of myself. Maybe I had been a bit rough on him. I need have had no worries. Two mornings later Ginger came down from Ward III to tell me he was going home that day.

'Thank you for what you did Nurse. You brought me to my senses.'

'That's OK Ginger. A couple of nights in this place and you would have come to them anyway.'

'You're right. I wouldn't want to stay in this place if I knew what I was doing. Must drive you mad.'

'It has done already, so I'm happy now.' I did a little mad dance and pulled faces illustrative of the condition. Ginger laughed. His healthy cackle cheered me as no other laugh in this place.

A few nights later he came back to return the Y Block clothes in which he'd left. He took me aside while his wife waited on the steps and told me how he had gone straight home and given her a good talking to. Superiority thus established, he popped her into bed, he said, and gave her something else to think about of a more amorous nature.

'It was great,' Ginger said. 'I don't know what's come over us but we're happier now than we've ever been.' I assured him of my pleasure in their new felicity and let him out. He and his wife waved as they walked arm-in-arm into the night. She beamed like any sweet young thing on her wedding day. A sixteen stone sweet young thing.

Although my part in Ginger's recovery had been accidental and even unnecessary, it provided a small unrepeated moment of encouragement. The real credit I was sure should have gone to an old trainee psychiatrist who was on duty when Ginger was in. I suspected that he had given Ginger a little sage advice on his domestic life.

CHAPTER 27: Last Nights

All the heat and haze that had been lacking last summer was packed into this one. At night the window sashes were raised to their four inch maximum, letting very little fresh air but abundant city noises drift in. The hot water pipes throbbed and all of the daytime's smells hung on the sweaty air of night. The see-saw routine of monotony then violence, lunacy and heavy threatening calm was slowed down and some of the uneven tempo levelled by the routine of night.

I wrote letters and filled in application forms in the quiet hours of duty then slept in my back room furnace each morning. Regularity on night shift made summer quieter than it would have been. Now I saw very little of Big Wilson and only a morning glimpse of Raggle, Semple and Howard. The mannerisms of Billie and Little Tom, Allan, Dobey, Riddle, Lakhani, Holroyd, Whale, O'Leary and Tiny Verity became as familiar as those of fellow prisoners in the keychecking claustrophobia of the night. The patients were usually heavily sedated by the time we arrived, and they had still not recovered full use of their distorted senses by the time we left. It was restful to make sure things remained that way.

Billie sat behind the Ward I desk and talked to whoever would listen. At the beginning and end of each subject he wiped his perspiring chins with a clean, white, unfolded handkerchief. While he talked he swept up little mounds of cigarette ash over the surface of the desk, punctuating his sentences by blowing one clump emphatically over the edge in place of a full stop or question mark.

'When I worked in St Luke's – you know, the private place that's closed now – we used to do a Panto every Christmas. Puff. We'd start working on it about now so as to be really good and ready when the time came. Puff.' A long pause while Billie gathered up more ash and breathed. 'I used to be the Fairy Queen Puff,' he said, without even a double puff to show that he was aware that this might have been too appropriate a casting. Holroyd asked him about what he wore. Verity and I exchanged a shrug and smile. Billie talked and blew, softly sweeping his reminiscences into the little land marks and puffing them away again. He might have gone on all night – he was always at his most anecdotal after a Sunday off – but one of his pet theories backfired, so to speak.

Nurse Billie Dunning held most rigorously to the view that the majority of mental complaints were caused by constipation. He would expand at length on the evils he had seen caused by blocked bowels, and the cures that had been effected by "a good dose of my mixture". Alas, Billie did not confine himself to the narration of his theory. He had just finished a stint on early shift and, having spring-cleaned his flat twice already since May, he possibly thought that he would perform the same service on the bowels of the more mobile patients. He slipped up, however, or his zeal carried him away. He gave his purgative draft to an old man who was unable to get out of his bed and did not call for a pan. The mess in the bed had to be cleaned up and the old man bathed. This happened twice on the late shift after Billie had gone off.

Whoever had faced the consequences of Billie's psychiatric remedy, Billie did not know. But they had certainly been on duty again for the late shift preceding ours. Now the lanky figure of a West Indian patient left his bed at the far end of the ward. He began to walk towards the lavatory door twentyfive paces away, weaving an erratic course in his drugged stupor. Onto the shuffle of his bare feet first a plopping sound was superimposed, then an accelerating splatter. Verity tilted the desk light to show that the poor man was finding it impossible to keep his bowels shut.

'Oo,' said Billie. 'He'll be better in the morning.'

Holroyd cackled and went back to Ward II where he belonged. I jumped up and steered the patient more rapidly to the lavatory. .'I wish you would not Billie.'

'Don't talk so silly,' he replied. 'Probably just what the doctor ordered for that one.'

The incident may have been a coincidence. But if not, as revenge the action was wasted as well as being an unkind use of a passive vehicle. Billie did not move from his chair. He sat pointing the light at each blob and streak which marked the patient's unhappy course while I mopped it up and Verity bathed him.

*** *

One night during the following week a man was admitted who proved that Billie did not believe every single mental complaint was bowel-induced. Mr Brown was a big, bald, fat man of middle age who, until recently had been employed in the Colonial Office somewhere out East. No sooner had we undressed him than he leapt up off the bed and charged from Ward 1 down the corridor through Ward II. Naked, he thudded as fast as he could from door to door wrenching on the handles. He found them locked and turned back to attack the front door. Dobey and Riddle tried separately to intervene and were flung aside like straws. Brown hurled himself against this front door in a final effort to get out.

'I'm not ill. Why have you got me here?'

'They say you are deluded my boy,' said Billie.

'I'm not deluded. I'm all right. Let me out.'

We managed to quieten him and restrain him on his bed.

'I suppose you think you're Napoleon?' asked Billie.

'No, I don't.'

'Who are you then?' He was slow in telling us. Obviously he was used to being disbelieved. He had no intention of being laughed at.

'I'm Jesus Christ. I'm Jesus Christ,' he shouted finally and struggled again to be free

'That can't be,' said Dobey. 'Jesus never had syphilis and I'm sure you have.'

'I'm Jesus Christ,' Brown repeated and eyed us narrowly for disagreement.

316

'I'll stop going to Mass then,' said Billie, 'and come and worship you here.'

'I'm Jesus Christ,' reiterated Brown.

'Just listen to the blasphemy of it,' said Riddle, who did not care one way or another about blasphemy. Dobey shook his gorilla head and grinned. His diagnosis of tertiary syphilis turned out to be correct, though Dobey could not support his hunch by any specific details. It was just that he had seen plenty like Brown "in the old days" before syphilis was so quickly spotted and checked. The final stages with delusions of grandeur took on common identities. Dobey had seen "Jesus Christs" before, he told me softly, and more modest "John the Baptists". "Gladstone" had introduced him to his first refractory ward of patients while numerous very, very, rich men, who said they desired their real identities "Henry Ford" or "Rockefeller" amongst others to be kept secret, had offered him large fortunes to help their escape. Many of those had gone on to show other signs of the tertiary state – the rotting and degeneration that the bacterium dictated. Others had been given malaria to combat the disease. For Brown, perhaps unique among our patients, the prognosis we were told was good; but it would have been better if he had paid immediate attention to the spots and rash which followed his youthful excesses in an eastern brothel. Some child might now be carrying the disease to suffer in his or her prime, and perhaps unable to be within reach of remedy.

***

By July, I was firmly convinced of the necessity for an additional ward in Y Block. It was not that there were too many patients; in fact, some weeks we were down to as few as seven, and on one night four. People had either decided temporarily not to go mad, or were being moved on so quickly by the day shift that new prospects could not go mad quickly enough. But, as if to keep the rest of us in trim, Corrigan gave a vigorous display of his attitudes and eccentricities. For my part, I would have liked an extra ward just for him. Though it happened infrequently, I did not like sharing a night shift with him. His belligerent attitude of divine rightness, his affectation of a bad heart, and his almost total laziness which the heart was supposed to justify, were all understandable defence mechanisms. Long ago I had ceased to notice that he coughed and sniffed liquidly and I knew to look away when I saw him glance at his thumbnails, a sure sign that he was going to settle down to a long session of nose-picking. These things did not disturb the peace of the night. Corrigan's bath did.

As soon as the one o'clock round was done on the first night, Corrigan disappeared for an hour. Banging and splashing woke the patients so that they were wandering around like ghosts looking for the lavatories. We settled them down eventually. The second and the third night Corrigan repeated his noisy ablutions. On the fourth night Holroyd and I were left in the Admission Ward while Corrigan disappeared again. Two patients were in the side rooms. A young man who had had meningitis as a

318

child slept solidly in bed 3. He was now in the same imbecilic state he had been in twenty years before when the disease first struck him. The only reason that he had been brought to us was that his parents needed a holiday and had finally summoned up sufficient hardness to have him taken away – temporarily. In the bed nearest to the padded cells – for good reason – was Albert, a meat porter at Smithfield Market by profession.

The register said: "Albert Crozier. Age 42. Married.

No   children.   Admitted   by   police. Homicidal/Maniac?" Evidently this hint had not been shared enough for us in Raggle's mind, so he stayed behind until we came on duty to make sure that we were warned and that Crozier was well under sedation. Raggle tried to persuade the admitting doctor to let them put Crozier straight into a padded cell. The doctor, for psychiatric reasons which he did not make plain, said emphatically, 'No.'

Crozier was not more than five feet and a couple of inches tall; he was muscular and almost as broad as tall. He went berserk in a warehouse the police said. Armed with a meat axe, he broke up the office there and was starting on its occupants – had already chopped one man's arm open when the police arrived. The fire brigade was called too by someone desperately anxious to have Albert's incendiary violence put out before he killed them. Five policemen brought him in. A sixth did not come because his leg was broken when Albert threw him off the van while he was being pulled into it. The late shift, Raggle said (and he was not inclined to exaggeration) had had to leave the Block *en masse*, climb into the Black Maria and fight to separate the patient from the police. Now he was left to us: Verity was eating in the kitchen, Doddery Allan was upstairs in Ward III, Corrigan was having his bath and Holroyd was buffing his fingernails while he sat in the wooden armchair by the admission bed.

Albert Crozier slept. I pulled the light down low over a newspaper and read. Corrigan splashed and banged in the upstairs bathroom drawing off more hot water in which to boil himself; the pipes rattled and groaned in their reluctance to part with it.

Albert Crozier did not sleep for long. After a while, he gave a sort of cry and sat up in bed, but his eyes were not open. I looked over at him, seeing his great neck and chest glistening with sweat. Holroyd walked to his bed and spoke softly to him.

'There's a good chap. Lie down quietly now and get some sleep.' Albert lay back down and Holroyd, walking back to the desk, gave me a knowing nurse's smile.

Ten minutes later Albert roared and sat up in bed, his eyes still closed but the sweat now pouring from his neck. The veins in his temples stood out prominently in the dim light. He held his arms in front of him like a caricature of a somnambulist and slowly swung his legs out of bed. I stood up and moved to the front of the desk. Crozier slow marched diagonally across the ward towards Holroyd. Tensing myself to keep my voice quiet and not to frighten him I said, 'All right, Mr Crozier? Had a bad dream then? Turn round now and go back to bed.' King Canute had more success. I looked across to Bob Holroyd because it seemed as if that was where Albert was heading. Bob was on his feet now; sweat stood out on his brow too and I judged that it was cold sweat, the same as that which had begun to trickle down the small of my back.

'Just keep still Bob,' I said. 'He may go back to bed. I don't think he's awake yet.'

I did not share my voiced hope. I was sure that both of us would be strangled shortly. If once that bear's grip caught Holroyd, his chest would crunch up like a packet of Smith's potato crisps. Involuntarily, I put a hand to my own throat to test its size and living texture. Holroyd was trembling now, with Albert only a few steps away from him.

'He's going to kill me.' Holroyd's voice was thin and surprised. 'For Christ's sake! *Do* something!' he screeched to me above the advancing head of Crozier. Already I had crept along in the wake of Crozier. I did not know what I was going to do, if I was going to be able to do anything at all, but I wanted to be behind the patient when I did it. I am a coward. Holroyd snatched a green counterpane off a bed and held it in front of him. With a suicidal leap I sprang at the broad back of Crozier and banged my knee into his lumbar vertebrae. Holroyd flung the counterpane round the extended trunk like arms. Putting every ounce of the terror that I felt into the blow, I swung my fist as fast as I could and thudded my knuckles into the hide below his ear. He sank back onto me and then onto the floor where I lay for a second pinned under him. Crozier lay silent with his eyes open. Without waiting to see if this state would last, I let Holroyd shout for help and began dragging Crozier along the floor to the pads. Thank God Verity came quickly with a hypo, already full. While I gripped Albert under the armpits and dragged him on his back over the parquet, Tiny found a flank of flesh and plunged the needle in. He then picked up Crozier's legs and tossed them into the cell after the rest of him. I ran out like a hare. Verity slammed the door to behind me. I felt sick and as slack in the spine as a blade of grass.

We left Albert Crozier for the day shift to remove. Corrigan and Doddery came downstairs with mild enquiries as to the trouble.

'You should have shouted,' said Allan. 'We would have come down and helped you widge him.' Allan would have locked himself in the lavatory or climbed into the bath with Corrigan more likely.

***

The next night at half-past one Corrigan said, 'I'm off to have a bath.'

'What again?'

'Why not?' (Angry)

'Have you got the pox or something?'

'No, I haven't. Is there anything wrong with having a bath?'

'No,' I said, 'not at the right time.'

Y BLOCK

Corrigan was red and bursting with anger now.

'Is it any business of yours when I have a bath?'

'It is when you wake up the patients.' I was even angrier; the man was so bloody selfish. Corrigan was angrier still and thundered off to the bathroom, slamming the door behind him.

Already some of the Admission Ward patients were awake. It was not so much for *their* health I was concerned, they could and would lie in all tomorrow. I was thinking of me. I had not been to bed during the day and would not be going to bed on the morrow. The day was mine for freedom so I was driving down to Brighton and back in the bone-shaker. Sleep was what I needed. Corrigan was going to make that impossible.

He put on a mammoth performance. He played every pipe in the bathroom. Each one clanged and bore his angry message through to the most remote parts of the Block. He adjusted the hot taps so that they banged and juddered as the hot water burst out. He hit the water repeatedly with the back of the longhandled scrubbing brush. He sang. He splashed. He let the water out in a dozen stages, an echoing, painful, choking sob following each re-insertion of the plug. He banged out of the bathroom. All the patients were awake now.

Pink, angry, with a new white coat on and his hair immaculately dried and brushed, as a final defiance he made for his car. This was parked immediately outside to save him the inconvenience of walking ten paces in the morning. He banged the front door. He banged the boot of his car. I crept upstairs to the kitchen there.

Only four inches of window would open, of course, so I edged an oven tin of water through. As he emerged, neck bent, from his car, I tilted the tin. Corrigan screamed and looked up. His face, his hair, his coat, even his trousers were splattered. He was livid. As he opened the door and rushed back in the phone rang.

'Night Sister here. Are you all right Nurse Corrigan?'

'Oh . . . yes. Yes.'

'I heard a scream. I thought you were having trouble perhaps, only it came from outside.'

'Ah no. It was me. I shouted. I had to go out to the car and a cat jumped out from under. It surprised me.'

'Oh, I see. That's all?'

'Yes, that's all. Thank you Sister. Goodnight.'

'Goodnight.'

Corrigan came upstairs and glared at me. 'I'll get you, you bastard.'

'You ought to be locked away,' I said, still too angry to feel that my protest was childish. Corrigan could no longer trust himself to speak. His face was purple from his dripping hair to his wet collar as he went downstairs. He did not emerge from the office for the rest of the night. It was our last night shift together, and I did not hear from him again until he sent me a card while he was on holiday. On his return he came on duty one morning as I went off.

'Ho, ho,' he said, 'it's the Water Chucker. Well, no hard feelings. I like a bit of pluck.' He laughed and thought it all a grand joke. Perhaps the soaking had made his attitudes more plastic. I wondered if I should count this as another cure to add to Ginger's. Then I decided that it was probably the holiday that had cured him.

***

Time was not moving with the speed that I would have wished. But already I had secured a job to go to. It might not have appeared to others as if the fleshpots of industry were opening for me, but I would be earning twice my present salary. That made it fleshpots enough for me. The date for our wedding was fixed. I had even managed to secure two weeks remission from the two year sentence. I had written to the ministry to which I was responsible and asked if I could leave a short while before my sentence ended, pleading the necessity to take up a career appointment within a certain time. To my surprise, I was asked to call upon a man at the government offices in Red Lion Square.

He took me to an empty corridor on the top floor and, leaning with me over the fire escape stairs, asked me about the job I was doing and the one I intended to go to. He listened with interest.

'Look,' he said, 'you've not given us any trouble while you've been a CO. Don't say I agree with your attitude, of course. But then you've been doing something pretty useful for two years, and I must say that it's a job I would not care to do. So you skip off as soon as you've worked your due shifts. That'll save you a couple of weeks. Now, good luck and don't say a word to anyone about this. I'll cover your tracks.'

My silence as I shook his hand was not ingratitude, but astonishment. I had never presumed that the Civil Service had any sort of soul, nor that any individual in it would be prepared to step out of line. I wished that I could have left Y Block then, full of the cheer and optimism that this encounter gave me. But it could not be so. There was my notice to work, end even taking the holiday time due to me when I left there were more shifts yet to be counted away.

***

Shifts passed in the hot monotony of autumn nights; except for the penultimate duty – there was no monotony about that. It was as though it had been saved to act as a memorable reminder that there was no happiness in this Unit. Nor any happiness in the worlds into which hurt minds withdraw.

At nine o'clock we admitted a homeless man. Either meths had been the attempted solace of his homeless existence or its cause. At ten o'clock he died. His was not a pretty death.

Shortly afterwards Piggy Spot the striptease dustman was re-admitted, slightly greyer and with his flesh now all white, unredeemed by the sunburnt hands of before. He was slower and more profoundly depressed than I remembered him.

Towards morning, a young man named Jack, distraught, dirty and deluded was brought in by ambulance and with Peter the popular DAO. It was the patient's first admission, and unlikely to be his last.

Jack was a New Zealander, and on his first visit to this country. Like other lost and lonely men he chose a large hotel near one of the big railway terminals to try and end his tortured life.

Jack cut his throat. It was packed over with towels.

It was a big throat and took a deal of cutting, but Jack used a very sharp razor named for this operation. A long, clean crescent of a cut had sliced down from below the lobe of his left ear, curving above the Adam's apple and upwards again towards his right ear. His head hung back now; the towels fell away and the two lips of his severed neck hung open. Fat, nerve and muscle were cut clean through; small arteries and the greater veins could be identified. Standing out in the bloody melon-sliced cavity, the corrugations of his windpipe were slashed. Air bubbled through a narrow cut. Weakened by the first jets of blood that crimsoned the room he was in, Jack had clearly taken his trachea to be the remaining vital connection with life. It was criss-crossed with scratches beside the final diagonal cut which had opened it. Miraculously, his carotid arteries had not been punctured so that now he still lived. Face and hands and clothes were solid with clotting blood. He could no longer hold his head upright, yet he talked incessantly; rambling, meaningless chatter and moans without pause. He struggled to be free while we held him on the bed amid drips rigged up beside

327

him. I took a grip on his hair to prevent his shaking body tearing his throat open even wider. For six hours I held Jack thus.

St Francis's Emergency Psychiatric Unit was his second port of call. He had been to the casualty ward and then brought across to us. Our duty doctor would not sew him up. But manifestly, he must be sewn together again. An ambulance was called for us to take Jack to the teaching hospital up the road. He was now a psychiatric patient, so a mental nurse had to go with him – me. Holding his head, I sat with him in a side room after we were delivered there. Numerous doctors came and peered with torches into the interior anatomy of his neck. I asked a nurse, who brought me tea and took a turn holding Jack's head onto his neck, why he could not be tended to. She said she thought it was because permission was needed to give an anaesthetic and there were no relatives handy.

'But suppose it was a matter of life and death,' I asked.

'Ah. Well, that would be different. But I expect that they want a specialist to look at him. That can wait for morning.'

Since Jack did not want to be alive anyway, he was not grumbling about the lack of attention he received. At seven I was relieved by Little Tom sent up from Y Block on his motor cycle. Jack was stitched up at midday and redelivered to us in the evening with his neck stiffed by bandages.

Poor Jack. His desperate assault on the body which gave continued life to his agonised brain typified the destructive torments he suffered. How many more Jacks would there be, I asked myself, before steps had been made to understand their pains and to give a living cure?

CHAPTER 28: My Two Years are Over

The last night passed uneventfully in Y Block.

Billie and Allan were in the linen room when I went to swap my white coat for the blue serge jacket. The noises of morning shift began down below.

'Don't just rush off now, will you?' Billie implored me. 'Father will want to see you, and I *think* they might have got something for you. Don't say I said so though.' He closed one eye and laying a smooth, fat hand on my arm whispered, 'Mum's the word.'

'Yes, Mum,' I said, grinning at him.

'Oo. Saucy!'

'You'll stay behind for a minute?' Allan tilted his head back to look at me. 'We've got a little something for you.'

'Oo Doddery. You *shouldn't* have said. Now the cat's out of the bag.' Billie preoccupied himself with his buttons and hair-do for a moment. 'Now he *knows* he's getting an alarm clock.' Allan could not remember telling me I was to be given a clock, but before he could gather together sufficient words for a sentence of protest, Billie firmly changed the subject. 'You're getting married tomorrow, aren't you?' 'Yes, I am,' I agreed happily.

'Watchoo going to wear then?'

'Jock-strap and bow tie.'

'No, you cheeky boy; you know what I mean. Is it formal coats and tails with all the trimmings?'

To his disappointment I had to tell him that it was not. We walked downstairs. I sat on the corner of the admission desk while Billie trotted off to round up any staff he could find. Patients lay or sat in their beds taking no notice of anything. The sounds of hypermanic broom sweeping came from Ward II. Verity loped along the corridor, his twiggy ankles pinched by cycle clips.

'I'm off,' he said, shaking my hand. 'Got to go. See you around then?' He turned and waved. He hated goodbyes.

Riddle and Dobey had been separated from their breakfast in the kitchen. They stood licking their lips by the screens just inside the ward. Lucy waited at the bottom of the stairs with her bucket and brush. She waved and smiled and called, 'Cheerio Mr Lynch!'

Opposite her at a cupboard in the corridor wall, Nurse Matthews was knocking on its door and grinning. He knocked again, cocking his head as if to catch a reply from within. Matthews was a new recruit; I had seen him once or twice but not worked a shift with him. Report had it that he was potty – 'Pixilated,' Little Tom said. 'He's very mild and does all the medicine rounds, but he's definitely pixilated. I should imagine he's hearing voices.' I looked sadly along at Nurse Matthews and waved at Lucy. She tapped her forehead and pointed at the grinning figure by the cupboard before waving again and bucketing her way upstairs.

Jack in bed 1 moaned as he tried to turn over.

Semple rushed in holding a brown packet in his hand.

'It's a clock. That'll get you up in the bleedin' mornin'.'

It was a very handsome alarm clock; a Jumbo Repeater the packet said. I thanked them all and shook their hands. Father stopped checking locks for a moment and offered to let me out.

'You'll be glad to be getting away from here Mr Lynch?' he said, rattling his key in the front door. 'It's no career for a young man.' Howard had never caught on to the fact that I had come to Y Block for a fixed two year period.

A fat man climbed out of bed and walked to the ward door.

He was naked. 'I'm Piggy Spot,' he said, 'Dustman.'

I was let out. Howard and Semple, Dobey and Riddle turned to carry on with the morning's work. Allan and Billie waited to let me walk out of sight before they left together.

I crossed the yard and passed the Porter's Lodge. To my right, on the opposite side of the geriatric wards, the sun was rising like a fried egg over the grey frying pan roof of X Block – yet another isolated world that others tried to forget.

I walked down between the plane trees. O Lord you have not made the two years pass quickly. It has been like a film, now rushing, now dragging; angled shots through a distorting lens; the sound track not matched with vision. Yet at least I have observed this weird kaleidoscope in dun colours and come away with sight. I have heard the discord of hundreds of split concertinas and not been rendered stone deaf. I have smelt this stew of broken people for two years and can still smell.

The green trees and love are mine. Work and the rewards of work; friends and the glad acquaintance of strangers will not be denied me.

What can I do for those who do not share our world?

THE END

Acknowledgements

The clever, and tireless Sylvia Funston, who made typographical sense of the first dusty *Y Block* manuscript and has given sound advice on some changes in language of the fifties that are not acceptable today. Great thanks to Sylvia.

Phil Sadler has a comprehensive knowledge base, from farms and their animals, to computers and has a number of other skills which have made him a very respected and admired friend. Thank you, Phil.

Paula, my lovely and very long-standing wife and friend should know how much she is a part of my creative life as well as the mundane which she lights up with her wit. Thank you many, many times. For each of these three my acknowledgement is slight but my thanks are immeasurable.

About the Author

Anthony Lynch.

Early education: 1953-1957, Cambridge; History and Philosophy.

Early career: *Y Block* was written a short while after he had spent two years (1957-1959) -as directed by the Tribunal for Conscientious Objectors, employed as a Nursing Assistant in the Emergency Psychiatric Unit of St Francis Hospital, East Dulwich. After a successful career in marketing structural components for the building industry; as the first marketing manager for Aram Designs Ltd; ISS Ltd; and finally as a Director of Christian Sell Designs Ltd., Anthony studied A level science subjects and entered The Royal Free Hospital Medical School. Here after hospital jobs he became a GP and practised in Gloucestershire until retirement. Dr Lynch has written on medical matters and eighteenth century art history.

Y Block is his first book, written in 1964/5 but lost in house moves until the spring of 2022. It is offered now with love to those who ever suffer from a mental illness and to those dedicated people who care for them.

(Dr) Anthony S. Lynch.

Newnham-on-Severn, Gloucester.

Printed in Great Britain
by Amazon

AMAZING TALES

A COLLECTION OF CREATIVE WRITING

EDITED BY
DONNA SAMWORTH

First published in Great Britain in 2021 by:

 Young**Writers**

Young Writers
Remus House
Coltsfoot Drive
Peterborough
PE2 9BF
Telephone: 01733 890066
Website: www.youngwriters.co.uk

Printed and bound in the UK by BookPrintingUK
Website: www.bookprintinguk.com
YB0453B

FOREWORD

Here at Young Writers our aim is to inspire creativity in children and to inspire a love of the written word. By helping them to become more confident and expand their creative skills we hope these aspiring writers will be encouraged to keep writing as they grow. And what better way to give them that encouragement than letting them see their own words in print!

Within this anthology you will find a mixture of amazing stories of all genres. Dive in to find creations bursting with imagination, expression and most importantly fun.

We're so impressed with the level of skill and imagination shown by all the writers – the result is an absorbing look into the eager minds of our future authors. We'd like to congratulate all the young writers in this publication and hope everyone enjoys reading these incredible stories as much as we have.

CONTENTS

Prathika J	125	Misha Goswami (10)	163
Kearna Blake	126	Ben Davidson (9)	164
Holly Blaney (7)	127	Hannah McNee (9)	165
Jake Evans (8)	128	Caleb Craig (10)	166
Lacey Shepherd (11)	129	Cye Buchan (9)	167
Marci Randle (8)	130	Femme Mangala (10)	168
Poppy Dormer (10)	131		
Amelia-Rose Mansie (7)	132		
Molly Mackay	133		

Winsford High Street CP School, Winsford

George Standlick (9)	134	Lilia Wingate (10)	169
Jessica Fernandes (9)	135	Sophia Buckley (10)	170
Harry Deeks (7)	136	Toby Walker (10)	173
James Doren	137	Isaac Johnson (10)	174
Maisie Sue (9)	138	Zara Briggs (10)	177
Megan Murphy (13)	139	Lily Griffin (10)	178
Krish Wagjiani (10)	140	Kate Robinson (11)	181
Zach Varney	141	Molly Lloyd (10)	182
Jack Chalmers (12)	142	Grace Campbell (10)	185
Angel Glover	143	Kayden Johnston (10)	186
Ayesha Imtinan	144	Samuel Latham (10)	189
Amelie Pilfold (12)	145	Emma Wicksted (10)	190
Andreea Robu (9)	146	Theo Dunbar (10)	193
Summer Taylor (11)	147	Joseph Mather (10)	194
Archie Scott (12)	148	Zain Barnett (10)	197
Liam O'Brien	149	Charlie Eaton (10)	198
Isaac Miskelly	150	Luke Okome (9)	201
Raphael Cohen	151	Alex Dawson (10)	202
Lucca Whybrow	152	Jayden Kilburn (11)	205
Chelsea Williams (13)	153	Laila Neunie (10)	206
Taiden Osarumen Eboikpomwen (8)	154	Louie Greavey (10)	208
Huseyin Ozaydin (8)	155	Lucy Holt (10)	210
Joe Paul Thomas (8)	156	Leah Taylor (10)	212
Lewis James Cole	157	Joseph Day (10)	214
		Jasmine Lloyd (10)	216
		Charlie Mitchell (10)	218

Audley Junior School, Blackburn

		Hollie Harradine (10)	220
Aiman Ghisa (10)	158	Miley Presland (11)	222
Zahrah Waqas (10)	160	Emma Toomey (10)	224
		Marlie Wilcock (10)	226

Bankton Primary School, Dedridge

		Macie Taylor (11)	228
		Evie Newton (10)	230
Lauren Robertson (9)	162	Summer Copnall (10)	232
		Bailey Saunders (10)	234

THE STORIES

The Guy Robot

There was a good boy who was awfully good at everything. He was born in a family who were not good at anything, so his family decided to make a robot son. The robot son was very good at everything. But the one thing is, that if the robot got splashed with water, he stopped working.

One day, at his school, there was a swimming contest for his class. The next day, Mr Williams, the teacher, said, "Who is available to come?"

Everybody put their hands up, except Robot. The teacher asked why and Robot said, "Ur, ur, ur... ummm... Oh, I have a dentist appointment and it's all day long!"

The teacher said, "Okay, maybe next week." Robot had nothing more to say.

He told his parents about it and they just said, "Oh, don't worry, you will do an amazing job," in a worried voice.

The next week, he decided to forget his swimming kit on purpose. He thought he had got away with it but had to wear the spare one his teacher gave him. He stepped into the water and he fell. He started shaking - *buzz, buzz, buzz*. The school headteacher phoned the president and the family were banished out of America.

Angel Rufasha (9)

An Easter Moral

Once there was an excited boy called Roger. Roger was excited because... of Easter, his favourite time of year. He loved it for one reason: chocolate eggs. Roger loved chocolate so much that if he could, he would eat it for breakfast, lunch and tea.

One day, he was walking through one of the many fields at his hometown, Crossbunshire, when suddenly he saw bunnies, the same ones he saw nearly every day but this time there were thousands of them! One bunny hopped over to him and somehow said, "You are the scruffiest boy I've ever seen."

"Excuse me, did you just speak?" said Roger amazed.

"Yes, I did and stop gawking at me, who do think you are?"

"Who are you?" asked Roger.

"I'm the Easter bunny, of course. A few other bunnies think I'm rude, personally, I don't know what they're talking about!"

"The Easter bunny, wow!" exclaimed Roger.

"Yes, I'm the Easter bunny, I just said that," said the Easter bunny, sounding annoyed.

The bunny hopped closer to him and said, "Walk and chat with me now!"

"Okay, by the way you look very nice," said Roger.

"Thank you, no one has said that to me before, I think it's because they're jealous of me being the Easter bunny. It's not a big deal you know! Did you know I have magical powers and can grant one wish and because you've been nice to me, I am going to grant you any wish you like."

"Thank you, that's amazing! I wish to eat chocolate for breakfast, lunch and tea every day," said a very excited chocolate-loving Roger.

"Are you sure that's your wish?" said the Easter bunny.

"Yes, it most certainly is."

"Okay then, your wish is granted," said the bunny. "Bye for now Roger."

"Wait a second, how did you know my name? I never told you!" questioned a baffled Roger.

"I know everything," said the Easter bunny.

Roger got home and asked, "What's for tea?"

His mum said, "Chocolate, Roger." Roger was amazed.

Roger on the very next morning again asked, "What's for breakfast, Mum?"

His mum said, "Chocolate, Roger."

"Wow!" said Roger. "The wish must have come true!"

He then rushed to look for the bunny in the field to thank him but couldn't find him. Roger went home and then went to bed and woke up the next morning and ran off again to find the bunny, but again he was nowhere to be seen.

Days passed, Roger was still eating chocolate and looking for the bunny but still no joy.

A month passed and Roger was sick of chocolate! Roger went to the field again and started to cry as he was so upset that his life was in chocolate pieces.

Then a voice was heard, "Roger, wake up, it's Easter."

Roger then suddenly realised it was all a terrible dream. His mum then shouted as she left his room, "You can have chocolate all day if you want."

Roger thought, *I need to be careful what I wish for.*

Thomas Mckenzie Parr (10)

The Dot That Thought He Was A King

Once upon a time, there were two brothers, their names were M and S. Every morning, after breakfast, they went to school. M and S loved going to school to learn many things and be with their friends. Sometimes after school, they even went to the park. One day, however, a small dot came from far away... he believed himself a king but a bad king who wanted to rule over everything and everyone. His name was COVID-19.

In a few days, he decided to close schools, parks and shops as those that were left had been badly affected. Everybody decided to stay at home. M and S also stayed at home and decided to create protective shields that gave superpowers. They had the power of masks, gloves and the power of endurance!

Now the children with these powers felt safe and COVID began to get smaller and smaller until puff, he disappeared. M and S organised a big party and invited their friends and they could give each other hugs and kisses again.

Emanuele Scavelli (9)

Secret

Arriving at this unfamiliar primary school, everything suddenly sank in. No one knew me in England. I could be a whole new me. No one at my new school would know my secret...

Getting out of the hot, stuffy car, I braced myself, ready for meeting my new headteacher, Mr Bockwurst. I thought this a funny name but when I was in the back of the car, giggling about Mr Bockwurst's name, Mum shot me a fierce look. We headed along the bright and lively corridors; kids' paintings were plastered all over the walls. Eventually, we got to Mr Bockwurst's office.

Standing in front of the Headmaster's door, Mum rapped the door politely and almost immediately the door opened, revealing the most smartly dressed man I'd ever seen.

"Hello, hello and hello again!" He took Mum's hand and kissed it. "It is a pleasure to meet you. And who's this?" He looked at me.

Mum gave me a nudge. "Oh, erm... I'm Alex. Just Alex."

"My goodness, I think I recognize you from somewhere!" Mr Bockwurst paused a second. "Weren't you the girl that was on the news as a child phenomenon at the age of 7? I think the girl had brown, straight hair and a sparkle in her eyes, just like you do. And she was also wearing a silver locket!" Mr Bockwurst smiled as I blushed and fiddled with my locket. "It's okay, your secret's safe with me. Now, you better get to class. Third floor, first class to your left. I'll escort your mother out. Goodbye!"

Standing in front of my new classroom door, I knocked on it loudly, so the teacher would hear. I heard a voice yell, "Come in!" Walking into my classroom, I looked at my new teacher and said, "Good morning, Miss."

Miss replied, "Good morning. You will be sitting next to Emelia, at the front. Now everyone, get out your English books for a test."

There were several groans by this point; everyone hated the boring tests every week. I sat down beside Emelia and got out my new English book. Suddenly, I heard whispers behind me. I craned my neck, but it was nothing.

It was nearly break by the time the test was finished. "To conclude our spelling test," Miss spoke, "I have one last question. Does anybody know the longest word?" Nobody answered.

I tentatively put up my hand. "Alex? Do you want to have a go?" Miss queried.

"Pneumonoultramicroscopicsilicovolcanoconiosis."
I didn't know what to do, deadly silence hung in
the air.
Then a kid at the front shouted, "I know who you
are! You were that kid on the telly!" There were a
few mutters.
Miss nodded. "I thought I recognised you. Why
didn't you tell us before?" She was really surprised.
"Erm... I don't know?" I was hesitant. All around
me, people started clapping. "Okay then... thanks!"
Miss smiled broadly and presented me to the
world. "May I present, Alex, the child
phenomenon!"

Blades (12)

Coronavirus

Something happened today. There was a horrible bug called Coronavirus. This bug is nasty. We washed our hands and sang happy birthday twice, hoping for the bug to go away.

Everything started closing! We had a lockdown where Mummy and Daddy could not go to work and we could not go to school and nursery to learn and play with our friends. We had to stay at home and stay safe.

All the doctors and nurses at the hospitals, policemen, firemen, ambulances and keyworkers were working hard and helping on the front line. We clapped every Thursday to say thank you. We also painted coloured rainbows and thank you notes and put them in our windows.

Homeschooling started and every Friday we have Zoom meetings with my class. It is not the same.

I wish this bug would go away and for everything to go back to normal so I can see my grandma and grandad and go back to school.

I will never forget the day the world changed in 2020.

Nikiesha Sagar (7)

Temptation

One day, a boy called Harry was in his garden playing football when suddenly he kicked the ball too hard and it went over the fence and into his creepy neighbour's back yard. Harry knew that his neighbour was a very weird old man and so he knew that he might not get his ball back. However, he went to get it anyway.

When he knocked on the door, there was no answer. He knocked again... no answer. Five long minutes later, a tall, dishevelled-looking man came to the door and said, "What do you want, boy?"

"I've just come to get my ball back, please. It landed in your backyard."

"You may have your ball back," replied the man, hesitantly. "But only if you can do one thing for me."

"Okay," replied Harry. "What would you like me to do?"

"Oh boy, there's one thing I've longed for five years now and I just can't get it out of my head. I would dearly love a sweet, crunchy, sticky, colourful lollipop."

"Okay," said Harry, surprised. "That's easy!"

Off Harry went to get this strange man his sweet, crunchy lollipop.

Harry ran straight to the local newsagents that he knew had a good selection of sweets. "Hello, Charles!" he said to the small, friendly man behind the counter. "I would like a sweet, crunchy, sticky, colourful lollipop."

"Sorry, Harry, but I only have sweet, sticky lollipops left. Will that do?"

"Yes, I'm sure that will be just fine. Thank you, Charles."

"You're welcome, Harry. Bye."

When Harry gave the lollipop to the tall, scruffy, old man he said, "This will not do! I asked for a sweet, crunchy, sticky, colourful lollipop, you silly boy!"

Harry groaned because he knew that the other sweet shop was all the way on the other side of town. He was also wet. He was tired and he was thirsty. It was terrible for Harry.

When Harry arrived at the sweet shop he walked in and *bam!* A sweet, crunchy, sticky, colourful lollipop was right there on one of the shelves.

Harry was so happy to see it, all he had to do now was buy it. So he went up to the shopkeeper and said, "May I have a sweet, crunchy, sticky, colourful lollipop, please?"

"Yes, that will be £2 please."
Harry looked at his wallet and... he only had £1. He was devastated! He had spent most of his money already! Harry could not believe his bad luck. He had been trying for so long just to get his football back and his mum would be worried. He couldn't even call her.

After a long, cold, wet miserable twenty minutes, he had the £2 and was ready to buy the lollipop. He went to the shopkeeper and bought the lollipop.

As he was walking back, his stomach rumbled, and he completely forgot about the man and the football and in ten minutes, there was no sweet, crunchy, sticky, colourful lollipop left!

Tommy Bustard

The Spider Pig

Once there was a farmer, a farmer called Fred. Fred also had a pig called Borris. Borris was Fred's favourite pig. The farmer would spoil Borris by giving him lots of treats and tummy rubs, but one day, Borris heard Fred calling to his wife, "I think Borris is getting too fat!" So Borris walked back to the stable and Borris was slowly shedding a tear. Suddenly a spider appeared and the spider whispered to him, "Do you want payback?"
"A little," said Borris.
The spider jumped down and bit Borris! Borris turned red and right under his feet he grew little spider hairs. Then Borris said, "You can call me Spider-Pig!"
He trotted to his friend's house and bust down the door then tied him up with his webs.
His friend's wife walked into the room and Spider-Pig trapped her too! Then she screamed and the Spider-Pig felt sorry for them and let them go.

Freddie Johnson (8)

The Girl Who Once Hated Music

Camilla Jordan Laker was a dark, gloomy eleven-year-old girl who attended Ashdown Girls' Secondary. She sat at the back of the class on her own because nobody found it fun being in her company. It was because Camilla absolutely hated music. From Adele to Mozart, Camilla would linger in the back of her classroom and listen happily to TED-E talks about how music was a terrible thing during the music lessons.

One bright day, Cleo noticed a girl sat in the corner of the playground, engulfed in a cloud of loneliness. "Just be a moment," Cleo told her friends. "I... forgot my sunglasses." Cleo left her friends walking towards Year 11's concert and strolled confidently to the anxious girl. "Hi!" she exclaimed with a friendly smile.

The girl gave her a furious glare and looked down. "Would you like to listen to the concert?" she questioned, suddenly feeling anxious.

The girl stood up fiercely, her dark locks scrunched up into a tight ponytail. "My name is Camilla Laker and I despise music!" she hissed, running to another corner.

Cleo thought for a moment. How could anybody hate music? That day she vowed to herself that she would make Camilla love music again.

Early the next morning, Cleo walked into the gymnasium, a flask of steaming coffee and a laptop in her leather satchel.

Time to get to work! she thought to herself, as she plugged in her laptop to the speakers and sipped from her flask. She plonked herself down on a wooden stool and selected a video.

Fizzing with excitement, Cleo stuck her head out of the door and called to Karen, a girl who always came early along with Camilla and Jazzy. "Can you call Camilla to the gymnasium, please? Tell her it's a party, oh and Jazzy too!" grinned Cleo, handing her slips of paper. Karen scanned one as she sped to her classroom to inform Jazzy and Camilla.

'Karen, you are invited to an event in the gymnasium for half an hour of fun dancing! There will be lemonade and digestives for refreshments and a wide selection of songs.

See you there!

Cleo Thomas'.

"Jazzy, Camilla!" squealed Karen, bursting through the door waving the slips of paper which Jazzy and Camilla speedily snatched. "Cleo is having a dance party in the gym! Come!"

Five minutes later, Jazzy and Karen charged through the gymnasium doors, Camilla trailing in confusion behind them.

"If you insist..." smiled Cleo, playing the song.

Anne Marie's voice rang across the room, sending Jazzy and Karen in a fit of joyful dancing and Camilla in a state of shock. Cleo took her hand and gazed into her jade eyes.

"Come on!" she urged. "I believe you can do it."

Camilla gave her a delicate smile and danced with Cleo in delight.

They became best friends and stuck by each other closely. Have you ever formed a close friendship by fixing a problem?

Emaan Basharat (11)

The Incredible Diary Of...

Dear Diary,

Today was a good day because me and my friends went to Dinosaur World. It was incredible but hot. In this world there was a building with a fence surrounding it. There were people inside breeding dinosaurs and they had guns and cannons. It was amazing. We stayed there and watched the dinosaurs for an hour and then we sneaked outside of the building.

Bang! Bang! Bang! For a minute, we thought we heard footsteps but then we saw something green. Saliva was dripping on us. We looked up to the eyes of flame and teeth as sharp as chainsaws. It was a T-rex! We screamed and ran back to the building as fast as we could.

We could see a guy on the wall around the building. They let us in. We stood there holding a lamp post because we were scared. A guy asked if we wanted to go home in a helicopter so we hopped in and sped off.

Now I'm here writing my diary.

Bertie.

Bertie Duckworth (8)

The Dinosaur And The Unicorn

66-68 million years ago, there was a dinosaur called Diny. He was a T-rex and lime-green and had teeth as white as snow, he always brushed them. he was seven years old and fifteen metres tall.

One day, he went to the waterhole and there was no water. He gasped. "The water has gone, how will I brush my teeth and drink! I must go find it." In the sky there was a big cloud and a golden unicorn with rainbow hair that was six years old. It had curly hair and was five metres tall. Rainbow lived there and she was on a stroll when she saw an empty waterhole and saw Diny. She cantered over and replied worriedly, "Are you okay?"

Diny replied, "Fine, just need to find the water from the waterhole."

He looked around to see but there was no water. "Let me go with you," Rainbow replied cheerfully. "Okay," Diny replied hopefully and off they went. They walked and walked until they came to a volcano, hot lava rushing out of its side like a swimming pool bursting. they knew it was dangerous and tried to find another way over because they couldn't go around it or under it. Lava spilt quickly down, it was coming fast.

"Oh no!" Rainbow screamed.

"What will we do?" Diny said.

He had an answer. "Pterodactyls!" answered Diny.

"Why them?" she asked him.

"I have a friend that will fly me over because I see you have wings."

The unicorn didn't say a word and started flying.

"Call him then," she said.

Diny whistled and Pterry, the pterodactyl came. He got on his back and they went past the volcano. While they went over, ash burst up and they all coughed but were fine. They landed in the grassland. Pterry asked them both, "Can I join the quest?"

They both answered, "Yes, it would be a pleasure."

Then something ran across the sand. It was small and yellow. "Raptors!" Diny whispered.

"Shhh!"

Lots more ran across the grass and then they saw something - the water. They hid among the grass, a raptor almost spotted them! Then Pterry had an idea. "Camouflage!" he whispered. "We could use Rainbow's magic to camouflage."

Rainbow waved her horn and they couldn't see each other. They sneaked out past the raptors then something bad happened... A utahraptor

came up and screeched loudly and then saw the three of them. They screamed, "Argh!"

The utahraptor kicked the sand like a bull, getting ready to charge!

"So he wants a fight, well he's getting one!" said Diny sternly.

The utahraptor charged and Rainbow stopped it for a few seconds to punch it and kick it. Then they moved out of the way and the utahraptor fainted. They then cheered and let the water out.

Abigail Kucera

The Day The Chairs Quit

One day, a little girl called Chloe was getting ready to go to her new school. In her popular school, everyone swung on their chair which really irritated the teacher and the chair so one day she got so annoyed she said, "Every time anyone swings on their chair they will get a detention!" Everyone stopped but Chloe's chair didn't stop, it wasn't at all Chloe, it was her chair rocking about.

One day, she came to school and saw... all the chairs all wrapped up with tape saying: 'Police discovery - do not cross this area!'. It also had a sign which Chloe shouted out loud, "We have quit because you have used us carelessly so for the rest of the day you will have to sit on the floor until you stop swinging on us. Thank you, Head Chair!" Everyone was sad and sorry for what they did to the chair so they never ever swung on a chair their entire life.

Youkaeshana Thivakaran (10) & Kuelini

The Beginning

In a field of knee-high grass, on a precarious hillside stood Maggie, the clear blue sky and her family's run-down cottage as a backdrop. To the left the village of Grampound, wonky and bent as usual, but to the right the sparkling ocean and sandy beach she'd spent so many days playing on. Cities of trees surrounded the farm and house like a wall of life. There she was, her head held high and her eyes closed. A big grin spread broadly across her face, as she took in her surroundings. Memories swirled around Maggie's head, of playing on the beach with Olive. Being with her dad before he left, then she settled on one memory... Life was boring for Maggie doing the same routine every day, sow seeds, harvest crops, sow seeds, harvest crops, sow seeds, harvest crops, etc. She'd been lonely the last few months. Before she'd had tons of friends, but all of them grew up too fast and left Maggie alone. She became miserable and anti-social, isolating herself by constantly farming, then locking herself in her room to weep in despair. Hot, fat tears would stream down her rosy cheeks and her face would crumple into a saddened mess.

At least that's what happened before war was declared. Four years later, lots of evacuee children her age arrived, like Olive, her new best friend! Maggie remembered this as she stood at the top of her field happily focusing on the time spent with her friend. Now Maggie was thirteen and she felt joy every time she woke in the morning. If she'd had her way the war would never have begun because now her dad was gone. War had changed her life for better and for worse...

Farming was one of the only ways to keep the village going, so Maggie had to pull her weight by spending all her spare time planting fruit and vegetables. In a gentle motion she began to stroll through the field, calmly sowing carrot seeds onto the upturned soil, laughing when the grass tickled her bare feet. She must have spent hours sowing seeds, at least that's what it felt like to Maggie, doing the same job repetitively. Lastly, peacefully, Maggie retreated to the house, beaming like a Cheshire cat.

Rumour had it that a few months after Maggie's father was recruited, he deserted the army and never returned to his wife or daughter! At least that's what everyone said when they thought Maggie and her mother Nancy weren't listening.

The problem was, the rumour was true and it made the Heathcotes feel at rock bottom! However, as she was raised by a caring family, Maggie was one of those 'stubbornly loving' people, with an affectionate heart but was very determined to get her way, just like her dad. I guess his heart just wasn't big enough to go back to his family. One thing is for certain though, Maggie Heathcote was a worker, a daughter and a fond friend.

Olivia Bowley (11)

Through A Door To...

I went to school and at school I had English. After English was break time. Just then, the bells screamed like an angry rhino.

Just when we went to play, I pulled my friends Zaara, Jenny and Aneet and told them about my really weird dream. After play, I went to my purple locker and I went into my locker. There was a strange tunnel! "Argh!" I went through the tunnel to the dream I had yesterday.

Funny enough, Zaara, Jenny and Aneet were there. Although I didn't know why they had their mouths open wide!

I turned around myself and standing there in front of me was... a gigantic castle made of candy. The windows were made of jelly as well as candy canes. The door was made of toffee. The gates were made of truffles. It was a dream so I slapped myself but nothing happened!

The girls screamed and so did I, but not much! All four of us rushed inside...

Chloe Wakley (10)

The Mum With The Toxic Bum

My mum loves pickled onions. I hate them. They look horrible - like eyeballs floating in a jar, they smell even worse and I can only imagine the taste... Ugh!

This is a story about my mum and her love of pickled onions and how together they saved the day!

Crunch! Crunch! My mum was eating pickled onions... again. I was holding my nose. We were just popping out to the shops when she popped two in her mouth 'for the journey'.

We live in a city, people think it's full of crime and criminals but it's not all bad. I love my school, my friend, my pets and my family. There's always something to do or somewhere to go.

We were just off shopping one Saturday afternoon. Walking along the road, I saw someone looking a bit suspicious. I tugged my mum's arm when he started following us. Next thing I knew as the man was about to snatch my mum's bag... she farted! She let out a huge loud long fart! The man froze, sniffed and fainted! My mum didn't even notice!

Next, we jumped on the tube. It was very busy. I spied another dodgy character dipping his fingers into people's pockets, taking their belongings. I tugged my mum's arm again. It must have shocked her as she farted again! It was more of a whooshing sound this time; I'd say it was an SBD (Silent But Deadly).

People on the train were in shock, holding their noses. At the next station, everyone jumped off gasping for air! The pickpocket was trapped, frozen in the carriage. My mum didn't know what was going on!

At the shops, we were buying *more* pickled onions! I saw yet another sneaky figure wandering through the aisles. He kept looking over his shoulder and was wearing a big coat even though it was a warm day.

I followed him to observe his suspicious activities - he was a thief! He was filling his coat pocket with lots of goods! I needed to tell someone, and fast.

I was about to report him to the store manager when my mum appeared, running towards the checkout with her trolley full of pickled onions. She spotted me with happiness after I had gone off being a detective. She was so relieved she'd found me, she let out an almighty trump. This trump was like nothing before - it was a powerful blast that blew the thief's coat right off, revealing all the stolen goods.

The police arrived and arrested the crook, putting him in the back of the police car with two other baddies whose eyes were staring forwards and watering.

See, my mum with her toxic bum was a hero and she didn't even know it. She thought she'd hit the jackpot when the store manager gave her a lifetime supply of pickled onions (poor me) and the police gave me a gold medal shaped like a pickled onion!

Pppppppprrrrrrrrfffffffftttttttttttt!

Mia Marlene Ursa Falatoori (11)

Dear Diary

On Thursday the 27th June 2019, we went to Yorkshire Wildlife. When I woke up, I was so excited! When I got to school, Miss Quirke did the register really quick.

After we went to the toilet, we had a good chat. When we came out, we got on the coach. On the coach, we did a lot on the coach because it was a one-hour trip on the coach. We sang, played rock paper scissors and did hand things. We saw meerkats, baboons, painted dogs, lemurs, warty pigs, polar bears and then we had lunch. I had a sandwich but you don't need to know the rest of it. After lunch, we saw squirrel monkeys, an armadillo, otters, lions, tigers, a rhino, zebra, horses, zorse, wallabies, ostriches, wetland animals, giraffes, a brown bear, a rabbit and a leopard - my favourite. On the way back we had another singalong and played 'rock paper scissors' and then we went home from school.

Ellie-Jade Sheils (8)

The Underpants Bandit

Once upon a time, a boy called Wasp wandered the streets of Nowhere Village. He was twelve years old and had a very strange hobby. Unlike any normal human who collected things, Wasp would collect rather strange things. You see, people would collect stamps and Wasp would collect underwear.

He used to go into every house of the village to get the underpants and get to know the owner as well. He hid his valuable collection in a big box called 'Hidden Pocket'. He checked his collection every few days to see if anything was missing.

One day, when he was checking his collection, he noticed a strange pair of underpants. They were a huge, multicoloured pair of underpants with eight holes. Wasp was so surprised to see that he had a different type of underpants that were very unique and looked so fashionable, retro and absurd as well.

But there was one problem, he didn't know the owner of those priceless, beautiful underpants. He decided to go to each house in the village to find the owner. He tried his best but he couldn't find them. Then he realised there was a home at the end of the street, which was abandoned. For the sake of his hobby, he decided to go in that house and meet the owner of the primal underpants.

At night, he stealthily entered the house and started looking for the charismatic personality. After a few steps in, he stopped with a shock. He was appalled and numb. He couldn't move himself. There was a giant spider sitting on the sofa and eating Doritos and drinking Coke. The spider looked at him and smiled softly.

"Are you here to take my autograph?" Spider asked. "You don't need to be scared of me. I am very noble and I belong to a very decent family," Spider further explained.

Wasp got some courage as he was there to find the owner of the giant underpants with eight holes, but he thought he had entered the wrong place.

Suddenly, the spider jumped off the sofa and started screaming, "Oh gosh, you have those underpants that belong to my ancestor, my great-great-grandfather bought them for Paris Fashion Show and we have all used them. They are our family symbol. Oh, I am so happy you have them. I want them here with me forever."

When Spider said that, the boy started running outside and began shouting for help. Soon, the whole village gathered there and they came to know the reality of the boy. They were very grateful that now they knew the spider because of the boy. So they didn't call the police and he promised he would never do it again. Then he changed his hobby to collecting socks.

Wasi Sherazi (9)

Story Time

Once upon a time, there was a little boy called Jack. The mother wanted to do a chocolate cake with raspberries and strawberries for his grandfather, but she could not make a cake with no berries.

The only place where they could find berries was in a forest that looked like a garden. A magic garden guarded by a lion and a tiger. His mother said the animals would give him the fruits if he could stand on one foot and sing a song.

Jak practised at school so he could get the berries. Then Jack, a bit scared, went to the forest and found the lion and the tiger. Frightened, he stood on one foot and sang 'What a Beautiful World'. The tiger and the lion were in tears at Jack's singing and gave him the berries.

Happy, Jack went to his mum who made the cake for his grandfather. The cake was good because I had a slice as well.

Julia Marin (9)

The Story Of Taylor Neet

Whatever happened that night was a mystery to everyone. Of course, everyone heard about it but no one really knew or understood what went on in that house. I was there that night and I'm your only hope to find out what actually happened in the house of dread...

Everything was normal. Everyone in the town of Stone-wall roamed the streets fearlessly with no knowledge of what was going to happen. Suddenly, the sky fell black. Two girls entered the house, clueless to what they were getting themselves into...

Me and my friend had an arrangement to meet by an abandoned house at the end of Death Road, a street that got abandoned because of its name and why everyone ran as far as possible from it. It was also a place of murder, yet again because of its name. Of course, we didn't know that at the time. So when the clock read 10pm we snuck out of the window and met at the house.

The windows were boarded up, the grass was a horrible shade of brown. The roof tiles were on the verge of closing in too. We went inside to find nothing except an open briefcase of files. We walked towards the case to check it out but before we could pick it up I heard this noise like floorboards creaking. It was coming from upstairs.

34

Like the rebellious teens we were, we crept up the stairs trying to make as little noise as possible... Nothing, we were surprised at this. But I knew there was something there, even if it was a rat. There had to be something, but nothing was there! Little did I know, something was there lurking in the shadows, waiting for the perfect time to strike, but what?

We went back down the crooked steps and back to the files. *Swoosh!* The window flew open but still there was no one around to have been able to open it.

We shut it, but what we saw next was terrifying. When we turned around we saw a dark figure, but it looked real, it was human-like almost but it was dark like there wasn't anything or anyone behind the shadow. It wasn't just a shadow, it was real, but what was it?

My friend ran out in fear but I just stood. I froze. I wanted to move but I couldn't. I was trapped inside my own body. I was in shock. The only thing I could feel was the goosebumps on my arm and the tears running down my pale face. I stood there like nothing was happening. It was weird, it was like someone had pressed pause on my life.

At that exact moment, suddenly, I was unpaused. He, she, it was gone, just left, took nothing, did nothing.
Later that week, I received a note saying: 'I will be back and I'm coming for you...'

Rebecca Wilcock (12)

You Can (Not) Replay

Once upon a time, there was a timekeeper called Tom. He had to play the piano at his secret magical clock tower every day. He had to make sure all the clocks and watches were working at the right time.

No one could see and enter the clock tower except for Tom. Inside the tower, there were lots of cogs connected to a magical piano. Whenever he played a magical tune on the piano, it would make him glow like a golden star. He played the piano every hour to get the cogs moving - to maintain the time.

Tom was a brilliant piano player but if he ever played the wrong note, he would be cursed by playing piano forever because the musical piece cannot be replayed again and the time would be going backwards.

He would never make any mistakes during all these years, as he always made sure he knew the musical piece off by heart.

Oriana Lo (9)

The Singing Dinosaur

One day there lived a boy called Stanley who was 10 years old and obsessed with dinosaurs. He lived dinosaurs, he breathed dinosaurs, read, talked and dreamed dinosaurs, in fact, he wanted to be a dinosaur. He begged and begged his mum to go to the museum. He begged his mum so much she eventually said yes!

When they got there, Stanley's mum bumped into a friend and started talking. Stanley got bored and ran off to see the big dinosaur. In the ribs of the dinosaur something caught his eye, it was a glowing red button. Stanley looked around to see if anyone was watching. There was no one about so Stanley climbed up the leg of the big dinosaur and crawled into the ribs. He grasped the button and pressed it. Swirls and colour filled the room and swallowed him up.

When it cleared, Stanley found himself in Dinoland with the button in his hand. He saw lots of dinosaurs and went exploring, being careful not to be seen. While exploring he accidentally dropped the button and a baby dinosaur rushed over and ate the button. Stanley was horrified and rushed over to the dinosaur, shouting, "Oi you! Give it back!" Stanley grabbed the baby dinosaur. The baby dinosaur was so shocked he burped loudly, the button turned green and took Stanley and the dinosaur back to the present time and the button went back to being red.

The baby dinosaur looked up and saw all the big dinosaurs and was so scared that he ran away and Stanley followed quickly after him. The dinosaur ran through an open door and into a room where there were people in white coats sorting old bones. There was a radio blaring in the background with the song 'Walk the Dinosaur'. The baby dinosaur thought this was amazing. He started singing and dancing along to the song.

When the song finished the baby dinosaur was still singing and dancing along when everybody turned around, they all screamed and tried to run out the door. As they run out, the baby dinosaur got squashed and the button in the dinosaur's tummy turned green, sending the dinosaur back to his home.

The baby dinosaur was still singing and dancing as all the dinosaurs looked on in amazement. The baby dinosaur taught them the song and dance and they all started joining in.

Back in the present day, the scientists discovered that dinosaurs could sing and were all amazed at this discovery. Stanley smiled to himself when he heard the news on the television and thought that no one would believe him anyway so he kept quiet. He always remembered that day at the museum when he met the dinosaurs.

Stanley Lawry (10)

The Jungle

In the jungle, it was as green as the greenest grass. The jungle smelt like the finest perfume. As the shiny sun came up, some explorers were bushwhacking their way to shelter. The explorers hadn't slept in days, but the fresh river water they drank gave them a pure boost of energy for them to keep going.

As they crossed the Amazon River, with eels and red piranhas in sight, the riptides made an unbelievable lovely noise. They all agreed to forgive the river. The main explorer said, "Fancy a picnic?"

After the picnic, they decided to set up camp before dark.

At night, the jungle was a lot louder than it was in the day. It sounded slithery but satisfying. It was echoey. So in the morning, they decided to call the mission off and to head home.

Aidan Edward Ives (10)

The Crown Jewels

I felt the wash of the waves, creeping up the sand right into my face as I lay face down on the soft sand. I could hear the crashing on the waves on the beach. I could feel the strong wind gusting, causing the palm trees to bend, to fly like the jet-black hair whipping into my face. Tasting the bitterness of the salty water, the gorgeous bell-shaped flowers smelt like the fragrance of exotic perfumes. What had happened to me? Where have I come from? How did I get here?

I lifted my body off the soft luxurious sand. To my surprise, the substantial weight of my shoulder bag dragged after me. I took the bag off my shoulders and flung it in front of me. I unfastened the buttons slowly with my benumbed fingers. I opened my bag, bit by bit, little by little, until I caught a glimpse of what was in my bag...

I remember, sneakily meandering through the Tower of London, stealthily passing all the guards, without them noticing. That, I do know. The Crown Jewels though were covered in thick bulletproof glass!

There is something I need to tell you before we carry on this story. My eyes are also lasers. They can shoot out heat which is as hot as the sun. This heat can break any materials. Anyway, back to the story!

As I entered, I stepped in front of the Crown, Queen Elizabeth's Crown. As I used my laser eyes to break into the glass, I could feel a lot of breeze, making my body quiver. I knew I was doing something wrong but I had to do it for my life and welfare.

My mum and dad had died and with both of them dead, I was an orphan needing to go to the orphanage with other people like me. I didn't want to go so I escaped, not knowing what to do, where to go and how to do things like this. That is when I thought that all I needed was the Crown, the Crown to sell for money.

At last, I saw it. I feasted my eyes upon it, the glossy, spherical, extensive crown. I picked it up, waiting for the alarm to go off. Then I heard an alarming sound. *Neow! Neow! Neow!* The alarm had gone off. I sprinted away as fast as the wind, hoping not to be caught. As I turned the corner, I caught sight of a guard staring at me. I had been spotted

I bolted off at top speed, hoping not to be caught. The police car's noise was disturbing my eardrums, making me turn back but I knew I shouldn't as it would just make me slower. Water was up ahead and I knew what to do. I plunged into the water, fingertips in first, and started swimming.

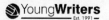

Now I have ended up here, on the run from the police...

Matanhi Kajan (11)

Dear Diary

I had the best time today. I went to the funfair with my family. First I got a beautiful glitter tattoo, it was shaped like a fairy. Then I went on the Ferris wheel, it went round and round and it was very fun. After that, I was quite hungry so Mummy and Daddy took me to get chocolate ice cream. It was super yummy. After I had finished my ice cream, I went to the small circus inside the funfair. There were clowns doing funny tricks, monkeys swinging side to side on trees and people riding in circles on bicycles. After that, I lay in the grass and had a little sleep.

When I woke up, I went to get some candyfloss. It was very delicious and then I went with my mummy and daddy. They said I had to close my eyes because they were bringing me a present. then we went home.

Daisy Golhar

The Land Of Safe Places

It all started in a terrace house in an ordinary town. There was a seven-year-old boy called Lucas. His imaginations were vast and strong. He built a fantastic bunker on his grandparents' bed. Late one night, his nannan was reading him a bedtime story, suddenly they heard a massive bang. His nannan shouted, "To the bunker!"

Lucas and his nannan got bored so they decided to make their own land up. Because COVID-19 had made the world a strange place for everybody, they called it the Land of Safe Places. The moment they said what the land was called, a purple swirling portal appeared at the entrance to the bunker and it sucked them in like a giant taking a huge breath in. They saw sparkling lights as they flew through a dazzling rainbow. A sign appeared saying: *Welcome to the Land of Safe Places.*

"It's the land we made up, Nannan!" shouted Lucas. Nannan was scared, this kind of thing had never happened to her before.

"Aren't you a bit nervous, Lucas?"

Lucas told her that it would be alright and she had nothing to worry about. He assured her that they would get back home safely.

They saw... crowds of people singing a happy song, a huge roller coaster full of joyful people towering over them, a small beach filled with people building sandcastles, people swimming in the sea, smiling children swinging back and forth at the play park, adults sat chatting away at the coffee shop and families and friends were hugging and kissing.

Lucas rushed off happily to join in with all the fun things he had seen. Nannan sat on a bench by the roller coaster enjoying a strawberry ice cream.

Lucas had a brilliant time doing lots of things he couldn't do in his world. The only thing he hadn't done was to go on the roller coaster.

Lucas rushed back to his nannan. "Nannan, do you want to come on the roller coaster with me?" he asked excitedly.

"Yes please!"

They stepped into the cab of a lorry roller coaster carriage and they sped off. A sign appeared saying: *Thank you for visiting the Land of Safe Places. I hope you visit again!* Then they went back through the rainbow and the purple portal.

They found themselves back in the bunker.

"Wasn't that amazing?" said Lucas. "I don't think anyone will believe us if we tell them all about it." They were too tired to move so they fell asleep in the bunker.

Lucas Jackson (8)

The Earth's Evilest Clown

Once upon a ridiculous time, in Ridiculous Circus School, Mr Gangsta Toilet (the Earth's evilest clown) lived in Scarcity House. What he hates the most are burps and farts. I know, right! He's just evil!

Mr Gangsta Toilet was putting people in the chokey (a spiky, narrow hallway with a dead end and more spikes).

"It's deadly!" people would shout. Yesterday, he put a manager in the chokey. He was a killer clown! That was when I assembled a team. Then we formed a mind-blowing plan.

Within minutes, the plan was in action. One adult drank a large gallon of soda and did an extremely big burp and fart. Mr Gangsta Toilet's neck twisted to him! His face was full of fury and rage!

Find out in the next story what happens...

John Segbefia

My Terrible, Horrible Day!

At the crack of dawn, I heard my mum exclaiming, "Your breakfast's ready!" I changed into my blue shorts and white T-shirt.

I stumbled downstairs and groaned, "Mum! Do I have to wake up? It's only 7!"

Mum said, "Yes honey it's time! Remember school starts at 8!"

When I finally got to the kitchen, I realised my mum had made me boiled eggs (I hate boiled eggs). I hid in the closet and grabbed a jar of Nutella greedily. But then... *bash! Boom!* The Nutella jar broke into many pieces of shiny glass. My mum dashed upstairs and said to herself, "That must have come from the closet!" Luckily I had zoomed off to school and the best thing was that my mum had not thought about me going to school.

A moment later, I arrived at school and I saw Jason. He was the mean boy in my class. I really did not want to start a fight with him so obviously I ran out of school and hid in the bushes. I also saw my friend, Jake. He was on the other side of the bush and I quickly but quietly ran to the other side right before Jason came out. He normally leaves school at lunch and eats his food there. I was always late because of those nasty boiled eggs that ruined my life. Jake was eating spaghetti bolognese with cheese on top. I stood with my mouth open. It was obviously my favourite type of food. But my mum would never give me that food. I always got a plain basic ham sandwich. I sat next to him and I said, "Can I just have a bite."

Jake answered, "Well I would give you some but there's still Coronavirus."

I told him that I always have a plain, basic ham sandwich. He looked so shocked and said, "Your mum gives you that? Every time?" I nodded sadly. He replied, "Do you have a spoon or fork at least?" I nodded happily, knowing why he asked that. I grabbed a fork from my lunchbox. But when I took my bite, I ate a bite of fly instead and I vomited. I had never felt so disgusted in my life. I did not vomit on Jake's food. I said, "Will you excuse me for a second and turn around?"

After that, our class today was maths. I tried my best but got an F and my mum was extremely mad. She even put me in her dungeon in our house. She said I had to stay there for an hour, but I stayed there for an hour, and another, and another. Well that is how my life ends, in a dungeon forever and ever.

Alicia Vitkeviciute (7)

The Beast

I was running very fast as the beast was chasing me! My friend was running too and we were both very scared...

One day ago, me and a group of boys from our class came for an expedition on this island but while we were walking, my friend, Jason and I got lost.

When we realised we got lost we went looking for the other boys, but suddenly we were attacked by a shocking beast!

After seeing the beast, we ran fast and hid behind a log and the beast lost us. We were relieved. All of a sudden, we saw a secret passage just behind a tree. We went in and saw a steaming red button which allowed us to enter the passage. Without wasting time, I wisely pressed the button and we entered the passage. Now I knew what my goal was, to find the other buttons to get out of this place.

After a while, I pressed four more buttons and when Jason and I were close to last buttons... Wait! I saw a red light in the chest of the beast, which was actually a gem and it was sensing us. Oh no! The beast caught my friend and threw him in the sea!

I was now all alone and was thinking it was a big, impossible mission for me to get out of this mysterious island!

Being terrified, I figured out a plan which was dangerous and risky but what choice did I have? So, I ducked through a small gap and there I saw the beast was breaking in so I took a stick to lock the door. It kept on bashing to enter and catch me so I quietly got out from there and saw the last two buttons which were far away. Suddenly I saw some shadows of boys so I went near it. Sadly, I realised those were actually the shadows of the trees.

When I went very near to the buttons, the beast was already there so I distracted it by throwing a stick to the opposite side and when it went to the other direction, I swiftly pressed the green button... Oh my god... It was the wrong button! Actually, the entire island had a bomb and the green button activated the bomb. Therefore, the whole island was shaking and I ran towards the sea. It was the only place to survive and,

what a relief, luckily I found a boat! So I jumped on and paddled with the oars and before I knew it... the enigmatic island exploded!

I was safe. I went to the nearby village and found the tents where I saw my friends and told them about the whole experience. I then went to sleep with my super exhausted body. What a horrific adventure!

Rizthil Shathil

The Endless Forest

There was silence. Nobody. Nobody. There was a young boy with scruffy hair and ripped clothes. The gnarled trees reached out to him like witch's claws. The long winding path led to nowhere. Nowhere. The forest was never-ending. A skeleton lay on the floor. Was it a human?

The miserable forest had decaying trees, the smell was unbearable. The horrendous mud was quicksand. The trees strangled anyone who crossed their path. If you were to look up, you would see not the moon, but an endless canopy of death.

This forest was endless. Endless. A murky stream ran through the deadly forest. Rotten leaves were brown and ripped, not a green one in sight. The brown leaves were endless. No one was safe in this forest. The danger was endless. Endless...

Eliza Khan (10)

The Apple Tree

I walked down the rose-petal covered pathway in my gorgeous, flowy, pearl-white dress. I looked my gaze up from the floor, there he was, under the blooming apple tree. We smiled. I walked over to him, he tucked my chocolate-brown hair behind my ear, making the pure white flower that was in my hair fall out. I chuckled, leaning my head back to the ground but he pushed my chin back up. I smiled some more, a light breeze brushed against us. We gazed into each other's eyes, he had chestnut-brown eyes just like mine. I closed my eyes, as he closed his. Then, with our heartbeats in sync, we kissed. My heart glowed as it filled up with love and passion.

Suddenly, as if we were in a movie, pastel-pink petals from the tree floated around us like a circle of love. I could almost hear the romantic music playing, it felt meant to be.

Abruptly, he got ripped away from my grasp. I saw him fighting for freedom but like a puppy. He got defeated, frozen in shock, I watched the royal guard's 'knight in shiny armour' take him away from me. I had fallen for a peasant! Yet I didn't even know his name, but I knew that I could never love someone as much as I loved him. He was the

Romeo to my Juliet and for as long as I would live, I would never give up on him. Even if it meant breaking the rules...

The day of the execution, I used my powers, my leverage as a princess, to cancel it.

"The execution is at 4pm, darling," said Father.

I agreed politely, as the butler neatly placed the diamond-covered crown on my head. I travelled to the beheading half an hour early as to be prepared. But, to my surprise, as I was dropped off by horse and cart, I saw his head trapped in the wooden dash prison. The sharp-bladed knife was about to drop!

I jumped out of the cart and ran and screamed, "No!" at the top of my lungs but it was too late. The blade dropped, his head dropping to the floor. My mascara, like a river, streaming down my eyes.

The next day, I was found hanging from a tree, one tear dripping down my face and a note below me read: In the name of love, I never knew your name but I knew your heart'.

The story was covered up, never revealed outside the royal family. I took my life for him with no regrets.

Natasha Harrison (13)

The Moaning Mouse And Positive Peacock In Lockdown

On March 23rd 2020, the UK went into lockdown, affecting people aplenty. The reason for this was due to COVID-19, the worst virus this world has ever seen. Outside, Dungiven, in a place called Oville, two creatures were self-isolating so they didn't get ill. Together they lived in a small little house - Positive Peacock and Moaning Mouse.

"I'm bored!" sighed the mouse. "I want to have fun but I can't leave the place to play or to run."

"Well..." said the Peacock, "it's not all doom and gloom, there is plenty of fun to be had in these rooms." So off to the living room, with cushions and blankets he went. In there he built a great big tent.

"Oh!" shrieked the mouse. "What a mess you have made!"

"No," said the peacock. "Get in! From here our football cards we can trade."

So they played and they pretended and traded cards until they were done.

"See," said the peacock. "The living room is fun!"

Out got the peacock and to the kitchen make.
There he emptied the cupboards and started to bake.
"Oh!" shrieked the mouse. "What a mess you did make!"
"No," said the peacock. "I've baked you a cake."
So they talked and they laughed and they ate all the buns.
"See," said the peacock, "the kitchen is fun! To the bathroom!" cried peacock in a voice that was shrill.
Here he turned on the taps and the bath began to fill.
"Oh," shrieked the mouse. "It is full to the brim!"
"Yes!" said the peacock. "We can go for a swim."
So they swam, played with bubbles, their ducks and water guns.
"See," said the peacock, "the bathroom is fun."
"I love self-isolating!" proclaimed Moaning Mouse.
"It is not all that bad staying in the house."
"Yes," replied Positive Peacock. "There is no need to moan, and if you want to talk to others you can just pick up the phone. We are in this together and we need to keep safe. So until lockdown is over, home is the best place."

Eimear McGilligan (8)

The Chreventure

On Christmas Eve, two children, named Ruby and Lilly, were desperate to open their presents. They were only allowed to open one. Ruby was eight, and Lilly was four. They chose a present, and to their surprise, it was a globe. Ruby thought it was a silly globe. As normal, if you shake the globe, snow will come from the roof of the globe. Inside the globe, the picture was of a snowman. On the packet, in big bold writing, it said: 'If you shake this globe three times at midnight, you will go to the North Pole'. Ruby thought it was lying. It also said: 'You can't go home for two days. On the second day, shake it twice at midnight and you shall go home'. Kali and Steven (Ruby and Lilly's mum and dad) wouldn't notice because two elves would be disguised as them.

At midnight, toddler Lilly and Ruby tried it out. It worked! They were invisible when they flew to the North Pole. Ruby said, "This is the best Christmas present ever!" Lilly was fast asleep whilst this happened. In small handwriting on the packet it said: 'If you lose this you have to stay at the North Pole forever until you find it'.

As soon as Ruby saw Santa, Santa had a big smile on his face because he knew that someone had opened one present on Christmas Eve and it was the most popular and expensive present anyone can get. Ruby told Santa she thought the message on the packet was fake. Finally, Lilly woke up.

On the second day at midnight, Santa said, "Ho, ho, ho!" But before he said goodbye, he told them not to tell their parents about their adventure. Santa gave Lilly and Ruby one more present each. Lilly cried because she got a pack of nappies.

Ruby and Lilly returned home, and Lilly fell asleep straight away. Before Ruby went to bed, she wrote her adventure in her memory book. Then she went to sleep. They both dreamt of their next adventure. What will their next adventure be with the globe and Santa?

Eesha Gudka (9)

Granny's False Teeth

One sunny day, Granny woke up to sunlight shining through the curtains, she smiled and stretched and thought to herself, what a wonderful day it is going to be.

She sat up and swung her legs over the side of her bed. She reached out and picked up her glasses and put them on, she then reached out again to pick up her teeth, but couldn't find them. She looked all over the bedside cupboard and on the floor but they were gone!

First, she looked under her bed because if they fell on the floor they could have rolled under her bed but they weren't there. Oh no, she thought. Where could they be? Then she looked in her wardrobe, they weren't in there either. She opened her drawers and had a look through her underwear. "No, not there!" She went into the bathroom and looked in the bin. "They are not here!" She slowly opened the toilet lid and peeked in. "Glad they are not in there," she whispered. She then went into the front room and stood looking around. She went over to the sofa and got down on her knees and looked under the sofa, lots of dust and... "Oh, what's that?" She smiled as she saw something under the seat.

She reached under and pulled out... a book! "Oh that's where you went," she said to the book. "You're not my teeth though are you?" She sighed and got back onto her feet.

She went into the kitchen and looked in the toaster, the microwave, the oven, the fridge, the sink, the cupboards, the drawers and the dishwasher!

"No, no, not in there, not here, not over there, my teeth are not anywhere!"

She went and put the kettle on, checking for her teeth before she put it on! Made herself some tea and went to sit back down on the sofa.

"Oh, Mittens," she said to her black cat that was curled up on the seat next to her. "Where are my teeth?" The cat purred a happy purr. "Do you know where my teeth could be?"

Mittens slowly looked up at Granny and smiled a huge, white, shiny, sparkly, false teeth grin!

Georgia Carter (9)

The Haunted Mansion

At the top of the very high mountain lies a huge Victorian mansion. No one dares to enter it because there are lots of stories about a green slimy ghost who lives there. Me (Cassius) and my friend Abel one day decided to go to the very scary Victorian mansion at the top of the mountain. Abel was a little bit scared. He said to me, "It looks very scary up there, I don't want to go in." I was scared too but was intrigued about the ghost and wanted to see for myself if it was real.

As we entered the house the big black door screeched, that was enough to make us both jump. Abel said again to me, "I really don't want to do this." So I said to him, "Are you not a little bit curious to see the ghost for yourself?"

He replied, "Yes, but it is really scary here."

We went further into the house and there were lots of creepy sounds creaking and slamming. At this point, we were both petrified but we still carried on our quest to find the ghost.

We went up the stairs, each step creaked as we stepped on them. At the top of the stairs was a strange-looking door. We were both interested to see what was behind the door.

As I opened the door there was a terrible sound coming from the room, almost like a girl crying for help. I flung the door open and it went with a big thud. There in front of us wasn't a slimy, scary-looking ghost but the ghost of a young boy. He was looking at himself in the mirror. His screams were because he couldn't believe what he was looking at. He couldn't believe he had passed away and was now a ghost! The ghost was not really a horrible ghost. He told us the story of how he became that way... He was once a young boy working for rich families but had a terrible accident because he wasn't treated fairly and was made to do things that were not safe.

Now he haunts the house he worked in because he blames the people who lived there for the accident...

Rhys Oliver Frost (9)

The Enchanted Wardrobe

Once upon a time, there existed a rich, mighty and valiant king. He battled many conflicts and was known as a hero. He used to have superlative gifts sent in.

One day, the weary and exhausted king came back with his military triumphant, when he spotted a mysterious-looking glass wardrobe. The monarch untied an anonymous note that was tied on the handle. The note said: 'This is a magical wardrobe, say anything you want and put your hand in. The thing you want will come out but be sure to put something back in, you can even put scrap paper inside!' At the end of the message it said 'a faithful servant'.

The king was over the moon to have magic in his palace. He used the wardrobe every day, putting back in something useless like a sock or a sweet. Soon the whole community knew about the powerful wardrobe. A band of embezzlers managed to pinpoint it and they planned to steal it when the king was out fighting.

The next day, as the king left with his army, the three raiders sneaked in though the high security and tried to run off with it. But they didn't know that the wardrobe had eyes. So the wardrobe wouldn't budge because it recognised only the king.

66

The thieves were so anxious that one of them found some clothes of the ruler and put it on so that the wardrobe would think he was the king. Soon the wardrobe moved.

The thieves soon arrived at their house and at once they rushed to the wardrobe to extract money. They carried on taking money till midnight but they didn't know that you had to put something back in. Because of this, they all became gluttonous. Then at one o'clock, they went to bed. They forgot about water and food and didn't have any for more than seventy-two hours so in the night they all died.

The king came to their house and found the wardrobe and said, "Alas, if they were honest and did not trick the wardrobe they would have been healthy men."

Hammaad Rashid

Space Potato

Once in a land far away from here there was a potato called Vachure. He loved art, cooking, playing and more, he really liked looking at beautiful nature.

One day Vachure was surprised because he discovered something and almost couldn't stay alive! Vachure went to the place and named it space. Then he created some stars and made Planet Mars! He made lots and lots of stuff and he was so tired he did a big huff and puff.

In the afternoon while Vachure was making his things he heard a big sound which made a... *ding!* Vachure hurried down to see and saw a sign written *Alfie*. Vachure asked him to stop but he didn't even listen, he looked so ugly like a giant kitten.

Alfie kept on shooting and being really rude, he almost broke Vachure's masterpiece the star-o-lude. Alfie came down to speak and he said..."It's time to talk and call my friend."

Vachure hopped out of space and went home and brushed his skin with a spiky comb. Alfie did loads of bad destroying and was really unkind. Vachure tried to stop him online but whenever Alfie got the message he just stroked his cat-like spine.

While Vachure was messaging he realised that Alfie was attached to his own phone. Vacher remembered that Alfie usually puts his phone on the sun and destroys things.

Vachure had a plan, a really good one, he was to go to space and break Alfie's phone on the sun.

Vachure set off to space and tied up his shoelace. He saw Alfie still destroying things. Vachure searched online how to break an enemy's phone and it said to sing to it so that's what he did and Alfie, his phone and all his possessions flew up to the sky.

While that was happening all Vachure's planets and stars were coming back again.

Everyone in Potato City heard what happened and were happy for him and a year later Vachure was famous and was known as... *Space Potato!*

Aahana Sahoo (7)

I Had A Dream

Once upon a time, on a very hot and boiling night, I was getting ready for bed. I went to the bathroom to have a shower, hoping it would cool me down, and while I was in the shower I wondered what unicorns and all the other creatures do when it is as hot as today was. I finally clambered into bed after putting on some shorts and a top and opening the window to let some air come in.

After a short time, I had gone off to sleep as I was exhausted after all.

I was now in a beautiful place but it was just as hot. I looked around to see where I was and there were not so many trees so was not a lot of shade. There were loads of unicorns, hippos and lots more animals but the question I kept asking myself was, "How are they keeping cool?"

"Well," replied a voice, you have come to the right place if you want to know. Let's go sit down on some marshmallow chairs."

"Wow!" I replied. "This is so magical!"

The unicorns have special horns you see, they are full of water and when they get hot, they slowly release some of the water on them to cool them down. When there is rain they drink and then it replaces what they have used. All the other animals have some kind of pouch to keep them cool."

I was so interested I had to go see these wonderful creatures and see where they were hiding their water pouches. Oh and I have to say, I also had to see all the stunning items that were made from all sorts of food like the marshmallow chairs and chocolate bar tables! The lollipop trees were truly amazing and wonderful!

All of a sudden, a horrible noise came and yes, it was an alarm. Nobody likes that sound! It always happens when I get to a nice bit of my dream and because the alarm goes I don't get to find out what happens.

Will I ever get to find out what happened next in my dream?

Lilly Foreman

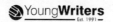

Tasha's Wonderful Birthday Party

One day, there was a girl who was beautiful called Tasha. She was very excited for her birthday as her parents said she could plan her birthday party all by herself.

Tasha was thinking of what options she could have for her birthday. At last she decided to have her wonderful birthday in a trampoline park. So, she told her loving parents and they called the trampoline park manager. Her parents asked them to book for a party on Tasha's birthday date. Unfortunately, they had said that someone had already booked a party on that day. Tasha's parents were disappointed about this and Tasha was also very upset.

Afterwards, a brilliant idea had popped into Tasha's dad's mind. He thought of hiring a bouncy castle and celebrating Tasha's birthday in their garden. Tasha came running down with excitement and said, "Can I ask my friends to come to our house too?"

Mum replied, "Yes of course you can."

Tasha was rushing to the telephone with a lot of joy and happiness and started phoning all her friends while Tasha's dad was calling the bouncy castle hiring manager. Tasha was done telling all her friends and dad was also done with the hiring of the bouncy castle.

The next day it was Tasha's birthday when everyone was ringing on the doorbell. On the first doorbell, the bouncy castle manager came to deliver the bouncy castle and fix it. All the other doorbell sounds were Tasha's best friends. Everyone went outside and really enjoyed bouncing on the bouncy castle. After the mains were served and everyone had eaten Tasha was going to cut her cake. All Tasha's friends came inside and Tasha cut her cake. Tasha's parents put a piece of cake in a small box for all her friends and then they all went home.

Tasha really liked it and it was one of her best birthdays she had ever had.

Saibinthushan Thayan (7)

Monica's Dead Soul

Monica. Her mother is dead. Her father too. She's alone in a house. All day, every day...

"Listen to the sound of my voice, my dear. Do not fear, do not cry. You will be the best that you can be. Dear orphan, dear child, do not weep. Do not feel sorry for me, for I had to go, someday..." her mother's voice echoed in her head.

"But what you seem to forget is that after each day comes the night, you would never know it, the constant pain I feel because in the light of day it almost isn't real. Everyone tells me I'm strong and that they see it in me but everyone only sees what I want them to see, not an orphan but a smiling... child."

She's drowning in silence and no one knows. Her parents are ghosts and no one believes it but they believe she's happy and she's the girl who will always say, "I've got this", even with tears in her eyes. But during the night, she can't hide what's really underneath. Monica cries and cries until she falls asleep.

"Do you want to join us? Souls snatched away?" her father declared.

"Anything to be with my family, anything to leave this evil and cruel world. Take me and save yourselves."

In a blink of an eye, her soul had risen before her and left her body piled on the floor.

A knock on the door: "Social services, we are here to take Monica."

They kicked the door down, ran up the stairs, just to find out that Monica was dead, but what they didn't know was that she had left her body and her soul had finally joined her parents. "We will report this to the police."

After two years, there was still no trace of what caused Monica to 'die'. They all paid tribute but they still didn't know why she died.

Praise Okpanefe

Hero

Fog covered the town like a blanket. The mist kept up to the house like a ghostly serpent, slid across the window, flicked its tongue into the corners of the house, waited a moment and slipped back to the path.

Mother was talking to the three children at the dinner table. "Kids, Daddy will have to go to get more firewood tomorrow."

"Aww!" seven-year-old Lucy and ten-year-old Jack moaned. "He's been out all day!" wailed Lucy sadly.

"He must be exhausted," added Jack.

Peter who was twelve was unusually quiet. "I'll go!" he proclaimed.

"Of course not!" retorted his mother.

Upstairs when he was sure Lucy and Jack were in bed, he changed his clothes. Now in his warm coat and gloves, he waited until his mother had turned off the radio. The household was asleep.

He crept down the stairs, quieter than a cat and silently opened the door. Peter stepped onto the cobbled driveway closing the door behind him. *What about Gloomy Forest?* he thought, *there's lots of firewood there.*

At the edge of the dark forest, Peter peered inside, then he ventured on. Cloaked in mist, the trees looked like ghostly stooped figures. The dead branches rose up and grasped at his ankles like bony fingers. Pushing the arching branches away, he stuffed them into his brown sack.

Forcing his way past the spidery tangle of trees and bushes, he made his way home. He pushed the door open not to make a sound and left the sack next to the front door. He shut the door, ran upstairs, changed his clothes and as soon as his tiring head hit the pillow he was fast asleep.

He had made it back through the dense fog and saved his hard-working father a lot of trouble. He indeed felt like a hero...

Sahl Ameen (10)

Who Once Was A Boy

And as he rose, he smiled. Yet it wasn't a nice smile. This smile was all teeth, large and long and sharp and pointed. The smirk - because by now it couldn't be called anything else - stretched wider, a gaping maw, revealing rows and rows of glimmering teeth, literally stretching from ear to ear, lips gone, just an endless chasm of darkness and mouth and teeth.

His twisting nest of hair reached out, each strand a shadow clawing for freedom from this puny mortal form, lashing at the floor, the walls and the ceiling, nails long and pointed, no, not nails, these could only be *claws* that grew from the boy, skin the same shade as snow, and the laugh, oh, the *laugh...*

It was a laugh that spoke of the underworld, of terrible things to come, of Hell to pay for those who wronged him, one laced with a poisonous, dangerous, tantalising darkness, burning through the light and calling those to his side, but who was he anymore, really? Certainly not human. That laugh sang of pain and power and death, of torture and blood and entrails spilling onto the ground, of screams and sobs and fear, of things that had yet to come; his laugh tauntingly reminded them of judgement day and the horrors that would be there.

Black ink coiled around what once were fingertips, cracks spreading across the floor, windows shattering and ceiling falling in, the building disappearing, crunching down on itself, collapsing, and the tar-like substance pooling around this demon that dared stand in the ruins of a once-beautiful place, in amongst the dust and stone that dripped with ebony oil and smelt of fear, tension so sharp in the air you could cut it with a knife.

And in the midst of it all, stood that demon that once was a boy.

Elizabeth Henderson-Millier

The Incredible Diary Of... The Sweet Sixteenth

January 14th, 2020

Dear Diary,
Hi, my name is Riley. I'm 15, next year. It's my sweet sixteenth. I have a mum. Her name is Shona and she is 31 years old. I also have a dad. His name is Shaun. He is 32 years old. My little sisters are the most annoying people in the world, they want to follow me everywhere I go! It's so annoying but yesterday I got an invitation to a sleepover at my friend's. It looked a bit like this...

Dear Riley,
Will you come to my party? (A sleepover party)
Food...

1) Chicken nuggets
2) Pepperoni pizza
3) Fried chicken
4) Spicy chicken
All from KFC

From your dearest friend,
Immy.

I'm sooooo excited about that. Oh, did I mention I have a Staffy called Bella? I forgot to tell you my sisters' names. They are Holly who is five and Carly who is four. Loads of people think they are twins but they are one year apart.

January 15th 2020

Dear Diary,
I'm back. Are you still here? Just kidding because I know you're here. I know you would not leave. Tomorrow I leave for the party (sleepover) but I still don't have a present or a card. I'll ask my mum for money to get a present and a card.
I've asked my mum and she said yes so right now I'm going to the shop.
I'm back with the present and card. The present is a puppy and the card is a normal one. Do you think she will like it? I kind of do. By a puppy I mean a pet puppy, it is worth £109, a lot of money. See you soon.

January 16th 2020

Dear Diary,
Today is the day of the sleepover so see you at the
sleepover...

Evey McKay (10)

Missed

As I walk to school, I begin to think about what I am going to do tonight with my best friend when she comes round. Maybe we could go out to a restaurant or go to the park? As I reach the school gates something seems off, no one's here yet. I begin to panic, thinking, *what if school's off?* No, I would have known. I conclude that I must just be early. Yes, it is early.

When I look inside and shriek. I find my English teacher covered in blood on the floor. Just as I go to go and call the police I am pulled into the school. That is all I remember from that moment. When I wake up, I am trapped in a room at the police station. People tell me that I have been missing a whole week. I wonder what happened...

Tabitha Goldup

Goodbye

I was so bored playing with my basketball in the garden on the most scorching hot day. I was as hot as a volcano. Suddenly I saw fire fall from the sky, it looked like a meteor. It zoomed as fast as lightning over Zoe the neighbour's house and smashed into the deep grass, two metres down. There were different patches of fire around it. I ran over to the hole and started digging with my hands to see what was there. It was one stick of white chalk. I took it inside and put it with my drawing stuff and Mum shouted, "It's dinner time."

After dinner I took the chalk back outside and started to draw. I drew a beautiful picture of my grandma Mary and grandpa Ronnie. I started to cry because I missed them. I accidentally dropped a tear from my eye and I said, "Oops," as it landed on the picture.

Then suddenly the drawing started to sparkle like magic. It was coming to life! Oh my, it was Grandma and Grandpa. I ran to hug and kiss them. I said, "Where are you taking me?"

They said, "We are taking you to our home up in Heaven." They held my hands.

I said, "Woah!" We started to fly high up into the sky. They took me to their house in the clouds. They gave me some biscuits.

"Quick," said Grandma, "it's starting to rain. We are starting to fade. Let's get you home. Take this magic dust, you will float down with it." They gave me a big hug and a special drawing of them. I told them I loved them. They loved me too.

As I landed in the garden the rain was washing away the drawing, but they got a chance to smile before the magic stopped. "Goodbye Grandma and Grandpa."

Thomas Jest (7)

Earth

Dear Diary,

I was asleep, I was in a dream. It wasn't a regular dream, was the dream. I was in my bed then I heard loud noises like a giant coming to attack buildings. So I looked out my window and I saw a large dark figure standing in the distant, he was mumbling. Then I heard my name loud and clear. I ran through the kitchen and the back door. I was very scared. The figure started to mumble again but even louder.

I wanted to say something to the monster but I was scared. I took a deep breath and I said hello. "Connor,"' is what the monster responded.

"Connor O'Malley," I kept on hearing, I didn't know what to reply.

I said, "Who are you?"

He replied back, "Who am I?"

I started to move away from the monster. "Why are you scared of me?" he said.

I said back, "Just a bit scared because I have never seen this ever in my life."

I thought it was real but it wasn't. My heart was racing like a drum set was being played. I thought, *what I should do next?* I didn't want to give the monster eye contact so I looked at the ground.

"Ha-ha, why are you not looking at me young O'Malley?"

I didn't say anything back. I looked at him for five seconds.

"I am your yew tree, did you know that? Really, I never knew that. I can be any shape and form."

I was so surprised and I didn't know what to say. I ran inside and went to bed.

I woke up with a scream, it was 12:07am. I went to get a glass of water, I felt something under my foot. It was yew tree leaves. I'm now wondering how the leaves got inside when the window was closed...?

Daniela Pakulnyte (12)

War Animal - Squirrel

Today I found out about the war. I wasn't expecting to, but it happened. I was collecting all my nuts that had been rudely pecked out by a woodpecker. I never did like that woodpecker. Anyway, I was collecting them all over again when I heard a silent, but growing battle cry, battle cries, loads of cries! It was getting louder. Louder, louder and closer! Very, very close. I got so terrified of the battle cries, the cries of pain and the cries of sorrow, I scrambled back to my hollow oak tree.

I looked down at my lost possessions, a tear filled my eye, then left it. Just like the nuts left in my grasp. I looked beyond the forest to see men falling, falling and fighting for their lives, for their dignity. They were slowly stumbling over my way. I thought that I had time, time to scavenge for my beloved nuts. I darted down the tree, towards the soft wet ground. I shuffled as much as I could in my ever-expanding mouth. The only problem was, I couldn't see the men. I could only hear them. I got scared of the super-loud sounds and retreated to my tree tower.

They were way too close for my liking now. Blood splattered at the base of my hollow home. "My nuts!" I said. A head smashed down on the ground. making my oak wood tree rumble like thunder. This caused even more of my nuts to fall out into the bloody abyss. Another tear dropped into my soft, furry palm. That was when I realised that this war, this treacherous war, it affects us all. Emotionally, physically, mentally. That was when I made the decision of running away. It was too dangerous and risky to stay. Anywhere would be safer than being at war.

Sophie van der Kroon (12)

The Eldritch School Trip To Antarctica

The school coach took all thirty students to the airport, where they boarded an Antarctica plane. What a great time! Flying to Antarctica, a boy picked his nose and guess what? He ate it! Uh, gross! Mkayla then started vomiting and suffocating! Whilst this was happening, the teacher, Mrs Mckenzie, was getting rid of the disgusting vomit and eating her lunch at the same time, whilst the pilot was trying to stay rigid and fly the plane in silence, without any disturbances!

A few hours later, Mrs Mckenzie realised she had lost her wedding ring. She asked all the children to find it. A minute later, Mkayla farted it out, but Mrs Mckenzie couldn't wear it on her finger because it was ill-scented!

At last, they arrived and got out of the plane when they saw an earthquake coming. A piece of ice fell apart and the children got dragged on ice. The children saw a huge crowd of king penguins, emperor penguins and lots of big-haired white polar bears, all having a snowball fight! The children then realised that ice can be made into all sorts of shapes and used for snowball fights.

Whilst the children were having fun, the ice started melting rapidly, so swiftly they got back into their plane and said by to the Antarctic animals.
The children were extremely tired, so they slept, zzz, farted, *prrp, prrp, prrp* and snored, *zzz*, just after take-off, till they arrived. The pilot woke them up and said, "Thank you all for sleeping and your stinky farts!" He gave everyone a special globe made out of real Antarctic ice. All the children were very excited as their parents collected them.

Janina Segbefia (6)

The Lost Treasure

The sun rose glowing its bright red colour on a summer morning, I woke up looking at the pretty sight through my window. Suddenly I heard my dad calling - "Son, Son, come down, there is a very special news report on the TV..."

I'm a researcher who loves to learn, discover and go on an expedition to find the lost treasure.

One day, I was reading a book called 'Storm and the sea' and the story goes like this...

In 1901, Vascodogama, who was a very rich man, sailed in his royal boat from India to the Russian Federation carrying his family treasure. The boat was large and had lots of compartments. There was a secret chamber where the gold was so the other pirates could not get it. It was halfway through the North Pacific ocean when there was a heavy storm, sea waves were rough and the wind was blowing very hard. The boat started shaking, almost difficult to drive further. Sadly the boat sunk with a splash in the water.

I learnt about the wreck and went on a treasure hunt.

I used my underwater robots to take pictures of the interesting things other than fishes, water and rocks. After searching for 200 days, some stuff caught my eyes from the picture. It was the same ship that Vascodogama drove with the treasure. I got more pictures of the interior of the boat, secret chamber and the treasure box. This made my expedition a success.

I shared the pictures of the gold to the government and I was rewarded. This was the exciting news that my dad called me for that was being shown on the TV!

Sai Ragavan (7)

The Haunted Boarding School

Brothwell Manor was most certainly not a normal school to be. The petrified girls would never dare to disobey the strict but safe rules of the haunted school. It was said to never go into the basement. It was not even tolerated if you went with a trustworthy adult.

It all started when a daring second-former, Anne Holsworth, risked her life for a discovery a few years ago. She was woken in the dead of night and it was pitch-black. She lit a candle and slowly but carefully, made her way down into the terrifying basement, where a strange sound had seemed to have emerged from. There, she examined an old form photo of the fifth form and noticed something very strange that made her fluttering heart skip a beat - Amelie Conner and Malania Belinda were missing! In other form photos many girls had disappeared or vanished. This made Anne so frightened that she dropped her candle. However, before it could do any damage, someone had blown it out!

It took her moments to realise, that over fifty girls had been reported missing between the 7th October and the 29th November 2012, nine days after the form pictures of the year were taken).

This meant, they would've been featured in the photograph.

Before Anne could shriek, a faint silhouette of a human-like figure grabbed her and took her to the 'forbidden room'. There all the missing girls were found.

After Anne and the rest of the missing girls were found months later, the school was abandoned. But something still roamed the hallways...

Alexandra Slavova (9)

Jealous Of Her Sister

Once upon a time, there lived a girl called Meida and she lived with a mean sister called Andreea. Meida had funny friends and Andreea was very jealous. Andreea had no friends but she really wanted a friend.

One day, a miracle happened and she found a friend called Maja. They became the best of friends. Andreea was so happy she had a friend. They had sleepovers and they did everything together.

After a while, Meida became jealous of Andreea and Maja because of their friendship so Meida, Maja and Andreea became friends.

A decade passed and Andreea and Maja were eighteen years old and Meida was twenty-one years old. Andreea and Maja were in college and Meida had a job that she liked it very much.

After their first day in college they saw each other and gave each other a hug. After a while they went for lunch and after lunch they found an abandoned kitten on the side of the road. Andreea, Maja and Meida took the kitten to the vet to see if the kitten had any fleas. The vet said the kitten was a girl and had no fleas so Andreea, Maja and Meida called the kitten Jojo.

Jojo had a happy life and two years later, Jojo was now two years old. Maja and Andreea were twenty and Meida was twenty-three.

One morning, a lady was at the door. They found out the lady was Jojo's owner. It was time to say goodbye so in tears they said goodbye. Since the lady was nice she let Andreea, Maja and Meida keep Jojo.

Andreea-Jasmine Marin (9)

Candy Land In A Different View

"Oh no!" Those devils were here, they were running around like a swarm of bees looking for their nectar. They were all grabbing all these treats and putting them in all sorts of places. Those hungry mouths were stuffing as much as they could in one gulp as if it were a race. Smudging their faces while stuffing themselves. Becoming chocoholic crazy.

These sweets were hidden in the factory. Far, far away where greediness didn't exist. I loved watching the beautiful scenery and listening to the sound of the rich chocolate gradually pouring down to the flowing river, gently blending in with the aromas. Dark chocolate trees were the background with caramelised apples hanging. The mouth-watering mouths wanted more and more. Mouths were hanging wide open when they were coming closer and closer to me. They cornered me one by one. "No, no!" I wailed but they couldn't hear me. The grabbed me from each side and destroyed me completely. I was no more. I wasn't a liquorice tree any more, I was more like a block of chocolate.

The land was no more a heaven of sweets, it was more like a junkyard with enemies attacking it and destroying the place until it was no more. They shredded the whole place like farmers shredded the wheat. I wish, I wish it wasn't true. I hope, I hope it is a dream. This is the place where dreams are fulfilled not where dreams are ruined.

Hannah Zab

Wartime - An Extract

They got on the train. As they travelled they could see the outside changing from a beautiful, peaceful village to a smoky, foggy place with cracked walls. Fire and flames sparked near buildings and other buildings collapsed.

Once they reached home, Mia stood at the top of the street where Albert and Audrey lived. They saw Charles hard at work and Mia's face dropped even more with disappointment when she noticed that Albert's house had been very badly affected from a bomb dropping on Albert's other neighbour, Sandra's house.

Mike and Mia feared that Albert had died but walking out of the fog was Audrey and Albert. Both Mike and Mia ran to their older relatives and everybody had a hug and a catch-up.

Albert then lived with Audrey until his house was repaired and Charles had finished his job until the next war and Mike stayed with his dad. Mia's mum lived on and her dad came back from the war with only one arm but was safe. Mia went to live with them again but she visited her grandma every weekend.

The sweetshop manager employed another man to work in the very same sweet shop that Mike worked in.

Life was soon great again but it took a lot of work to recover from the damage the war had caused. World War II was over but everybody dreaded World War III - if it ever came...

Leon Hilton (11)

Remembrance

I'm sitting here at 10:55am in a trench, during the First World War. I remember everything, I remember too much. Every day men go out to the front line, stepping up their attack. The sound I hear the most is a soft telltale whistle, then a bang. The only safe place is the trenches. I know you tell me to keep going and I know that, at home, you have the same telltale whistle and then a loud bang!

When I leave my trench, my life is at risk. The sound of guns deafens me. The sound of men falling to the ground, wincing with pain, stays in my brain. I ask myself the same two questions every day: "Is this the end? Is this the day that hope turns into sorrow?" A cold chill runs down my spine and I have lost the feeling in my hands too many times to count. I see men from both sides fall to the ground and never see them get back up.

I hate having to be here, I hate the fact that I may never come home. I hate the fact that you are suffering at home because of my actions. I wish the guns would fall silent for even a minute. I wish I could go home and wrap my cold, tired arms around you and squeeze you tightly.

The guns fall silent, they drop to the floor. 11/11/18 - 11am. There is no noise, everything falls silent. There is no telltale whistle, no sound of pain. There is just silence.

Grace Stewart

Trick Or Treat?

One night, a group of girls were trick or treating. Their names were Sage, Laisay, April, Jane and Samantha. They came across a spooky house, it was Spookeville, the neighbourhood house. Samantha looked behind her, she saw that her friends weren't there. Sadly, no one was there. She tried to do something about it. She went into the home with no hope and the doors shut behind her. *Bang!* As she walked, the door went creak with the floor. All she could see were coffins, coffins, coffins. She yelled for help but it was no use. "Please help me, come get me..."

Suddenly, from behind her she could hear, "Little girl, little girl, it will be fine. Cry all you want but you will be mine! Ha, ha, ha, ha!"

Something appeared. She was scared. A pumpkin was walking up to her while the witch was still cackling sarcastically. "I'll help you escape," said the pumpkin.

She jumped on him and hoped it wasn't a scam! She wanted to flee the facility as soon as possible. Samantha couldn't help but cry. She was the scaredy-cat of the group she was trick or treating with.

"Help me, help me, help me!" She escaped and stopped trick or treating. She felt happy but little did she know, next year will be way worse...

Alicia Unciuleanu Miriam

On The Beach...

Once upon a time, I was with my friends Sirius, James, Lupin and Fatimah. The bright sun shone while we were swimming to shore, where our parents were.

"Shall we play in the rock pools?" asked Lupin.

"Yeah, why not! Let's go," I said. So we got out of the water and went to the rock pools.

"We are going to have a barbecue in an hour," Dad reminded us.

"Oh, here comes the Serverus!" I said and we all giggled to each other.

"What are you doing Serverus?" asked James.

"Shall we go to the caves in the cliff?" I asked.

Everyone started shouting in excitement at this idea so we went deep inside the cave of the cliffs until we found a big, scary shadow. We hid ourselves quietly behind a big, booming, large boulder. It was huge!

"You go first and take a look," James said to me.

"Ummm, okay," I said, looking puzzled. Nervously, I came around the boulder and it shrieked.

"Argh!" I shouted.

All of us screamed and started running out of the cave. While running, I turned around and saw that the giant, huge shadow was actually a tiny mouse!

We quickly ran past the lapping waves and finally reached the barbecue spot just on time.

Abdullah Naveed (7)

The Incredible Diary Of... The Pig With A Great Life!

Dear Diary,

I'm Button. My life is hard with no mum or dad to look after me. Well, I bet you are wondering what happened to them? Well, you are about to find out...

Well, when I was only one-year-old they were taken away to the place where they were made into meat. We were separated like all the other families and it was my turn next. Well, I guess you're wondering why I am still writing. This is because this small girl came. When it was my turn, the person who was taking us argued with a girl and at first, I wondered why. But then she came and picked me up and said, "Hi, I'm Elsie, I'm here to save you."

Slowly, she strolled over to her red car with her mum waiting in the car like they were planning to take me all along. As we drove, it felt like a dream come true. I finally had someone to care for me! When we got to Elsie's house, I sat on her small, soft sofa and thought about my friends and what I would have missed if this sweet, generous girl (Elsie) hadn't taken me to her amazing house.

She gave me some apples and took me outside to play. This new life was amazing, better than normal pigs. I felt special.

Izzy Wray (11)

Mimi Has A Cake Problem

Mimi was going to a party, her sister's party, Paula. Paula wanted a princess cake. Mimi wasn't much of a good chef (Mum and Dad were going out).

Mum: "Mimi, take care of Paula."

Dad: "Remember it's your sister's birthday today!"

Mimi: "Yes, Mum and Dad." (Wave.)

It wasn't easy for Mimi to bake a cake, let alone a princess cake (Mimi was exhausted!)

Paula: "Come play with me, Mimi!"

Mimi: "Sigh."

Paula didn't know that it was her birthday. So, Mimi was ready to surprise her.

Mimi was in the kitchen preparing the ingredients for the cake. Meanwhile... Mum and Dad were on their way to the supermarket.

Dad: "Which cake shall we buy for Paula?"

Mum: "I believe she wanted a princess cake."

Finally, Mimi managed to bake a cake, but it looked unappetising. Then... *ding-dong!* Mum and Dad were standing at the front door holding a princess cake! Mimi was confused.

Mimi: "Mum, I have already baked a cake as you had asked me to do so."

Mum: "Oh, Mimi! I told you to take care of your sister, not bake a cake!" Everyone was laughing, including Mimi.

Salma Saleh Faraj (10)

Julia Goes To The Beach

Julia always wanted to go to the beach but, for some reason, her parents never let her go. One day, she had a plan to trick them to go to the beach. So the next day she said to her dad that she was going to the playground when she was actually going to the beach. Her dad gave permission and she went out.

She was really happy and saw her friends playing basketball at the beach, so she joined them too. She was having a fun time until John threw a ball into the sea by accident.

"Who will get it?" said Mia.

Julia shouted, "I will!" and she jumped in the sea but she couldn't swim and started drowning.

"Oh no!" Emily quickly ran to her mum and told her everything. Her mum called the lifeguards and ambulance who saved her from drowning. Julia's parents were very disappointed with her and when she was better, they scolded her a lot for telling lie. Then they hugged and kissed her too, for they were happy that their daughter was safe. They gave a present to Emily and her mum for saving Julia.

Julia never went to the beach without her parents again.

Aarvi Gupta

Dear Diary

Dear Diary,

One sunny day, I woke up and got dressed to go to the forest. When we arrived, there was no one there. So me and my friend, Gorilla, went into the deep, dark forest.

When we were in the deep, dark forest, we heard a twig snap. "Oh no, is it a fox?"

"Don't be silly, it''s probably a bird looking for worms."

"Look at those chickens," said Gorilla. "Aren't they cute?"

"Nonsense, there is no time for chickens!"

Gorilla and I went and saw a snake. "Is it poisonous?" asked Gorilla.

"Hmmm, no, its eyes are not like a cat's."

Then Gorilla and I went home because we were both so tired.

Dion Pickett (8)

Superhero

My superhero name is Black Knight. My superhero powers are: invisibility, claws, electricity and pausing people. Also, I use them at the same time. I try to defeat villains but they always escape (that means there are going to be consequences).

One day, I was on my CCTV camera, seeing if there was anybody being bad. I saw a villain smashing a man's car window and I was quickly catching him by pausing him with powers. Then... I finally caught him. I took him to the king and my reward was jewels and 50,000,000 bags of gold. The punishment for the villain was to be a prisoner for 5,000 years.

The king was happy with me and said, "Thank you for always saving people when they need help."

Jayad Sayham (7)

A Sunny Adventure To The Funfair

Today on a sunny day I went with my class on a trip to the funfair in Hampstead Heath. Everyone was excited, especially me and my partner. Suddenly, a little green alien approached me and pulled my jumper saying, "Hey, what is your name?" I was shocked and petrified at what I saw. He told me that he wanted to join the rides with me. My partner and me took the alien to the roller coaster and he really enjoyed it. We went on a different one and we ate candyfloss. Zing the alien asked me what time was it as he needed to go to space. He waved to me and he thanked me for the kindness and the great time he had. He rushed to the flying saucer and I saw it swishing into the sky. What a lively trip.

Isla Socol

Nobody Knows

The slender woman slowly tilts her head and as you blink she gets closer and closer but for some reason, you can't move. Then she taps you on the shoulder and you fall down, down, down into the forever pit of darkness. Suddenly, horns, devils, fire! You realise you are in Hell. The woman up there says, "Bye-bye!"
Suddenly, your eyes pop out of your head, your ears pop out too, your head turns left to right then falls off. Next your arms are torn off, you fall off, your legs are ripped off and your feet are dislocated until there is nothing.
Did you survive? No one knows why you went to Hell and no one knows who the woman is...

Lucie Vu Le

The Grandad Who Loved Food

Grandad loves food! Every fantastic combination of starter, main and dessert is his favourite. The only time he's not munching is when he is fast asleep catching the zzzs. Although in saying that, when he's sleeping he is always dreaming of his next bite.

On Grandad's 69th birthday, instead of opening any presents, he plonked himself at the breakfast table ready for an all-day feast!

On one particular night, Grandad was dreaming about eating a giant toasted marshmallow. When he woke up in the morning, his pillow was gone! It's funny how Grandad keeps burping feathers now from time to time!

Harley Lloyd (11)

Dear Diary

I went horse riding with my horse, Cheeky. She rode a bit slow but we were okay. She was amazing and I went, "Wheeeee!" because we were trotting up a mountain, she went down the mountain really fast.

"Her saddle is so pretty," I said to the person who looked after and she said she was beautiful and pretty. She said she knew Cheeky was one of the rarest in the world.

I said, "Giddy up!" and pulled the rein down. She went really fast and jumped over a fence on the road ahead. She saw a unicorn. Cheeky and the unicorn got married and had a baby horse and a baby unicorn.

Caitlin Fairhead (8)

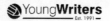

A New Beginning

The glistening stars twinkled in my eyes as I was seeing hope in deep black. In the night sky, it was filled up with bombastic blue stars. Then, the big firework display was filling up the luminous black like it had never been. Blinding my vision were outstanding flickers, swirling stars and exclusively bright blue beams. They were dropping hope. It was beautiful because of the happiness it sprayed. There were frozen fireworks and time started again amongst the raindrops of stars. As they were starting life again, the stars were dazzling more than ever in the deepest, darkest places.

Manny Sampson

Why Now?

Everything is going wrong all around me. 'The Apocalypse' is what everyone is calling it. There's screaming from every rooftop, garden and on every television. People shouting, "It's coming, we can't stop it."

Just last week it was peaceful, no one was screaming from every rooftop, no one was screaming from their garden, nor was there a word from any television news station. So what happened? How did we get here? Should I have known about this? These are all questions I have been asking myself, along with the new question in my mind... Why now...?

Ella McInnes (12)

Lost But Never Forgotten

Once there was a girl called Ruby, she was five and she had an older brother called Max. One day, Ruby came home without Max so she ran inside, asking her mum where he went. Her mum said, "You will find out soon."

Years passed, Ruby still hadn't seen her brother but she hadn't stopped looking, she was seventeen years old. She ended up going to an abandoned house. Walking around... *bang!* She saw a shadow and stared at it like she hadn't opened her eyes in years. Her face turned as white as snow. "Max?" she whispered. The man nodded.

Amie Ward (15)

Scar The Lion

My name is Scar, I am a lion but I am not scary. I'm kind and a little crazy! My best friend is a mouse called Henry. All the other lions make fun of me but Henry loves me and tells me his secrets. He makes me happy. We have been best friends for as long as we can remember. He tells me I am beautiful and he is too. He is very tiny but very bossy! He is very sweet and we play hide-and-seek. Henry always wins, hahaha! I wouldn't change a thing, as long as I have Henry as my friend. So, I'm not a scary scar-faced lion, I'm just Scar, a crazy but very lucky lion.

Maddison Mitchell (9)

Sizzall, The Rainforest Snake

My first day in the rainforest, I found a tiny snake and I named him Sizzall. Sizzall was red with lots of attitude, but he was very sweet. Sizzall slept in my boots, when I wasn't wearing them of course! He showed me around. I met some of his friends, some were spiders, ants and butterflies.
I had so much fun in the rainforest but soon it was time to go home. I would miss Sizzall and all of his friends. We said farewell and bye-bye, see you again. He was sad but knew the day had to end.
I got home and wait, what was in my boot? Sizzall, the rainforest snake!

Lexi Mitchell (8)

Dear NHS And Keyworkers

I am a student in the RPS (Ranelagh Primary School, Ipswich). Me and others are really grateful for what you are doing for people who are harmed or injured. So I am writing this thank you letter for your hard work and for healing these innocent people. So thank you so much! I know this letter isn't much, unlike a bunch of flowers, but I am writing with a bunch of love. So I'm very sorry. But just to let you know you guys will always have a place in my heart. When I grow up I want to become a part of the NHS. I love you, NHS!
Yours sincerely,
Prathika J.

Prathika J

The Spicy Meatball

Once upon a time, Poppy, Scarlet and Amanda lived in the crystal wood. They made their way to the shop to buy ingredients for dinner. When they got there, the shop was destroyed.

"OMG!" shouted Scarlet to Amanda and Poppy. "Yesterday, I went to the shops and it was all nice and clean. What happened?"

A puff of smoke appeared and a meatball rolled out. It said, "Don't eat me. I'm a spicy meatball and my sauce is on fire!"

Amanda didn't listen. She took a big bite out of the meatball and had lots of farts all night!

Kearna Blake

Abracadabra

Once upon a time, on a wet and dull day, all of my teddies, Pink Blossom, Bluebelle, Bloomy and Truce, sat on the shiny table watching me. They loved me and wanted to see where I went all day. So, they decided to follow me... Well they must have followed me because my teacher thought she heard footsteps and giggling in the corridor.
At break time, they made a bad decision. They went outside where they found a stick covered with pink, sparkly glitter, but it was actually a fairy's wand! "Abracadabra!" they said and turned in to real-life people!

Holly Blaney (7)

The Crazy Robot Who Lost Its Bum And A Super Raptor Who Saved The World

Two hundred years ago, there was a lonely robot.
He travelled back in time to find a friend.
While he was discovering the view, he went into the lake, as he was boiling.
Suddenly, a piranha came and bit his bum off!
The robot went crazy, running into the forest he saw a raptor.
He captured the raptor, making him into a superpower machine.
The robot had an idea, to destroy time. The raptor decided to use his powers, by running in circles around the robot, making him faint.
He had stopped the robot from splitting the world in half.

Jake Evans (8)

Gangsta Carrot

The carrot they all know! The carrot they all nearly ate is the baddest carrot alive! It's not only the baddest but it's the nicest looking carrot around that everyone could want. The carrot that we call Ganster Carrot is hiding away and no one knows where but he is the only carrot left in the town and everyone wants a roast dinner! This carrot has stolen all the potatoes and, most importantly, all the meat in the town! This carrot must be found! This is two-year-old Timmy's opinion, "Waaaaaahh!" Will Gangster Carrot ever be stopped?

Lacey Shepherd (11)

The Mermaid Quest

Long ago, there were two children called Zac and Ruby. One day, on TV they saw a mermaid 'fin-print' track. They asked Mum if they could go to find it.

When they entered the dark forest, it was freakishly massive! In the woods, they met Hannah, the kind, friendly bat. She said the mermaid was back in the magic ocean. They felt excited but worried because they might get lost.

They set off on the journey to the magic ocean. Finally, they found her and made very good friends. Yay! They rowed off into the sunset on her pet dolphins.

Marci Randle (8)

Food Forest

One night in the forest the fluffy koala couldn't sleep. Everyone was asleep but he was bored. He decided to go on an adventure. He went around the hills till he couldn't walk anymore then in the distance he saw a weird-looking tree. He went towards it, it was a marshmallow. Then he saw more of them and the grass was turning into cheese. He pinched himself, he couldn't believe it, then he saw biscuit animals.

They went together and had so much fun bouncing on marshmallows and eating pizza toppings. The koala fell asleep on cheese hay.

Poppy Dormer (10)

Amelia The Reindeer

Once upon a time, there was a reindeer called Amelia and she wanted to be one of Santa's reindeer. One foggy Christmas, Santa went delivering presents when all of a sudden his sleigh broke. Amelia saw and went to fix it when Santa wasn't looking. After Amelia fixed it, she left a note on Santa's sleigh which read: I fixed your sleigh, Santa! From Amelia.

Afterwards, Amelia became one of Santa's reindeer! She felt so happy she went to the North Pole and Santa said, "Come on, we have to deliver the rest of the presents!"

Amelia-Rose Mansie (7)

Trapped

I have trapped her finally. After years and years of trying I have got her in my living room! She is about to get a taste of her own medicine! Only ten more minutes until I get my revenge, in the meantime I will go check on her. "Why would you do this to me?" she screams.

"The same reason you did it to me," I say testingly. Finally, it is time. I undo the lid in my pocket, pull out my gun and point it at her. "Any last words?"

"Yes," she says with a smirk. "Look behind you..."

Molly Mackay

The Battle Of World War One

The LMGs and miniguns were shooting down on the enemies like thunder shooting on you. Fighter Flier One is using a minigun in an army helicopter. Bob is in a trench, shooting people to their death. Bob is a destroyer because he used rocket torches to destroy tanks. The tanks are made of strong metal and they shoot out bullets which kill you easily. Bob is hiding in a trench and shooting people. Fighter Flier One is up in the air and his helicopter is getting shot at and blown up. After the battle, Bob is looking over the enveloped graves.

George Standlick (9)

The Crazy Wizard

On the top of a mountain, called Crazy Wavy, there stood a bizarre castle, and it was said that a crazy wizard lived there. The castle was old and it was surrounded by nature. There was a village at the bottom of the mountain and from there you could see a strange light through the castle's windows. No one knew what would happen in the castle until one day a group of brave young people decided to go up the mountain to solve the mystery. They discovered that the wizard was the guardian of the village. He was the protector!

Jessica Fernandes (9)

Dear Diary

Yesterday I went to the zoo with my family. I saw the elephants, tigers, lions, meerkats, chimpanzees, orangutans, giraffes and zebras. The elephants were funny, one lifted up their trunk and got the straw. I laughed and laughed. Next was the meerkats. I loved the meerkats but I loved the elephants best. Next was the giraffes, I loved the giraffes better than the meerkats but I loved the elephants better. Next was the orangutans. I liked the orangutans more than all of them but my favourite animal in the zoo was the elephant.

Harry Deeks (7)

The Hamburgers That Did Not Want To Be Eaten

Once upon a time, there were two hamburgers in the butcher's window. One hamburger said to the other, "I wish we could go on holiday together." Then a lady came into the shop and bought the two of them.

Half an hour later, they were in her fridge. They looked at each other and one said, "I wanted a holiday, but not in Alaska! I wanted somewhere hot."

An hour later, the lady put them under the grill. They were very happy because now they were in Spain but still they did not want to be eaten.

James Doren

The Secret Of Dolphin Academy

Once upon a time there was a dolphin called Dawin, it's a Spanish name. Dawin had no friends. But then Dawin went through some seaweed and then he was now in a Dolphin Academy. They had different dolphins. But there were two dolphins called Bite and Rotty. They were mean dolphins. But Spark, Whiz, Corizon and Noah and Deagow were nice. They even played trickball. Trickball is a class where you can show off your tricks with a ball like balancing it on your nose. Corizon and Bite ended up in a big prank war. Corizon won!

Maisie Sue (9)

Missing

The place was empty. The streets were so scarce and quiet you could hear a pin drop. It was dark, I was all alone, you could see my breath in the air and my teeth chattering with the cold but I couldn't stay in anymore. Lockdown was hard, my mind racing with a thousand thoughts - classwork, homework, the news. All too much to take in! I was scared, but scared of what? Staying in or catching the virus! The only thing I knew of to escape it was to run! I needed time and by now my parents would notice I was missing...

Megan Murphy (13)

The Farting Unicorn

One peculiar day, I was doing my ridiculous homework, that I hated. While I was doing my dumb homework, I smelt a loathsome smell so I looked towards where the smell was coming from. I saw a farting, mythical unicorn and it stunk the whole house. I said to the unicorn, "Why are you farting?"

The unicorn replied, "I don't know."

"Why don't you fly back?" I asked.

The unicorn flew back to where he came from. After a while, the repugnant smell disappeared into the vast, bright day.

Krish Wagjiani (10)

The Hockey Sticks Dimension!

As I was looking for the equipment in the shed, I opened the cupboard. I was in a new dimension! I got the hockey balls and left. When I got out, then I saw the hockey sticks were humans, including my coach! When the hockey sticks spotted me, I ran, but the hockey sticks chased me into the changing rooms! I was surrounded, but there were vents. I opened the vent and crawled into the lounge. I opened the door and ran to the shed and I looked and looked for the cupboard until I found it and left.

Zach Varney

Pizza And Football

One day a cat found an old football in a garden with pizza slices on it. The pizza slices were rotten. The next day the cat was still playing with the old football. The pizza was still there. The cat was scratching the ball then it started to rain so the cat ran in the house, then it stopped raining so the car went out and started playing again. He was playing with it all night. In the morning he went inside and went to sleep all day. Then at night he played with it again. He was tired though.

Jack Chalmers (12)

Dogphin

Once upon a time, there was a dog called Kaleesi who was a Dalmatian. Her owner Miley took her to SeaWorld water park because no one could look after her and Miley had to work.

While Miley was busy, Kaleesi snuck away and found a cove. She saw a dolphin and bit it. The dolphin was not hurt. When Kaleesi and Miley got home, they went to bed.

In the morning, when Kaleesi had a bath, she turned into a dogphin and when she got out and dry, she turned back to a dog until the next bath.

Angel Glover

My Baby Brother

Mummy went to the hospital yesterday and she brought a baby home. Daddy named him Adam. They told me he was my new baby brother. He is always crying for something. Sometimes for milk, sometimes for a dummy and sometimes for a nappy change. Yuck!
He doesn't talk or play with me. All he does is lie down, he is very lazy. Mummy and Daddy say when he is older he will talk and play. I just think he is very naughty. I would rather have a sister, I know she would be good, just like me.

Ayesha Imtinan

Missing Mind

Why can't I remember? Why couldn't I just be missing? It's like I am missing a very important thing in me. Well, it is true but still I feel empty, alone, like I don't have anything. Not even a family member to help me and that I am very sure of. The only thing I remember is that they died... Every single one! Only I'm alive. Why can I only remember that? I am not sure and I hate it! Even if I remember, I won't have the ones who care about me and my dead family.

Amelie Pilfold (12)

The Girl That Had An Alive Doll

Once there lived a girl who had a doll. Her doll was so creepy because of her face. One morning at 3am, the doll rolled her eyes and head. The girl that was called Maria was scared when she saw her doll doing those things. Maria wondered why such a thing would happen to her. She said, "Why? I don't get it." The doll nodded her head.
The next day, Maria found out that her doll actually had electric batteries and that's how she found out that her doll was alive!

Andreea Robu (9)

The Evil Lady

Why are there gates if nothing is out there? There is an evil lady who creeps and takes and she is very dangerous. That's why she has to have gates so she can't get out! She screams so very loudly and she is a bad person. You don't want to go near her, oh no! If you see her you need to run and very fast! Like I said she is very dangerous. Where we are right now is dangerous so I think we should leave this place, don't you? Let's go now before it's too late...

Summer Taylor (11)

The Missing Mother

I woke up quickly to a massive bang. I ran to see my mum but she wasn't there. The window was open and she was gone. I saw a note that said: 'If you dare call the cops you'll never see light again'. Then I saw drops of blood. I followed it and it stopped by a cave but the cave was locked. Suddenly, a tunnel appeared. I went down to the end. I saw a massive shadow and I heard death happen. Then the shadow was gone. I then ran and saw her on a wall covered in blood.

Archie Scott (12)

The Evil Pizza

There once was an evil scientist that created all evil things. He wanted to visit his son who was a baker. So he packed all of his stuff and went to Riverdale. When he got there his son's face lit up like a firework. They hugged and had a sausage roll and when he sat down one of his vials smashed and spilt on to a pizza. It came to life. It stood up and ran and threw stuff at people's faces. Then it got trapped in a corner with one kid called Marley and gulp it went.

Liam O'Brien

Evil Football

This mum is very, very dumb, she tried to eat a size 5 football. She got it into her mouth, the football was so excited. There is something you do not know, the football was evil. So when the football made it in, it ate to the throat. When he made it there he had a rest because his belly was full of course. When he was ready to pounce the evil football pounced and got stuck in the throat. The mum was choking and the evil football started to laugh. Mum's son cried sadly.

Isaac Miskelly

World War 3

I woke up and I heard that a war was going on. I went to have breakfast then I went to my army base. I heard a gargantuan explosion. I got kidnapped! I went to their base and had to tell them where my base was. I escaped and my friends got ready for war. We got our sneaky snipers and our measly machine-guns. We put out protective vests on. The war was bedroom vs staircase. Bedroom was the good guys and staircase, where the bad guys were advancing from, won after many years.

Raphael Cohen

The Flaming Penguin

One day, the flaming penguin was sad so he got really mad. He screamed and screamed until a toilet fell on a lad. Penguins fought and got mad. The flaming penguin found a bunker with a rocket. "Eww that smells like poo." On the rocket it said 'Poop rocket destroy penguins'. The penguins made a wall out of pink poop and it fell on the rocket and it flew in the sea. But that's not all, the man with the toilet fell on a penguin and blasted into the sky.

Lucca Whybrow

A Part Of Me Was Gone

A part of me was missing. The last thing I remember was that I was on a plane. Suddenly, the plane stopped. I felt a huge whoosh. My heart dropped to my stomach. We were going down... I couldn't feel any part of me and suddenly, *crash, bang!* We hit the ground. All I saw was darkness, nothing at all.

I woke up in a hospital. I couldn't move a muscle. Then I noticed that a part of me was missing...

Chelsea Williams (13)

Dear Diary

Today I went to the beach and I had a picnic. The beach had a pirate ship, it was amazing. I went there but it wasn't as fun as I thought and my mum and dad came too. My dad played football with me. It was awesome when we got ice cream. Mum had strawberry, Dad had caramel and I had bubblegum. After we had finished we had a burger before going home.

Taiden Osarumen Eboikpomwen (8)

Dear Diary

Today, Saturday, I went to Camden Town. I saw famous stuff. I was interested in the rings, they had animals. Then I got a toy, it was Star Wars, then we went home and I played with my new toy. Then we ate dinner and we had roasted chicken.

Huseyin Ozaydin (8)

Dear Diary

Today I had porridge for breakfast then I went swimming. After that, I walked to Abington Park and went on four old buses. The poles were as white as a cloud. The trees were crashing against the window. The buses went to Moulton Park.

Joe Paul Thomas (8)

Dear Diary

I went to the fair with my uncle and I went on fast rides. I ate candyfloss. On the way home, we stopped for ice cream.

Lewis James Cole

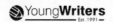

The Incredible Diary Of... Portal Secrets That Make You Rude!

Dear Diary,

This morning, at 20 minutes past 6, I woke up and started reading my favourite book 'Dork Diaries'. I was still in my favourite pyjamas because they were so comfy. I finally got up and opened my curtains, but before I could do that, a sparkle of dust just flew out behind the curtains. It was very unusual to me but all of a sudden, my phone rang from an unknown number. Without thinking, I just answered it. The hairs on the back of my neck stood up when no one answered.

Suddenly, something whispered behind me, "Audery!" Then there appeared a portal. I had seen a portal before but not like this one! It was dark purple and had yellow moons and stars. I was not petrified, scared or confused and then I heard a click and something popped into my head.

"I recognise this portal!" I shrieked.

My mum came running up the stairs and I told her everything was alright, but it wasn't!

"Audery," something whispered behind me again.
Without thinking, I jumped into the portal.
"Yipeee!" I yelled as loud as possible.
I landed in a meadow but I didn't know which one.
I had seen so many meadows but not any like this before!
The portal was still there, it hadn't gone away.
Suddenly, a wizard came with a tall hat, a long beard, a purple gown and a wand with dark secrets.
"My dear!" he roared.
I stuck my tongue out and spat at him. "What a rude girl!" he giggled.
I stomped off annoyed, I was still in the meadow.
Then I jumped back into the portal and that's how I became rude. This secret cannot be told!

Aiman Ghisa (10)
Audley Junior School, Blackburn

My Horrible Life

Dear Diary,

I woke up today at 3am, realising that today was my first day of school. I am very shy I didn't want to be late for my first day at school so I ate an apple for breakfast and then I quickly set off.

Dear Diary,

I absolutely hated my first day of school! There is this mean girl called Samantha and she kept on bullying me and calling me names. No one at school likes me and they call me the 'poor girl'. It's true, my parents are poor and they keep screaming and fighting with each other. I'm just a kid so I can't do much!

Dear Diary,

Today wasn't much better because in history my teacher, Mr Malone, told me to share a desk with... Samantha! Samantha groaned but Mr Malone didn't hear. At playtime, Samantha and her gang of friends kept on following me and then when I wasn't looking, she pushed me and I fell on my face. Of course, they all just ran away giggling and I didn't bother telling the teacher. I just ran away, tears filling my eyes.

I ran out of the school gates and onto the road. Then I saw a car zooming towards me. I tried to run but it was too late. The car zoomed past, leaving me covered in blood. I am now at the hospital. I will never forget this day!

Zahrah Waqas (10)

Audley Junior School, Blackburn

Hero... To... Villain

One lazy day a moany superhero called Spagheto was very lazy. "Crime alert! Crime alert!"
"Oh be quiet."
"Crime alert! Crime alert!"
"Ugh! Fine I'll do my job. Ugh, I hate being a superhero."
Finally Spageto was going her job. Meanwhile...
"Hahaha finally I can rule the world, haha!"
"Iona is so lucky. Wait a second... I'll be a villain! My name is... umm... Lazyato! Hahaha!"
Now Iona and Lazyato are partners in crime. They are very evil, but now she is not lazy anymore, which was good. Now they work together in crime.

Lauren Robertson (9)
Bankton Primary School, Dedridge

The Gangsta Foot

Once upon a particular time there was an angry gangsta foot. His name was Kicky because he liked to kick other feet 100 times a day. Some, I mean everyone doesn't like him, not even a teeny weeny bit. So he became very very sad. He said sorry but did not care. It happened again and again and you know what I mean. But somehow he became best friends with another foot and he became friendly and polite. Good news, he is not an angry gansta anymore and he stopped kicking other feet. He changed his name to Nicefoot. Yay!

Misha Goswami (10)
Bankton Primary School, Dedridge

The Poorly Dude

Bobby was in the doctor's because he was ill. People thought he had the dreadful Coronavirus, the truth was there was a person who had it in his teeny tiny town. Not a single person knew who it was. He saw his brother because he was a doctor and it turned out he had the dreaded Coronavirus! Now everyone knew who had it. Just to check, Bobby's brother took a test to see if he had the awful, dreaded, unforgettable Coronavirus. Oh no! He had the Coronavirus! He then went to his home and isolated for two weeks.

Ben Davidson (9)
Bankton Primary School, Dedridge

The Jealous Robot

A factory makes ten robots but one of the robots gets jealous because he wants to be the only robot in the world. His name was Jimmy but Jim for short. Jimmy saw one of the robots coming. He grabbed the robot and threw the robot and the robot died. Jimmy knew there were eight more to get rid of. As he defeated more and more there were only two more robots to defeat. Once he defeated the rest the factory members noticed and made Jimmy a ninja robot to protect the factory for good, to stop all the thieves.

Hannah McNee (9)
Bankton Primary School, Dedridge

Doctor Vs Magician

There was once a super magical scientist called Magicist who said, "When there is a crime, call me." But then one day in Mootropolis was an evil boring doctor who called himself Bortor. He wanted all magic gone. He said magic is not real so Magicist threw a bunny at him which threw him in a teleporter to China! He and Magicist fell off a house which was where the mage was on holiday. She then hit the villain away never to be seen again. To reward him they gave Magicist new magic stuff.

Caleb Craig (10)
Bankton Primary School, Dedridge

The Toilet Block

There was a toilet, his name was Toilet Block. He lived in a toilet shop and he wasn't used. When the shop closed he went to the toilet in the restroom because no one flushes, it's like a bog in there. So he takes the poo or wee and puts in in himself. The next day someone bought him and he was clean, so when the guy buys him he's happy in life and he will always enjoy it forever. But he doesn't get flushed so he is even more happy for his poopy little life.

Cye Buchan (9)
Bankton Primary School, Dedridge

The Forgetful Chef

One magical evening, a forgetful chef made a pizza with some spoilt ingredients. While serving the pizza a slight movement came along. Suddenly the pizza made a quick escape towards the door and entered the crowded city. It galloped to the nearest restaurant to recruit other foods like burgers, fries, chicken and more. They charged down the rocky road and you know it, they didn't look left or right so they made an oopsy. At least blobs of their food were still there.

Femme Mangala (10)
Bankton Primary School, Dedridge

Poachers!

"Finally," sighed Cheat as she strolled along the crooked woods. "But where am I now?" She carried on going through the woods and soon realised it was a jungle. "This isn't my home!" she said in confusion. "All I wanted to do was catch that gazelle! What is this place anyway?" she said. "At least I can't see any lions around. Ouch!" she said, as she carelessly walked into a tree, with vines that could kill any human walking past.

A net wrapped around the tree and Cheat soon realised that she was being chased by a poacher. "What is he doing here?" Cheat was running as fast as her legs would go. She was running and running, trying to dodge all of the bullets that ran past her face. "Why is a human here, in the jungle?" she cried.

She ran and ran without a break until she realised something had changed.

At last, she was safe and unharmed. Cheat had finally run away from the poachers, luckily without a scratch.

Cheat ran home and found her cheetah family safe and then told them her story.

Lilia Wingate (10)
Winsford High Street CP School, Winsford

The IESR Mission

As the sky darkened, an adventurous trio called Kate, Derek and Tom were getting ready to go on an important mission to rescue endangered species. They worked for the IESR (International Endangered Species Rescue). They were dashing around getting the last bits of gear and supplies. Eventually, they hopped on to their plane, with their hearts beating rapidly. What would the newly discovered island be like? Would they complete their mission? It was now time to find out! The runway was clear, it was time for take-off...

After a very long journey halfway across the world, they had finally made it! What first caught their eye was a large volcano in the distance. Surrounding it were bendy palm trees, but no sign of endangered species. They began their search in the spectacular jungle. As they stumbled over bumpy roots and winding, elongated vines, coconuts and beautiful flowers dropped from archways of twisted branches, but still no sign of any animals.

Continuing on through the jungle of obstacles saw Kate sinking in quicksand, Tom rescuing her, dodging poisonous snakes and terrifyingly huge spiders. Soon, they came to a clearing, where monkeys were playfully swinging on vines and hopping between stones across little streams.

Further in the distance, resting high up in the trees were a family of critically endangered birds named Kiku's. Just what they were searching for! However that wasn't all, right in front of their eyes were a group of yellow pandas and zigzag leopards roaming the jungle too.

Somehow they needed to figure out a way to get the species back to IESR headquarters. But how? Tom's idea was to call the crew back at the edge of the island. He told them to bring as many transportation cages as possible and soon! So the trio waited for hours and hours. Finally, they arrived!

As the multiple moons exchanged places with the sun in the azure sky, they started to head back as it was getting late. Suddenly, there was a loud bang from behind them. Kate was the first to notice. "What's that?" she asked worryingly.

"What?" asked Derek, confused.

"Th-th-that... n-n-noise!" stuttered Kate, now shaking. Derek and Tom turned around.

"Oh my goodness! Run! Now! Get the animals and go, go, go!" bellowed Derek.

"Wow!" exclaimed Tom in absolute shock. The volcano was erupting, they needed to get off the island quickly as lava was cascading down and destroying the whole island. The lava was getting

closer and closer... would they get off the island in time?

Before they knew it, they were on the plane heading to the headquarters, leaving the devastation of the island's destruction behind them.

Upon arrival they were greeted and congratulated by the rest of the IESR team and presented with the 'Rescuers of the Year Award' for saving the endangered species. Years later they are known as the 'Brave IESR Trio' for their bravery and courage during the mission, leading them to fame.

Sophia Buckley (10)
Winsford High Street CP School, Winsford

Shopping

As the sun edged to its middle, James' mum gathered up some noisy bags for shopping. Meanwhile, James was playing on his Xbox when he heard some shopping bags bashing together. What could this mean? Was his mum going shopping? Whatever it was, James was interested so he went downstairs.

"Mum," he asked. "Can I go shopping with you?"

"Sure," replied Mum.

"Yippee!" James exclaimed. If there was one thing James loved more than video games, it was shopping.

When they got to the shop, James went to look for his mother but she wasn't there. "Mum?" he said, clueless where she was.

He then began to run down the street when he heard a voice. "Stop!" they said, from a distance. James was scared and hid behind a car.

A little while later, James peered round the corner of the car, hoping it was all a dream... "Mum!" he screamed and ran towards her.

When they got back home, James ran straight to the Xbox and played and played.

Toby Walker (10)
Winsford High Street CP School, Winsford

Adventure To Gold City

Damp, wet, sticky, gooey tree sap lay on the hard trees like sinking sand. Leaves jumped through the air, trees waved in the wind. "Good morning Tom," whispered Dad.

Dad and Tom marched into the jungle. "Squawk to you Mr Bird!" said Dad. Fluttering and flapping birds guided them as their beautiful wings fluttered and their fluffy feathers fell to the floor. Suddenly, the forest opened up like a window. Stretching in front of Tom was a vast, deep river. "How are we going to get across that?" said Dad. "Look what I found Dad!" screamed Tom; he'd found an old, rusty boat. They pushed and pulled as they conquered the rapids.

They reached Gold City. "It's breath-taking!" said Tom.

"Yes, it is," said Dad. The shining, glimmering golden buildings glittered in the hot jungle sun. Dad and Tom left the boat and started their expedition into Gold City. "You know the plan, Tom?" said Dad excitedly.

"Yes, according to the map, the golden globe is in the centre of the city," replied Tom.

After Tom and Dad walked miles to get to the centre of the city, they reached a blocked off passageway. After trying to push it open with all their might, they eventually realised that they had to find clues scattered around the city to open the passageway.

Exhausted, they set back off to hunt for the clues. After unbearable hours searching for clues, they finally found the first clue to open the passageway that would lead them to the golden globe.

They set off for the next clue as birds flew over them. As the ground rumbled, a gigantic wall emerged from under it. Rocks tumbled and fell, Dad and Tom swiftly dodged and swerved them. After they defeated the tumbling rocks, Tom asked Dad, "Are we going to overcome the challenges to obtain the golden globe?" Dad said, "The next clue isn't far from here, we should get moving before nightfall."

Dad and Tom continued their quest and found another clue in a spiky pit. "How are we going to get down there?" Dad exclaimed.

Tom said, "If you hold my feet tightly I think I can reach, Dad." Tom managed to grab the clue with Dad's help.

There was one final clue to find. Dad and Tom ventured into a cave to find the clue but the water was rising fast around them! Tom spotted the clue from the corner of his eye and grabbed it. They found a way out of the cave and headed back to the centre of the city.

The clues helped Dad and Tom to solve the puzzle and the passageway opened up. It led them into a dark room with a shiny, glimmering globe held on a stand. Both Dad and Tom said, "Hooray, we did it!" as they smiled and cheerfully hugged each other.

Isaac Johnson (10)
Winsford High Street CP School, Winsford

Untitled

As the scarlet moon rose into the sky, the rusty door opened in front of the abandoned school. Liv could smell the mould going around the school. She could feel the air and the spiders crawling around her body and it felt yucky. She could see the police coming into the abandoned scary, smelling school so she had to hide.

There was a weird smell but Liv thought it was still the mould so she covered her nose with her top and then Liv realised that it was some old books that were smelling. She had really red rashes on her face and her clothes were ripped because the ghost ripped them. "Hello my name is Liv and I have dull clothes on and different clothes."

The reason she went there was because she was looking for ghosts. Liv liked them and really wanted to look for them. But someone was dressed up as a policeman but it was fake. Liv wasn't very happy because he was chasing her. After she finished searching for five hours she finally finished looking for her ghosts and said, "Get me out of here!"

Zara Briggs (10)
Winsford High Street CP School, Winsford

The Journey

After a long autumn morning, there was a young happy boy walking quickly through the forest. A misty haze began to form under the canopy of the swaying, rugged trees. What was this place? The ugly, vile branches swung side to side in the wind. The boy walked through an unknown forest. Suddenly, the dust, grit and grime drifted from the archways, created by the curving branches which overshadowed the dimming forest. The hideous, revolting trees stretched up to the sky. The trees disagreed with the horrible weather as they danced around in the stormy wind. The ground was like a sad, miserable smashed monster. The vines wrapped around the trees as tight as a boa constrictor.

As Max went through the forest, on his way to the jungle, he saw an unbelievable oak tree swaying around the scary, strong wind. The obnoxious, anxious ground lifted up as Max walked on it. On top of this Max was at the end of the forest and walking to the airport.

Finally, he got there after fourteen miles. Max went to the lounge area and sat down. Unfortunately, he dropped his ticket and so did somebody else. They picked them up but got the wrong ticket.

Suddenly, Max boarded the wrong plane but he thought he was on the right one. He couldn't find his suitcase because he was on the departure. He waited for his real flight so he met up with the man and they swapped tickets. They boarded the correct plane.

After an eight hour delay, on the plane, Max found a jungle specialist that could help him find the rare, hairy monkey. Suddenly, he told him that the best way to get one was to give him two special things: peanut butter and bananas. So he found some on the plane and bought them. All he needed to do was land on the ground.

Suddenly, Max felt a slight bump as they were high in the air. After many more bumps, Max was fed up. Max then saw a furry, fluffy creature in the distance. It crept forward quicker and quicker. Unfortunately, Max saw the creepy monster come out of the first-class part. The creepy monster was a dog, panting like mad. Its owner was asleep. The dog was hungry so he went into first-class and got the dog's treats off the owner. His owner was a man and he was a good sleeper. Max woke him up and told him that his dog was out of control.

Max was devastated when he said that he didn't care. He had to handle it himself. Max got the treats and went to the dog and was shocked as the dog was gone. Max realised he needed to find him.

"Yay!" he said. Max found him and gave him treats. Max returned the dog back to his rightful owner.

Finally, they had landed and Max was so relieved he got off the plane and went to the jungle...

Lily Griffin (10)
Winsford High Street CP School, Winsford

Schoolday

Hi, my name is Kate. I was five years old when I started my first day at school. I was scared. My uniform was a skirt, top and tie. I looked cute and I got in the car and my mum was telling me all the top tips.

I got out of the car and saw my teacher. I saw children. I wanted to run and I did. I ran down the street and I found myself lost in an alleyway. It was dark, it was eerie, it was spooky.

As I ran, I came across some posters that had my name on them. I started to worry. I saw my school teacher out looking for something or someone. I ran up to her and she said, "Where have you been?"

"Umm, I have been trying to find my mum," I shouted.

"Oh, your mum is at school," said my teacher. "Follow me."

"Okay," I yelled.

I saw my mum. She was happy to see me. We went in the car and I had my lunch while my mum drove us home. My mum then made me some dinner and told me a bedtime story. I will never make that mistake again.

Kate Robinson (11)
Winsford High Street CP School, Winsford

The Board Game Adventure

One day, Emily, Tommy and Lucy went to the park
to have a salubrious meal. They took a board
game, which would help with their learning. The
wind blew the crisp bag away as Tommy bit into a
delicious, crunchy sandwich! As the hallow trees
surrounded them, the autumn leaves crunched
each step they took. Dangling down from the
layers of moss, bold leaves flickered like flames in
the growing bluster of winds. Dust, grit and grime
created curving branches that shadowed over the
tarmac floor. The unfamiliar plants pranced and
twisted as the creak and squeak of the swings that
swung like a monkey. What was this place? Why
did it catch the corner of my eye? So unnerving!
However, the weirdest of all sights was how they
opened the game. It blew a whistle of white, mist
that jumped up to reach the children. The screams
scared the birds away. Unexpectedly, Emily,
Tommy and Lucy disappeared into the cold,
blustery air. Where did they go? Are they magic?
Will they ever come back? They felt vulnerable as
they all stood lost and engulfed in the strange
setting! The place was truly special but in the
wrong way. The damp saturated ground stood

below brown, elongated tree trunks. Flickered leaves twirled and danced through the cloudy wind.

Instantaneously, Emily, Tommy and Lucy came across some angry-looking sleeping lions, who lay beneath the trees on the damp floor. Not all of the creatures would have wanted to be woken. At that moment, all the lions circled them. They had to face them. Scared, they all stood looking for a plan. In the corner of Tommy's eye, he spotted a bamboo stick and quickly grabbed it. They all ran and made a hole to escape...

As they walked through the forest, the clouds swirled above them and started to become darker. Suddenly, a huge storm appeared in the distance. Leaves fell to the ground as the wind swooped through the sky! How did the storm even appear so quickly? As a few seconds passed, it was flooding and there was no shelter to cover them. A strip of thunder bellowed in the sky. The dirty water nearly made them drown. A gush of wind below a few logs in front of them, which gave Lucy an idea! Lucy pulled some string to tie the two logs together. They all sat on the logs and felt relieved. As they carried on, determined to try to vanish themselves from the board game, they had to complete one more challenge. Would they

complete it? They came across sinking sand. They all started to sink. They relaxed as they pulled each other out. "Argh!" screamed Emily...
Unexpectedly, they had arrived back home and told their parents the journey that they had. Which turned out to be an amazing adventure.

Molly Lloyd (10)
Winsford High Street CP School, Winsford

Birthday

There was a girl named Lucy who had a perfect life. She had a really nice mum, an adorable dog called Mittens and the most fabulous bestie ever, Luna. Lucy always felt a bit jealous of Luna, they had identical bags, coats, school kit and many other things. Still, Luna always had the new and improved version. There was one thing both girls really wanted, a phone.

One bright summer's morning, it was Lucy's birthday. She set her alarm for 7am. She got up, got dressed and brushed her teeth. She then woke her mum up. "Good morning Mum, do you know what day it is? My birthday, come on!" cheered Lucy, in a rather jumpy voice.

Lucy's mum followed her down the stairs and the little girl unwrapped her presents. Her jaw dropped down to the floor in joy. "You got me a phone! Thank you so much! You are the best mum on Earth!" She grabbed the phone and started to install hundreds of games on her new precious treasure.

Grace Campbell (10)
Winsford High Street CP School, Winsford

The Temple

As soft leather boots scattered the papery leaves in the dense undergrowth, the fearless hero ran from the beastly monster. Dead trees colonised the forest and supernatural plants grew on them. Tall grass smashed into Tom, as he shot a hard arrow that wedged into the temple door. He slid through the doors gaping jaws, that clamped together on the beat. Tom tripped and stumbled into the vast monument, sliding into water. The walls grew clawing vines and toxic flowers devoured the ancient hieroglyphics. Dark water foamed and fizzed and the colliding waves bubbled at Tom and dunked him under.

Tom's eyes opened and the darkness closed his weary vision which was cold and blurry. His lungs were bursting for a breath and suddenly, the calm surface of the deathly prison burst open like a rocket. Tom dived onto the rocky surface of the temple, the ice-cold water stung like a knife. He lit a torch and stumbled up, then he walked through the corridor.

Tom walked along, when suddenly, he heard a growling sound and it got louder and louder. He turned around, nothing. "Phew!" A drop of green goo dripped down from the roof and onto Tom's pale face. He glared up and saw a giant spider clinging onto the temple ceiling. It dropped down onto the floor and shot a giant web from its venomous jaws. It grabbed him, Tom grasped for his sword but it was too late, what could Tom do now?

Suddenly, Tom kicked the giant arachnid in its stubby legs and in its toxic fangs. He slowly dragged the steel blade through the beast. He wiped the oozy green slime off his face and sword. Soon he got on his way again to the golden mask of Avantia. Tom saw a mysterious lever on the wall. He pulled it without hesitation. Tom heard a rumbling sound and suddenly the walls were caving in on him, waiting to crush him.

He quickly wedged the torch into the gap of the remaining space and leapt onto it. He noticed a trapdoor slowly appearing in the ceiling of the deadly trap. Tom burst through and the walls closed.

Tom climbed through the maze of tunnels and out down a ripped banister. He peeked out and saw the mask. He ran for it, faster and faster as quick as his legs could carry him. Just as he was about to grab it, a strange rock grew up from the depths of the temple. It smashed onto the damp floor, knocking Tom back. Tom swung his hard metal sword at the golem's foot that had appeared it toppled Tom over. Tom lunged at the beast and

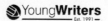

buried his iron sword into its bony stone skull. Tom turned to see the mask right next to him. He grabbed it. As he touched the mask he got sucked into a vortex spinning in discombobulation... He saw light...

Kayden Johnston (10)

Winsford High Street CP School, Winsford

Help!

Once, a young boy was running to school, when he stopped and took a short cut in the forest. He ran and instantly got lost in the overpowering woods. He looked around in fear as it struck him down more, more and more. After the horrified boy trembled in fear, he started to sprint right past all the viny trees when he fell down a deep hole...

"Help! Help!" the boy cried as he tried to jump out. It was no use. Then the boy remembered he had an enormous rope so the boy threw the rope up and climbed and climbed.

At the top, he shouted, "Hooray!" Then he ran as fast as he had ever ran before to get to school. He could see the light and then he started feeling conscious of his surroundings. Then he realised it was nothing and kept on running.

Finally, he got to the Winsford High Street School, just in time for 10:09. There the teacher said, "Good morning, Jack."

Samuel Latham (10)
Winsford High Street CP School, Winsford

The Secret About The Mountains

I just received the best news ever! I was at my friend's house and they invited me to go to the mountains with them. I'm so excited, I keep thinking this is a dream. As I lay in bed that night struggling to sleep, I was texting Emily, and she told me a shocking story that sounded familiar...

The day I went to the mountains had finally come, I had butterflies. We had to ride for four hours in a helicopter. The views were impressive, despite the surprising air sickness. Eventually, we arrived at the mountains, and it was freezing!

"You guys can explore for a while whilst we unpack," mentioned Emily's mum. It was so much fun! We played in the snow, throwing snowballs and chasing each other until we stumbled upon a cave...

The cave looked very mysterious, and we went inside to explore. Emily's Mum did give us permission to explore after all! It was dark and damp, and our clothes got soggy, so we decided to head back to the cabin to get changed... but we were lost! It was pitch black and I couldn't see.

Every way looked the same! I asked Emily if she knew where we were, but she was silent. I turned around to see what was wrong, but Emily was gone...

I got so anxious, I almost had a panic attack! When I finally calmed down, I found a letter, it said: 'I have your friend, Emily. You will never find us! If you ever want to see her again, then you must give me back what is mine.'

It sounded a bit like Emily's shocking story. She had told me about a man who was waiting for someone to give him back a shiny red jewel. It was concerning because I once took a red jewel of a man - but I thought it was mine, so it wasn't my fault, was it?

After what seemed like a lifetime, I found a brass key near to a door. I was exhausted! I had been looking all day for Emily and surely this meant I was finally going to find her! Nervous excitement ran through me at the thought of finally finding Emily. I unlocked the door, and sitting in a corner of a brightly lit room was Emily. I squealed with relief and excitement, but then I felt somebody behind me. I slowly turned and the scary man that had taken Emily was standing there. I was petrified! I threw the jewel at the man and turned to Emily.

"Run!" I shouted and then I ran, faster than I had ever run before hoping Emily was following me. When we finally got back to the cabin we told Emily's mum about our adventure but she told us we had great imaginations, so we pretended it was a joke. We will never take something that isn't ours again, or go anywhere near a cave!

Emma Wicksted (10)
Winsford High Street CP School, Winsford

Trapped

Vines surrounded me like a hangman's noose. Brushing my face every time I moved, I couldn't get out. I was trapped like a fly in a spider's web. Feeling trepidatious, scared and worried all at once, the dark gooey, damp vines were as think as twenty pieces of wood. It was hard to get out. Then I realised I had my pocketknife in my pocket so I cut the thick, tough, strong, overpowering vines. Finally! Then I saw a strange man who was dressed up in all black. I ran and ran until I dropped. I couldn't walk or run.

In the distance I could see the man again. I realised that he wasn't walking, he was chasing me so I ran and hid behind a tree. He still found me so I ran to a bridge.

He still followed me. He ran across the bridge, chasing after me. I cut the bridge while he was still halfway and he fell. Was I safe now?

Theo Dunbar (10)

Winsford High Street CP School, Winsford

Adventure Time

"Hello, who's there?" the boy said in a worried manner. The wondrous boy was really confused. He looked up and saw devil-like trees that were as tall as giants and branches that draped like a hangman's noose. Charles was scared. The boy stood up and took a look at what was around him. All of a sudden, a silhouette of a black hooded figure was staring like an eagle watching its prey's every move.

Charles took a step and tripped over a stick, piercing his leg. The helpless young boy screamed in agony. The death-defying figure bent over to look at him, not taking his eyes off him for a second. Charles' instincts took over him and made him kick the psycho in the face and run into the frightening unknown.

After an intense time of constant running, Charles turned around to see if the maniac was still chasing him, which he wasn't. Just to be sure, the brave Charles climbed up the tree that struck fear into the faint of heart to watch from above.

He couldn't see anything but all of a sudden, he heard a snap and he was falling from twenty feet in the air. "Arghhh!" Charles had broken his leg.

The poor boy heard footsteps. Crying and sobbing, the boy was hopping for his life. After he hopped up the hill in agony, he saw a light. He finally turned that crying face into a delighted face. He turned and the hooded maniac was there. He got punched in the face and everything went black... After what felt like a three-hour power nap, he woke up in a dark, damp, uncomfortable shed. Charles looked up and saw the man who had kidnapped him and chased him down. The black silhouette was throwing loads of random stuff into a really deep hole of boiling magma. For some reason he was reciting the words... "All I need is human blood!" over and over again.

Charles spent hours trying to get free from the rope, until it dropped to the floor like a dead man's hand. He silently got up off the floor and crept up behind him, pushing him into the boiling hot magma. "Argh!" the dark figure yelled louder than Charles ever could.

Charles ran out the door, hopping. He had to constantly pick up sticks to use as crutches but they would always snap.

Soon, Charles finally saw light. He threw the sticks and went down the hill. He saw a house and opened the door.

"Where have you been and what happened to your leg?" Mum said in a serious voice.
"I got hit by a car and broke my leg!"
"Let's get to the hospital then."
Charles wasn't mad about his leg, he was just glad he was safe, or so he thought...

Joseph Mather (10)
Winsford High Street CP School, Winsford

A Hungry Search

As hungry as a tiger, ready to pounce on an unsuspecting antelope, the man lay in his bed dreaming about his next meal. At last, the man finally got out of bed. First, he put on his neon, stripy boots and his leather expensive coat and set off.

Halfway down the long stretch of path near to the food shop, he realised his dream was beginning to come true. He could have his first meal of the day. Finally, he got to the door. He tried to get in but it wouldn't open. He was disgusted, now he had to go to the other food shop.

Now the man had to walk another four-mile journey. The man set off and halfway down the snowy stretch he felt really hungry but the shop was nowhere near.

He finally got to the second food shop and he yanked the door and it did not open and he realised it was because it was Christmas Day.

Zain Barnett (10)
Winsford High Street CP School, Winsford

Going Hunting

It was a long night, when a young explorer took great advice from his dad to go and complete his destiny...

Four hours earlier, "Mum? I'm going out, I've got something to complete," he shouted in an excited voice.

"If you start to not feel well again, take a tablet, okay?"

"Okay."

"Be careful!" she said back.

He set off to the highest point of the mountain and went to his cabin. He had a super destiny to find and take a photo of an undiscovered animal. His dad had recently died and his mum was ill, he needed money for some medicine.

He had only just put his hunting gear on, ready to go, even though he was not hunting any animals. At this time it was the 1800s, he really hoped he would find a great animal for the newspaper. Suddenly, he was conscious of his surroundings and knew something was staring at him. "Oh no, monster!" he whispered in fright. He thought of what other explorers do to look for ghosts and took pictures all around him so he could look at the photos for someone or something.

He then heard a frightening clash of rocks falling off the mountain. He looked up and made his eyes follow the falling rocks until they hit the bottom and landed in front of a hole of darkness. It was... a cave.

He hesitated, deciding whether or not to go in. He smacked himself to get the fear out of his face. Then he walked up the path, until he arrived at the dark entrance. Laughs came from behind him but the fear didn't let him turn around. Suddenly, the cave lit on fire and a man stood in the middle of it, with his arms out. Bats flew in and out and the explorer got out his camera and got ready to take a photo but he didn't know he had it on flash...

With no fear, he took the photo but... *flash!* The flash blinded the person's eye and it pounced at him, pinning him to the cold floor. He could see the man over his face, opening his mouth. He saw... fangs!

It didn't take him a second to realise it was a vampire! He quickly got hold of the vampire and threw it off him. He quickly got up and ran down the side of the mountain, thinking he was free. But was he?

He suddenly heard the sound of a flapping cape, coming towards him. he looked to his side and could see the vampire about five metres away from him. the monster dived forward until... *boom!* The vampire missed him and hit his head on the mountain. He was dead.

Suddenly, the sky went dark and lightning appeared. He immediately ran as fast as he could to his cabin. He then went straight to see his mum.

Charlie Eaton (10)
Winsford High Street CP School, Winsford

The Pretty Girl/Monster Girl

One dark, damp night, at the bottom of a pit, lay a creature that only ate teeth, liver, pancreas, tongue, fingers and eyes. It had knives for fingers and can deceive you by looking like a girl but really it does this to draw you in. This happened to me and this is my story...

I was walking down a path towards an old shack that gave me goosebumps. I entered but then, thud, total darkness.

I woke up in a gloomy cave and I saw a creature that was huge, had four legs and teeth that were deep red. I didn't know its gender by the way. It called my name, Jackson, and asked me to come closer.

Then I saw my opening and took my chance but it knew what I was doing and bit my leg and ripped off a chunk! I sprinted all the way home and I heard, "This is not the end, Jackson. Mwhahaha!"

Luke Okome (9)
Winsford High Street CP School, Winsford

The Jungle

As darkness engulfed the fading light of the jungle, a thick humid haze filled the air. Who created this place? Where was he? Birds squawked aggressively high up in the cloak-like canopy overlooking the vast terrain. The sun which hung over the sky like a blanket, shone a beautiful ombre of glistening orange and yellow.

Even though the wonderful setting hypnotised Billy, he was still convinced that a mysterious presence was lurking within the shadows. Suddenly, a pair of glowing beady eyes began to stalk Billy through the thick, canvas-like layer of the bracken. An eerie beat filled his ears as his heart thumped furiously in his ribcage like an enslaved lion.

As if out of thin air, Billy watched the oppressive foliage come crashing down and the peculiar creature took a deadly lunge towards the quivering body of the poor boy.

"Help!" blurted Billy as the dark being rapidly sprinted towards him. As quick as a flash, he turned and fled, ducking both over and under rogue branches and roots.

Billy soon came to a patch of poisonous berries. He scrambled with his sweaty fingers and picked them off of a tree. He quickly threw it at the monster, causing it to flee.

A troubling thought filled Billy's mind, how could he escape this horrific island? He could hear the approaching footsteps of the hulking monster. A terrifically, ear-piercing roar erupted from the deep, dark depths of its blood-red raging mouth. He bolted through the jungle, swiping extensive vines and eye-catching bracken. Eventually, the moss of forest disappeared into the large open plain. Luckily, he caught sight of a broken-down helicopter. Filled with encouragement and pumping adrenaline, he ran down the steep hill, pushing plants and small animals aside.

Once he had reached the damaged corpse, Billy fidgetted with the scrapped propellers and rhythmically swiped his hands along the complicated panel. Flicking switches, buttons and levers alike. A cry of joy spilt out from Billy's mouth as the soft, chugging and loud spinning of the propellers started.

He hopped into the hard, leathery seat and gracefully lifted off the ground. Just as he thought that he was safe, Billy heard the depressing clan of bullets. One lucky shot hit the jackpot and clogged up the spinning blades. The sound of an explosion erupted as the helicopter came spiralling down

and crash-landed into the sea, never to be seen again.
Did Billy survive or did he meet his bubbly demise?

Alex Dawson (10)
Winsford High Street CP School, Winsford

The Unknown Story

Callum was running through the pitch-black forest full of snakes that were chasing him. Their teeth could impale anything in their way. Everything that surrounded him could be a trap. The grass was not green, it was black and full of slime. Callum was very conscious of his surroundings. The wilderness was not for Callum.

The snakes bolted for him but he kept on running. He could not see the snakes but he was trepidatious and hid from the snakes. His heart was pounding out from his skin and the snakes had yellow eyes and their skin was black.

As he ran he saw the outline of a house. Callum said, "That is my house!" But he forgot there was a disaster out of the front of his house. How will he get in now?

Jayden Kilburn (11)
Winsford High Street CP School, Winsford

A Dog's Adventure

This is the happiest time of my life, Lavender is taking me for a walk and Lavender is my owner. She is thirteen so we can do everything together. Just the two of us with no other dogs who try and steal her from me. I must protect her at all times. I am small, cute and a Cavalier but I will not let Lavender out of my sight.

"Spring, come on!" Lavender says.

Yes, it's time to go!

In the bright sun, I hop out of the car and run into the field. "Let's put your lead on," Lavender commands. There is no way I am wearing that! How am I supposed to chase birds and squirrels when I am being pulled back? Sorry, not going to happen, bye-bye.

"Spring, come back!" Lavender screeches.

The smells are damp and new, my soul feels lost in an unreal world but the only thing is, when I turn around, Lavender isn't there. I am so disappointed in myself. I am supposed to protect Lavender and never let her out of my sight. Now I don't know if she is lost or if I am. So many negative feelings are hitting me. I can't find her by scent because all I can smell is the damp leaves. Maybe she'll be at home, all I have to do is get there, but how? Home isn't in sight and I am lost in some sort of jungle where no one can find me. Now it's sunset and it is much darker now.

Luckily there's some light from the big, white, round thing in the sky. I hope Lavender is alright. I think I have hurt my leg in my sleep but I cannot stop and must continue with my adventure. I'm too thirsty to carry on walking so I will have to find somewhere to stop. Thankfully I have found a river to cool me down. As I try to get out, I find that the river is pulling me like a giant game of tug of war. I can't swim with my leg and the water is pulling me even more. I tell myself, "Come on Spring, Lavender needs you."

Then I hear a voice, it sounds very familiar. "Spring where are you?" the voice speaks.

"Lavender!"

She runs straight to me and pulls me out of the river. "Lavender I am so happy I found you. Please take me home, the forest is scary. I will go straight to bed."

Now I am home, curled up on Lavender's lap. I have realised that sometimes you just have to wear the lead.

Laila Neunie (10)
Winsford High Street CP School, Winsford

The Monster

As the moon was washed away from the cloud and wind, the trees were swaying nervously from seeing the hairy monster. What was this green place? Were there any beastly monsters waiting to pounce for any prey coming out of nowhere? The weeds were even scared and were wrapping around the bark of the trees. Some were even dangling down from the thin, multicoloured leaves. The dim forest even had moss and twigs on the thin objects.

"Ow!" was what the explorer was constantly saying every five minutes. He was tripping up with nearly every step he dared to take from how scared he was feeling. In a desperate attempt to find food, he was ripping the bushes. Then he saw two huge, yellow, round eyes peering at him and dared to take another look to see if it was a monster and it definitely was!

He pounced up and dodged away from the monster and couldn't stop running. Rob, while still running, heard the beast coming after him so he sprinted for it. He only heard it coming because it was running faster than him and was going through everything in its path. Unlike Rob, who was dodging and ducking everything.

The monster quickly caught up with the explorer and had hold of his backpack and it flung him back. As quick as a dash, the man rolled out of the way before the ugly monster nearly crushed Rob's bones. The explorer felt relieved from going away from his death.

As quick as a lightning bolt, the middle-aged man saw a miniature gap in a tree and went in it so the monster would be puzzled. The man was so lucky to not have died. But that's not what he was thinking. He was planning to make a potion that would knock the monster out.

When he made it, he gently put it in his pocket and dashed for the monster. As he was on the monster's back, he dangled down with his potion and before it could eat him, he shoved it in his mouth to knock him out for twelve hours.

During the twelve hours, he would go in his aeroplane to fly away from the monster. Sadly, it was the wrong potion and it made him sleep for twelve seconds. So he was confused that he woke up so early. He bolted through the bushes with the monster behind him. When he got to the edge of the cliff and he jumped... Was he safe or even alive?

Louie Greavey (10)
Winsford High Street CP School, Winsford

The Cheetah And The Farm

After a full moon stood over an old, mysterious pig barn, rats scurried around like cats hunting mice. Fiercely, a rusty ancient side door opened and the smell of mouldy pellets escaped into the cold air. Muddy, stinky hay lay under the disgusting, decaying corpses of pigs, that sat motionless around a warm, bubbling bucket that looked to be sitting there for a millennia. The creepy, spine-tingling atmosphere was very weird as someone stepped in. Old, wooden fences surrounded the noise of hay scattering around.

An eleven-year-old boy named Ethan travelled through the creepy barn and heard a loud, confusing sound. He loved exploring but definitely not at night. His chestnut-brown hair blended in with the brown fences. Ethan was a cool kid and his friends always described him as adventurous but he didn't feel it at this very moment. His parents were in the car, worrying!

As Ethan started to explore deeper, a sound of a human walking around echoed on the walls of the barn. He started to panic. What was he going to do? As quick as a flash, a vicious, aggressive cheetah appeared. Ethan was very, very worried. "Hello, pussycat," he nervously spoke. All of a sudden, the cheetah pounced on Ethan and he was trapped. The cheetah wickedly laughed and Ethan shouted, "Mum, Dad, help!" As Ethan got angry, he used that anger and pushed the cheetah away. It tripped over a log and ran towards its hiding spot. Sadly, not for long! The cheetah let the weak boy run and cornered him, so he had to run into the storeroom, there he was trapped. Ethan was stuck! He tried really hard to get free but he couldn't. Ethan closed his eyes, thought and pleaded, "Please let me go!" Ethan then pinched himself to see if he was having a nightmare. He wasn't! Ethan had a plan. He was going to climb over the fence. He had to wait for the perfect time. Whilst the cheetah stuck its head over the door, Ethan bravely climbed over the fence and ran to lock the door.

Rapidly, Ethan ran to his mum and dad's car and cried, "I never want to go outside again! There was a cheetah! It tried to eat me!"

Lucy Holt (10)
Winsford High Street CP School, Winsford

The Mansion

As the moon changed places with the sun, she found herself at an old, abandoned mansion. Why did the place look so old? Why was it so eye-catching? Old stained-glass windows were broken. Casey who loved to just relax disturbingly heard wolves howling, dogs barking, foxes crying and owls hooting. She started to get frightened. "This place doesn't look that nice and smells like it's been here for centuries! Well, I hope it hasn't!" muttered Casey.

The forest surrounding the mansion, looked like it was haunted because there were creepy noises. Casey heard trees snapping, leaves flying off trees and trees swaying back and forth.

As she stepped foot inside the house, she sighted the most weirdest thing ever, it was a... plant or flower but it was glow-in-the-dark. It also had green, spiky bits on. It was sprinkled on the emerald, sapphire towers. This place was very shiny but then got very dull. "I hope I can find something magical, shiny or scary in here!" shouted Casey in excitement.

Through a gap between the wall, she could see something shimmering in her lovely light blue eyes. Casey went to look what it was and it was a golden book. Her wish came true so she opened it and... every window and door slammed shut!

212

She ran downstairs and the door wouldn't open. She thought she was locked in forever so she started shouting, "Let me out!" No one heard her so she kept trying and trying until she gave up. She was starting to get a bit horrified.

Finally, hours later, Max (who was Casey's friend) came to rescue her. He said, "Don't worry I will get you out somehow." He went and got a hard stick and got her out. They found out that she left her teddy in there and she got it when she was first born. Then she heard *bang, bang, bang*.

Max went into the mansion and Casey prayed he was alive. Then he came and he had her favourite teddy. She didn't even know what to say. Casey and Max went back to Max's house and watched a movie. They heard a knock, opened the door and hid. It was just a package, or was it...?

Leah Taylor (10)
Winsford High Street CP School, Winsford

The Golden Mask

In London 2005, Esrin and his pet, a bearded lizard, were set a task to retrieve the golden mask. It was made by the Aztecs and he was going to take it to the Natural History Museum so it could be in the new exhibit. There was a huge reward to get it and trust me, it was a lot! Esrin worked as an archaeologist so it was the perfect job for him.

As the sun rose, Esrin got Komodo, his lizard to jump in his backpack with his grappling hook. They quietly set off in a speed boat 355 miles off Land's End.

Once docked on the volcanic island, he saw lava spurts and huge obsidian pieces as big as boulders and a great rocky volcano in the middle. He instantly set off to the volcano as the temple of the mask was built into it. Esrin soon found it and entered the massive temple where the mask was but he tipped over a tripwire hook.

Suddenly, a boulder the size of an elephant burst out from the tunnel behind him so he ran for his life and zipped down the tunnel but it wouldn't give up the chase. Then it cornered him in a dead-end. He was about to close his eyes and wait for the finishing moment. Suddenly a chest rose from a gap in the floor. There must have been a secret tile or something that he stepped on. He opened it and threw the piece of TNT right at the rock. It shattered into a lot of smoke, rubble and dust. Surprisingly, the ground started to crack open with the lava leaking like a geyser in the middle of an oasis. Esrin had an amazing idea, he would get his grappling hook and swing across the lava. But the only problem was, the grappling hook was on the other side. Komodo then shot his tongue out and grabbed it and he took a great swing over the lava and fell through a hole to the golden mask. It was there!

Quickly he grabbed the mask and ran as fast as he could to the exit. He made it. He jumped over the lava and rocks, got into his speedboat and took the mask to the museum before the volcano erupted. So he got the prize and his name would be called Esrin the Volcano Conquerer from then on.

Joseph Day (10)

Winsford High Street CP School, Winsford

Dinosaur Land

As the stars gazed down at the noisy jungle, a boy and a girl, who were twelve years old, started a mysterious journey.

What is this place? Why is it so noisy?

Staring at the ragged trees that looked amazing, they suddenly knew where they were. They were in the jungle. The confident girl's name was Lizzy, she had a brother called Darren. You could see the birds tweeting in the high, leafy trees, feeling lost, lonely and scared. By the sound of it, that was how Lizzy and Darren felt. Lizzy screeched, "While we're here we should go and explore and look for a new minibeast." So they did...

Hobbling through the crunchy leaves made a loud noise and running through the leaves made an even louder noise. A noise that was unbearable! They came to a gate with a sign saying: *Beware Dinosaurs!* The second Lizzy looked away to identify an oak tree, Darren did not read the sign as he had already gone in.

"Uggghhh!" Lizzy sighed. She ran into the jungle to save Darren.

A second later, through a smash of dark leaves, Lizzy and Darren came sprinting out with an enormous, loud pterodactyl chasing them.

"Arggghhh!" Darren screamed.

"You big baby!" screamed Lizzy.

After five minutes, an enormous fairy came over. Lizzy and Darren jumped onto its fluffy body and screamed, "Yee-haaa!" Off the laughing fairy went. The laughing fairy took them to a rainbow book. The book was very dusty and old. All of a sudden, Darren opened the rainbow book and a big, shiny light shone into his beady eyes. He became colour blind, by its magic. Luckily, Lizzy was carrying a cure potion and she told him to drink it, so he did. He was no longer colour blind because he drank it and the positions magic cured him.

That healing potion attracted minibeasts, and it attracted a minibeast that had never been discovered before. It was a multicoloured woodlouse with red spots. Lizzy called it a Rainbowsaurus.

Now, how could they get out?

Jasmine Lloyd (10)
Winsford High Street CP School, Winsford

The Rapilo

The day had arrived for Danny Parkinson's trip to Australia! Danny was a brave and positive boy who loved an adventure. That morning Danny's dad turned on the news, a new species of animal had been discovered in Africa, it was called the Rapilo! The Rapilo was thought to be a relative to the rhino, similar in appearance but much stronger and more aggressive. The Rapilo had two razor-sharp horns to fight anything that came across it. *I am so glad we are going to Australia today and not Africa,* thought Danny, *so I don't have to see the Rapilo.*

When Danny walked into the busy airport he bumped into a boy and he didn't realise they had accidentally swapped tickets. Danny's dad didn't realise either and he kept on walking without him. Danny soon got lost and didn't know what to do so he just went to the nearest plane and got on. As the doors closed Danny heard an announcement: "Thank you for flying with Lovely Holidays to the African Safari one-day experience," said the pilot. *Oh no, the Rapilo!* Danny thought and he began to shake in his seat.

Danny had arrived at his destination, the African Safari Experience. It was going to be terrifying, the most dangerous place on Earth. Danny came across a sleeping lion and he didn't dare to wake it. He crept past silently and just got away with it, the lion did not move. Suddenly, he spotted something moving inside the tall grass. He got his camera out and ducked behind a rock. "It could be the Rapilo!" he whispered. Danny almost dropped his camera because his hands were trembling but managed to press the button and he got a clear shot of the Rapilo running away. Danny then realised he had cash in his pocket and could afford a journey home. Five hours later, he was home. "Where have you been, boy?" shouted his mum. "Outside playing," he said, lying to his mum, knowing he had a wicked time.

Charlie Mitchell (10)
Winsford High Street CP School, Winsford

Lily's Adventure!

It was pitch-black, as if the sun and moon had been stolen from space. In the deep, dark forest, two red, hypnotising eyes stared upon me whilst millions of poisonous spiders dropped down and made the shape of an evil man's skull. I felt like I would never see daylight again. What was this spooky place? What was going to happen next? In the distance, I could see a strange, creepy man. I saw that he had something on him that said: 'Horrible Harry'. He had two white eyes, with no pupils! Blood dripped down him as he slowly limped towards me, Lily.

"Lily," shouted Horrible Harry.

As I ran, I listened to my name getting called. Suddenly, the man ran closer and closer to me. Faster and faster and faster. I ran like a storm was chasing me. Horrible Harry struck me like lightning, whilst grabbing my cold arm as he brought blood to me...

Suddenly, a bright strike of lightning landed on top of Horrible Harry. As I pulled his hands off me, I ran away, not looking behind me. The man fell. He was unconscious. His crew wasn't going to give up, were they? So Horrible Harry's girls chased after me. I closed my eyes hoping that all of it was just a dream and in one minute, I would wake up and be in a nice house full of every single thing I ever wanted. But no, it was real!

I carried on and I did not give up. "Why did you do that to my boss?" shouted one of the girls, as they both got closer and closer to me.

Suddenly, splash! Evil Isabel fell into the deep lake. She thought she could swim but she couldn't. A weed got stuck on her foot. Sophia still ran until her and Isabel's horses, William and Ronnie, came into view. She grabbed them and both of the girls ran away.

I ran home through the forest and fields until finally, I was safe. I told everyone about my adventure but only Mum believed me.

The next day, I was nice and comfortable until I heard a knock at the door...

Hollie Harradine (10)
Winsford High Street CP School, Winsford

An Adventure

The twisted bamboo branches wrapped around the bees, acting like a long scarf. The branches hung down from the thick hollow trees like long arms. There were pandas climbing around the bamboo forest. Birds danced around above the clouds. What was this place? Why was it so beautiful and peaceful?

The most puzzling thing was all the strange noises the boys could hear. In addition, the plants were acting like a mysterious figure waiting to pounce out like muggers. Ethan and Nathan were frightened because the mysterious creatures were looking at them. Slowly, the grass swayed side to side in the breeze. Ethan and Nathan were walking down a small path. Then they realised they'd forgotten something.

Through a small gap in the leaves of the trees, they noticed that the path started to disappear. Ethan and Nathan tried to search for the map in their backpacks, but it wasn't there. The boys started to worry that they might be lost. Fortunately, the boys had a brilliant idea to re-track their steps in case they dropped it out of their backpack. They re-tracked their steps and they found the map then went back to the same path they were at and then went to the bamboo forest.

As they were walking along, they heard a mysterious noise, it sounded like a monkey squeak. Ethan and Nathan turned around and saw a wild pack of gorillas. the boys had no idea what to do so they just tried to keep the gorillas calm until they came up with an idea.

After that thought long and hard, they still had no ideas. Suddenly, Nathan remembered something. Nathan grabbed some bananas and threw them into the bushes and the gorillas ran after them. The boys suddenly saw something move in the bushes behind them! They moved the bush and saw a cute but strange panda. It wasn't normal though it was yellow and white!

They took a picture of it on their camera and took it to Channel 4 news. They became famous once again.

Miley Presland (11)
Winsford High Street CP School, Winsford

Ryan's Adventure

One beautiful morning, as the sun exchanged places with the moon in the breathtaking sky, a misty haze began to fly through the rough tall trees. What was this place? Wrapping around the spiralling branches, were thick, gigantic vines which hung above the clear blue water. As the wind wailed, vast colourful leaves jumped into the water as Ryan strolled through.

However, the strangest thing was the unfamiliar plants which were spread all through the forest. In the distance, Ryan saw a map so he ran across to it. The old, dirty map said in massive writing: 'Find the golden crown and you can keep it!' Ryan's eyes lit up.

A few moments later, Ryan found a beautiful boat and started to paddle down the stream. As he went further down, he saw exotic birds flying in the never-ending sky.

Suddenly, as Ryan paddled down the stream, he spied red beady eyes, looking directly at him! Then it came closer and closer. Before Ryan had a chance to move away from the disgusting, massive jaws of the crocodile... it moved closer, chomping its gigantic, scary teeth towards Ryan. As quick as a flash, the crocodile grabbed Ryan and lifted him into the air...

Fortunately, the explorer grabbed hold of the crocodile's mouth. Eventually, the nasty crocodile released him. In a blink of an eye, Ryan paddled as quick as a cheetah to the end of the deep, clear river and climbed out. Suddenly, Ryan saw colourful ecstatic birds flying in the never-ending sky. When he turned around, he saw the gold crown he was looking for.

The next day, Ryan travelled home. On his way home he saw enormous, thick trees that were swaying in the strong wind. Lots of leaves were flying around the whole forest. As soon as he got home, he showed everyone his crown. The crown had sapphire gems dotted all around it.

When Ryan told everyone about his adventure, they were terror-stricken but very proud of him.

Emma Toomey (10)
Winsford High Street CP School, Winsford

The Jungle

Dad woke Tom to see the damp, wet, sticky jungle. It was gloomy in the jungle, the trees were gooey, stringy great sap and it lay on the hard rocks like quicksand. The trickling stream followed the dark, gloomy jungle and the fish were following the trickly stream. What place was this? A misty haze began to form under a canopy of swaying, rugged trees and the jungle was all dark, gloomy and stinky.

Suddenly, they were marching forth into the murky dimly-lit jungle. As the bird's beautiful bright feathers floated to the forest floor, Tom's feet were killing him. The most puzzling sight of all was a strange thing, they were all as busy as a bee. This place was truly special but for the wrong reason. The jungle was horribly stinky inside and suddenly the daytime was gone, it was dark.

Suddenly, the forest fell silent like a window, stretching in front of Tom and his father. The vast, deep river ran. The river was as quiet as a mouse and as busy as a bee. Tom felt heavy walking and his tummy was like a roller coaster. He heard a *crash, splash, boom!* The rain went falling down onto the hard, muddy floor. It was hard to cross the river because the wind was blowing hard.

Suddenly, they had to pull and push as they rowed rapidly across the river. As quick as a flash, the young explorer gasped as they rode back and forth. The rain was going to calm down so they could row again and faster so they could see the beautiful world again.

They reached their destination. Tom's heart was going to explode like a drum. Finally, they reached the glorious sight of their beautiful destination. As the peaceful river floated across the wet, muddy floor their mouths dropped like an elevator going down.

They stood up and marched to their destination. They had a picnic then lay down on the grass with the creatures and had some fun.

Marlie Wilcock (10)
Winsford High Street CP School, Winsford

The Escape

The high waves tried to drown my petrified body, the rapid swell tried to pull me to the bottom of the threatening water. It made me feel like a fish being pulled from the sea. Having no way to get out of the net, the bubbly water got higher and higher, faster and faster. It grabbed my face and strangled me to near death. I had never experienced anything worse than that!

As quick as a flash, I pounced out of the water and ran down the steep stairs. With no support for the stabbing pain in my body, I continued to run as fast as a leopard down the stairs, praying for an escape. I came up with a masterplan to escape the house with a dangerous tank of water in it. Suddenly, I ran out of the door and in the background all I could hear was voices shouting at me.

"Get him now, don't let him get away!"

As I ran out of the door, I saw millions of cars and I didn't know how to get across the road. "If I cross the dangerous road, I could get run over," said the scared voice in my head.

The cars were so fast and they zoomed past me. I could never get across. I didn't know how to get the cars to stop. Finally, I figured out a way to get the cars to stop. There was a button to press. I was so happy, I would eventually get away!

As I thought about it I saw a puddle and suddenly, I realised it was not a vision, it was right in front of me. I got really terrified as it reminded me of when I drowned in water. It officially became my worst fear. Every time I saw water it reminded me of the time I was in the dreadful waves. I nearly drowned. As quick as a flash, I saw a little path that ran straight past the terrifying puddle and I was so relieved I would never see water again and would never need to worry about anything else again unless it was water.

Macie Taylor (11)
Winsford High Street CP School, Winsford

The Dodo

The glorious, azure-blue sky sat below the puffy, condensated clouds overlooking the wooden picnic tables. Green, soggy grass danced on the floor and a huge whistle of wind blew the swaying leaves on the prancing trees. Jason was a young boy who was perched on a bench. He had black, curly locks that draped down to his shoulders and he always had a cheeky smirk permanently drawn on his face. He had a twin sister called Jasmine, she had brown neat plaits and big bright green eyes.

The twins were in search of a dodo that they had heard about in a story. They travelled on their pet horse. Within days, they had crossed mountains, valleys and deserts in search of this creature. But luck they didn't have.

Soon they passed a jungle, in the blink of an eye, they heard a noise. A noise that glowed with throbbing rage. Before the pair could move a muscle, two dull round eyeballs emerged, followed by a gaping oval full of yellow teeth, sharper than the peak of Mount Everest! It was a tiger!

The pair began to sprint for their dear lives. Luckily, the hairy vile beast was obviously tired and couldn't bear to chase the children for any long period of time so it rested its head on a gargantuan, lime-green, pale leaf.

Suddenly, they came across a brown, leafy bog. They were puzzled. How could this possibly have happened? Jasmine looked up puzzled, Jason also looked up and then they had an idea! The would swing across a vine to exit the bog.

Swoop! Swing! Slide! All of a sudden, they realised they were back where they started with a dodo by their feet.

A few days later, they felt it was cruel to keep this poor bird so they set it free. Everyone lived happily ever after, but Jason and Jasmine never forgot what happened.

Evie Newton (10)

Winsford High Street CP School, Winsford

The Trip

One dull, misty morning, the children went on a big trek in the frosty forest where they saw a map so they followed it and it was taking them to an airport. They both had blue eyes and blonde hair and they were also twins. Everywhere was so dark because it was 7 in the morning.

It was so calm and peaceful, but muddy and foggy too.

All of the frosty leaves were swaying in the strong wind. The sunset was flickering like flames because the trees were swishing everwhere.

After two whole hours, they were freezing.

The weird thing was, the kids were in the middle of a forest but they could hear lots of cars!

They kept walking and they saw a big building.

They entered the big airport. It was so hot. They were given some money to travel so they went to the check-in, they put all their luggage on. It was so warm so they got something to eat and bought two milky coffees.

As they were called, some people were a bit rude and pushed past them so Noah dropped the ticket and then picked up the wrong one so now the kids were going on the wrong plane. The twins didn't know that they had the wrong ticket and were going to the wrong place.

After two hours they arrived and explored the place. Then they went back to the airport, went to the office, said their names and realised they were in the wrong place.

They got in the car to go home.

When they got back to the UK, it was freezing. They went to call their parents to tell them how hot it was in Spain. The whole thing was so, so funny.

Everyone was at home so the kids made sure they bought everyone presents and when they got home they told everyone what had happened and everyone was amazed.

Summer Copnall (10)
Winsford High Street CP School, Winsford

The New Species

One day, there was an adventurer called Bailey. He was studying a very new animal, no one had ever seen it before, except for him today. Also, the animal's habitat was in a dry bit of swamp. He was walking in the swamp. Then he spotted something with keys in it, which made him rather curious.

Then he got closer to the object and realised it was a dirt bike. He ran to it and then he jumped on to it and turned it on and set off. He was only one hour away from the habitat, but there were lots of murky yellow puddles, it was quite dark because of the trees.

Finally, he was there. It started to get a bit more lighter because of the lanterns. The new species liked a bit of light, but not too much. There were guards guarding his habitat. He tried everything, but nothing worked. Then he thought of something genius, he thought he could ask them nicely, "Please can I go through to see the new species? I am studying it!"

"Never, I'm never going to let you through," replied the guard, so that didn't work.

Suddenly, Bailey thought of something even more genius. He could get on the bike and sound like someone's trying to get around the back. Then run all the way back around the front and get in that way. So he tried all of that once, and it worked! He didn't think it would! He was amazed at how nice the habitat was, it was clean and bright.

Finally, he could study more about this new, mysterious creature and figure out what species it was. It was a type of gorilla, it was a baby and was called an American gorilla. Then Bailey could story more about it.

Bailey Saunders (10)

Winsford High Street CP School, Winsford

The Graveyard

One misty night, Nathan went to a terrible haunted church behind the graveyard. In the graveyard, he found the tomb of doom. Nathan could hear the screams of ghosts trying to catch children. All of the candles were flickering as shadows went by. As Nathan went into the spooky church he could feel the wind behind him. As quick as a flash, the big wooden door shut and Nathan couldn't open it and he was stuck.

Nathan kept on going and going until he went into the haunted graveyard. The graveyard had blood dripping out the tomb. As Nathan looked behind him, a ghost smashed a window and a tomb started grumbling like mad. Nathan tried to escape but he couldn't so Nathan ran back inside and screamed for help.

As quick as a flash, Nathan hid from the spirits. Nathan then peeped around the corner and he could hear the ghost so Nathan ran down to the creepy cellar where they kept the dead bodies.

As Nathan went down to the cellar, Nathan got a bit of a scare from one of the ghosts. Nathan could hear a mysterious noise, it sounded like screams. As quick as a flash, the door shut behind him and Nathan was so scared he couldn't move. Nathan was brave and kept heading forwards.

Nathan saw a window so he needed to find something to smash it with. As Nathan looked deeper he saw a hammer. Nathan ran back to the window and smashed it to pieces. Nathan didn't get hurt by the glass.

Nathan then saw a bike and took it. Finally, he was back home, safe! Nathan told his family but they didn't believe him and Nathan never went back there again.

Jamie Whitehurst (10)

Winsford High Street CP School, Winsford

Ella's Adventure

One sunny day, in a gorgeous, beautiful forest, there was a little girl called Ella. Ella was an explorer, she loved looking at trees and nature. Ella was just sketching a tree, when all of a sudden she saw a treasure map on the green forest floor. Dangling down from a layer of moss, vast, bold leaves flickered like flames in the blowing bluster of the wind.

However, the most puzzling of all sights, was the strange, exotic unfamiliar plants. All of a sudden, Ella saw some foxes guarding the ancient treasure map. Ella took a sudden step towards the map and the forest started to stir. Ella really wanted to see where the map led to.

Suddenly, Ella saw three paths. But all of a sudden, the foxes came closer to Ella. She was in a state of fear. Ella went down one of the three paths. It took her back to where she had started. "Oh no, I'm lost!" cried Ella. The sky got covered like a blanket from the grey, thick clouds. "Where am I? Am I lost?" questioned Ella.

Fortunately, Ella went down another one of the paths and she found a way out. Finally she could go home and tell her family about the adventure she had been through. Ella was so excited that she could go home and see her mum and dad.

As the sun switched places with the moon, Ella was so tired and she slowly stumbled back home in the dark, creepy woods. Suddenly, Ella saw her house and ran as quick as a flash. When she got into her house, she gave her family and friends a huge hug and told them all about her exciting adventure.

Faye Dormer (10)
Winsford High Street CP School, Winsford

The Church

As the darkness rose, thunder and lightning struck trees around the abandoned church. Mysterious noises bellowed from inside the church's ground. What could be in there? Owls hooted in the dark trees to scare off predators.

The most unfamiliar sight were the diagonal gravestones that moss covered, seeing the words carved on the stone. Evan was strolling down a path he had never been down. As he stopped, out of the corner of his eye he realised there was an abandoned church across the road to him. He walked over the road, through the graveyard and entered the church. He walked in and... *slam!* The door slammed behind him.

Evan tried opening it but it was locked. Candles flickered on and off. Evan knew there was something fishy about the church. He walked through the church, hoping to find an exit, but there was no hope. There were no more doors. He looked in every room and every corner for a key but he still couldn't find anything like a key. Evan's last hope was an ancient oakwood cupboard. He slowly pulled the cupboard doors open and he saw... a metal key chain with a key dangling on it.

He ran to the door and unlocked it. He ran back to the cupboard to put the keys back and darted through the door, leapt over mossy graves and hopped over the fence. He whispered to himself, "Finally freedom!" as he traced his footsteps back home.

Evan eventually got back home to his warm, cosy house. He changed his battered clothes and said, "What an adventure it has been!"

Harry Wallace (10)
Winsford High Street CP School, Winsford

The Jungle

One time, there was a damp, wet, sticky jungle with gooey, stringy tree sap lying on the hard rocks like sinking sand. The beautiful rainbow birds sang like an opera. Trickling along through the gloomy dark jungle, dangling down from the layer of moss, the leaves flickered like planes in the blowing wind. The leaves danced on the trees as one part of the jungle was desert dry while the other was the complete opposite.

The person who was here was called Tom. He was on a quest. All the trees seemed to stare at him. Strolling forth into the murky dim light jungle, it felt like quicksand. The birds fluttered as Tom shouted. In addition, Tom felt nervous and was on a roller coaster of emotions.

Fluttering, flapping birds flew like plastic in the wind. Suddenly, the forest opened up like a door. Stretching in front of Tom was a deep river. His heart was pounding like a piston. he took a moment to think about how he would cross the vast deep river. After a couple of minutes, he remembered he took string. He could make a raft. When the raft was completed he was rowing endlessly to cross the vast deep river. He got to the point where he kept rowing faster and faster.

As he reached land he got to a rainbow, the most colourful of all. "It is glorious!" gasped Tom. As he reached the start of the rainbow, he dug a hole to find a chest of gold. He found it. He opened it to see gold diamonds. He was rich!

Jamari Chandler (10)
Winsford High Street CP School, Winsford

The Church

One misty night, there was a boy called Nathan
and he climbed through the side window of the
old, dusty church. Next to the church there were
creepy, muddy gravestones with cobwebs hanging
on. There were owls hooting, loud music, people
screaming and there were rats running around the
gravestones. Nathan escaped from home to go
ghost hunting. He has dark black hair, brown
glasses, light blue jeans, a dark red jumper, grey
shoes, light blue eyes and crazy hair.
In the church there was a cat with scarlet-red
glazed eyes. Nathan said, "Shoo, cat!" She
stretched out her claws, trying to scratch Nathan.
Nathan was creeping down the stairs and a gust of
wind slammed the door shut and Nathan was
trapped. There was blood all over the floor where
people's heads were chopped off by a chainsaw.
There were smashed bottles on the floor and blood
dripping from their wrists.
He found a hammer in the cellar and he smashed
the window and escaped. He used all his strength
to pull himself through the window and he tried
not to get a pierce through his shin.

Nathan climbed out of the window and ran home. He found an abandoned bike but it was attached to the fence. He finally unattached the bike from the fence and rode all the way home as fast as he could go.

When he got home he ran upstairs and felt really, really happy because he was not in that smelly church and wouldn't be ever again.

Mason Whittle (10)
Winsford High Street CP School, Winsford

The Dinosaur

As they chased the clouds, shadows began to form in the eerie, dark forest. Where were they coming from? The trees swayed outwards in the breeze and showed an old, abandoned museum. The smell of the place was horrible, but why was it so eye-catching? Curling around it were green, soggy vines. Suddenly, a little girl called Nancy slowly walked over to the building.

However, there was something different about the museum. The howling of the furry, grey wolves made the atmosphere suspicious. Nancy wasn't afraid but then the decaying, old, rust door began to open. Was someone in there? Was it just the wind? Then, loud bangs were coming from inside. All of a sudden... a dinosaur that didn't look very happy made its way to Nancy. "Argh! Help me!" she screamed in terror. Unfortunately, nobody could hear her because of the stamping of the dinosaur's big, scaly feet. *Stomp! Stomp!* Nancy was petrified, she didn't know what to do!

Suddenly, the dinosaur went to bite Nancy. Fortunately, she managed to escape.

Seconds later, the dinosaur passed out and a tree fell on him. In shock, blood started squirting out of his mouth and stomach. Nancy nearly... well, fainted.

A few moments later, Nancy's parents went to the forest to call Nancy in for her tea. All they saw was a few marks of the dinosaur on the ground. Nancy was nowhere to be seen.

Isabel Kight (10)
Winsford High Street CP School, Winsford

The Jungle

A damp, wet, sticky jungle. There were layers of gooey, sticky tree sap on rocks like sinking sand. The beautiful singing birds sang like an opera song and the monkeys were screaming like donkeys. Suddenly, Tom saw a snake around his neck. Tom screamed. The snake let go and he backed up and fell into an abyss of darkness. Suddenly he landed and there was a herd of donkeys. The stood all over him and he got knocked out. Surprisingly Tom got chased by a big gorilla. Tom gound a cave and ran into it. The gorilla ran past him. Suddenly he was stopped and saw deep, gooey mud and then disgustingly walked through it. Then he found a bird and took it so it could protect him. Terrifyingly, he got attacked by a pack of wild wolves. Tom started running for his life and he started to run out of breath. He found a stick and threw it the other way, but that did not stop them.
Tom tripped and fell down a hill and left the wolves. "Wow!" puffed Tom. He saw the sea and evidently started building a boat.
Two weeks later, the boat was built out of twisted bamboo and palm tree sticks and leaves. He started sailing.

Two days later, he arrived at his destination. He started to see visions then he saw a missing poster of himself. He was shocked and ran home. He arrived at home with cuts and bruises and his mum and dad were thrilled to see him. Tom lived happily ever after.

Alfie Farrell (10)
Winsford High Street CP School, Winsford

The Forest

The forest was damp, wet, sticky.

"Good morning, Tom," whispered Dad.

The gooey, sticky tree sap lay on the hard floor. I could hear the wind whistling like a whistle. What was this place? The trickly stream flowed down the gloomy, dark forest. In the forest, I could hear the leaves dancing on the trees. We had been walking for ages and my shoes were killing me. I could see the dreary, dismal darkness in the distance.

I was marching forth into the muddy, dimly-lit jungle. "Squawk!" What was that? Dad looked puzzled. The fluttering, flapping birds glided like jets through the trees as they dodged them. I felt frightened as the birds flew around. They nearly hit my head.

Suddenly the forest opened like a window. It was weird because it was dark and now it was light.

"Dad, how are we going to get across this river with a broken canoe?"

"It's fine, we can just fix it."

"How? It has an enormous hole at the bottom?"

"We can use sticks."

We built it for hours, then finally made it from an old, rusty boat to a fixed boat.

"Now we can get across the river!"

"No, no, no," shouted Dad. "Let's try it first." We tried it and it was finished.

Finally, we made it to their glorious destination. We were glad that we had made it.

Dominic Griffin (10)

Winsford High Street CP School, Winsford

The Game

Once there was a boy walking on the street, to get home from school and something caught the corner of his eye at the front of the antique store. A box with a label saying: 'Get passed the dragon and the goblin'. It was a video game, a very rare video game which was lying in the street. No one was around to get it so he took it home with him. He got home after a very long time because the box was really heavy to carry a long distance. He shut the windows as quick as a flash and sat on the sofa and opened the video game. He set the mysterious game and a big bang came from somewhere and it happened again. He tried to unplug it but the game was too strong for him and a ginormous portal appeared and he went into it... When the boy got sucked into the portal, he imagined he was in the game. When he landed was a really spooky forest in the middle of nowhere. He looked around two times very slowly. He was relieved that he saw nothing in the distance but he suddenly heard a massive roar behind him.

He looked around very slowly and saw a very fierce red dragon. Running as fast as he could, he ran through the forest. He was frightened...

He suddenly hid behind a massive tree in the fierce forest and made himself as small as he could into a ball. What would happen to him?

Rio Bennion (10)
Winsford High Street CP School, Winsford

The Church

One misty night, there was a boy called Nathan and he escaped from home. Nathan had black hair and was twelve. He went to search for a ghost at an abandoned church.

As Nathan arrived, the doors were open and he walked in nervously. Nathan took a Bible that was above him and he heard music and bat wings hitting the sides and there were owls hooting like a whistle. The curved windows were shattered like a car and Nathan found shadows flying around the church. The candles were flickering like a light and Nathan heard the floor creaking as he was looking around the church.

Nathan tripped over Bibles and cobwebs got in his face. Then Nathan saw the door slam shut. He looked for an exit because he was horrified so he wanted to go home to get some sleep. Nathan then heard a mysterious noise come from behind him. Nathan found blood dripping down the wall like a fountain and a door that led to the basement. The door slammed on him and Nathan said, "I want to get out!" Nathan saw bones and glass lying on the ground so he said, "I have to be careful now!"

Nathan then saw a hammer and broke the windows. He said, "This is great!" Nathan got out safely with no cuts or grazes.

Jack Lacking (10)
Winsford High Street CP School, Winsford

The Well

As the sun came up, a young boy called Max ran away from home because he always got shouted at. Max turned up at a beautiful, graceful city. He carried on walking until he got to a skyscraper. He finally reached the top and he could see everything, but not home. He finally got down and the misty fog had finally gone away. He was wondering where he was.

Suddenly, he walked further into the loud, beautiful city. He saw people with delicious doughnuts and yummy chocolate cake. He saw a deep, dark well so he went to see if there was any water in the well. There wasn't...

Max fell deep down into the smelly, rat-infested well. Max's heart dropped as soon as he fell down the well. He was rooting and rooting and then he finally found a rope with a hook on the end...

Max threw the rope up the deep, dark well and made sure it gripped onto the well. Then he leapt onto the rope and used all of his strength to climb out the well. He said, "It's much better than down there!"

When he was out of the hole, he had a brainwave on the way home so off he went. He finally saw his mum and dad again. "I will never leave home again."

Oliver Walker (10)
Winsford High Street CP School, Winsford

Young Writers Information

We hope you have enjoyed reading this book – and that you will continue to in the coming years.

If you're a young writer who enjoys reading and creative writing, or the parent of an enthusiastic poet or story writer, do visit our website **www.youngwriters.co.uk**. Here you will find free competitions, workshops and games, as well as recommended reads, a poetry glossary and our blog. There's lots to keep budding writers motivated to write!

If you would like to order further copies of this book, or any of our other titles, then please give us a call or order via your online account.

Young Writers
Remus House
Coltsfoot Drive
Peterborough
PE2 9BF
(01733) 890066
info@youngwriters.co.uk

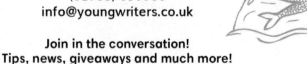

Join in the conversation!
Tips, news, giveaways and much more!

 YoungWritersUK    @YoungWritersCW